Dedication

This book is dedicated to my family, who are the most interesting group of all.

Acknowledgements:

I would like to thank my colleagues in the supervision group for all their insights and support. Thanks are also due to my teaching colleagues, Dr. Peter Shanahan, Course Director, and Dr. Pauline McClenaghan, Course Co-ordinator at the University of Ulster, and to the many students I have been privileged to teach at the university.

I owe a great deal to the group members I have worked with in my role as group facilitator and as group participant, over the past ten years. It is impossible to exaggerate just how much I have learned from my experiences in these, and other more informal groups.

My thanks are also due to my former teachers, Suzanne Redding and John Redmond, who are both aware that many of my early experiences in group training were difficult for me personally, though never dull, and always educative.

Finally, I would like to thank David for all his support and encouragement, and for the illustrations he did so willingly for the book.

Contents

◆ Chapter 3: Communicating in groups

◆ **Chapter 6: Individuals and their conduct in groups**

◆ **Chapter 8: Behavioural and Cognitive-Behavioural groups**

◆ Chapter 9: The Humanistic Influence in Groups

◆ **Chapter 10: Principles of good practice in groups**

Introduction

This book is about groupwork skills, theory and practice. It is written primarily for students on group counselling and therapy courses at certificate and diploma levels, although students on post-graduate level counselling courses with a groupwork component could also use it. Because of its additional focus on the characteristics of groups generally, including group dynamics, developmental sequences, and group member behaviour, it should also prove informative and useful for anyone wishing to learn more about groups and how they function. The book is addressed to students or readers directly, and encourages them to pay close attention to what is happening in their own class or group, and to link these experiences to theories about groups and research in this field.

Throughout the text I concentrate on an *interactive* approach to the reader. By this I mean that the reader is invited to consider along with me (through the use of exercises and Case studies) many of the issues raised in the book. There are over fifty exercises included overall, and many of these require that the reader/participant should actually experience some of the impressions and feelings that group members are likely to have at key stages in the life of a group. This kind of experiential learning is sometimes disconcerting and challenging for students of group counselling, but is nonetheless an integral part of developing insight and skills. Some of the exercises are addressed specifically to groupwork trainers, since it is they who have responsibility for organising programmes in a way that is safe and suitable for their own particular groups.

In writing the Case studies I have included much of my own experiences in groups. Also included is material gleaned from the experiences of other group facilitators, trainers, group participants and students on various courses, all of whom gave me permission to use the information supplied. My method of using this kind of material is to work on it creatively, so that all identifying details are changed or altered, while still retaining a central idea or focus necessary for illustrative purposes.

This creative approach is important from the point of view of confidentiality, because it ensures that client anonymity is protected throughout.

Though the main emphasis in the book is on group counselling skills and theory, the first chapter deals with more general theories about different groups and how these have evolved. It seems to me important to include these general aspects since they have a direct bearing on our present knowledge about group dynamics and processes. The difference between a large group and a small one is a case in point here. We know that a large group may be very creative, for example, but it is less likely than a small one to generate a feeling of belonging among members. Additionally, information about homogeneous and heterogeneous groups and how these differ is useful, because it tells us a great deal about the advantages and disadvantages of certain group compositions. The second chapter deals with the practical aspects of planning a group in a variety of settings, including health care, the community and counselling. This means that the reader is encouraged to translate some of the theories discussed in the first chapter into a more practical framework, and to consider all the attendant minutiae such as practical planning entails. For anyone intending to become involved in group counselling, a sound understanding of theory is a vital component of training and should always underpin practice and participation in groups. Though learning through experience is rightly emphasised (in my view) by groupwork trainers, the need to understand accompanying theory is not always given the attention it deserves. My intention in writing this book is to bring these two elements of theory and learning through experience together, and in doing so, to address what I perceive as an imbalance of focus sometimes present in groupwork training. I would further suggest that all students of groupwork, especially those at post-graduate level, read as much as possible about the subject, including academic journals and papers that highlight recent research and experience in groups.

In the course of the book I return again and again to the subject of leadership in groups. This is because many of the students or readers using a book like this will be required to work in that capacity at some stage in the future. It goes without saying that the role of leader is an immensely important one, with its own particular pressures and demands. Because of these pressures and demands, prospective leaders need as many opportunities as possible to think about, experience, and discuss every aspect of the leader's role and function. Chapter five looks specifically at the group leader's role, and discusses the different ways group members are likely to respond to different leaders and their styles. The term 'leader' is also discussed at length in this chapter; this is because there are now so many titles used to designate this role, and students often find these variations confusing. When referring to the leader in the text, I often use the different titles interchangeably, depending on the context of the reference and the Case study or work I am describing. More than anything else, however, I am concerned to highlight the responsibilities that all group leaders have. These responsibilities include ensuring that group practice is based on respect for members, and a dedication to increasing self-awareness, supervision, further training and personal therapy when needed.

The psychological dangers of group participation are also highlighted in the text, but these are discussed in the context in which they are likely to occur, and not as separate issues. In addition, many other ethical issues are discussed in context throughout the book, though some of these, confidentiality, for example, merit special attention and are addressed in more detail in chapter ten. Certain exercises in the book ask students to engage in some degree of self-disclosure. However, when this level of involvement is requested, I suggest that group trainers make their own decision about the suitability of self-disclosure for their particular students or participants. I do this because what is right for one group at a particular time, may not necessarily be right for another at a different stage of development or learning, and only those in very close contact with group participants are fully aware of such variables. Overall, however, I do think that students in an experiential group (as any good training group should be) need to disclose some of their responses, at least, to what is actually happening in the group. If they are not encouraged to do this, they can't possibly learn anything useful. They certainly won't get any feel of what it might be like for clients in groups to make themselves vulnerable in this way. This does not mean that students are asked to disclose their personal problems; a learning group is not a therapy group, and students are not asked to become clients in group counselling.

In addition to the basic skills and theory that constitute the foundation of all groupwork practice, this text looks at the principal theoretical approaches to counselling and therapy, and considers how these have been incorporated into groupwork practice. These theoretical approaches include the broad categories of Psychodynamic, Humanistic and Cognitive-Behavioural. The concepts, skills and techniques that are integral to individual theories are described, and their merits or usefulness discussed. Students are encouraged to look at the advantages and disadvantages of different influences in group counselling, and to assess their therapeutic effect in specific situations and with specific group members.

USE OF LANGUAGE

As far as possible, I have tried to ensure that the language of the book is both inclusive and respectful of all groups and the various members who participate in them. This respect for diversity is a cornerstone of all therapeutic groupwork, and is one of the first principles that students starting on courses should learn. We all have experience of belonging to different groups throughout our lives, including family, school, friendships and social groups. What we often lack, however, is a true understanding of, and respect for, the other people we encounter in some of these groups. Through study of group theory and practice (in particular theory and practice as it applies to counselling and therapy groups) it is possible to increase our own self-awareness and knowledge, and in doing so, to learn more about other people and their experiences.

I would like to add one final word about my use of terminology when I refer to groups and the people involved with them. The words counsellor and therapist are used interchangeably throughout the text, since any distinction between them is now regarded minimal or even irrelevant. Other titles, including facilitator, leader and groupworker are used in a similar way, though obviously these designations are not as precise as the terms group-counsellor or therapist. However, I hope that the context in which all these words are used will show that they are relevant and suitably descriptive.

1

Groups: What they are and how they have evolved

INTRODUCTION

This chapter is about the way group study has developed over time. It is also about various group types, their composition and the many functions and purposes which they serve. Although the chapter opens with some observations and questions about groups in general, a more specific focus is placed on those groups which are dedicated to therapeutic outcomes. Special emphasis will also be given to aspects of early research in the field of group theory and practice. Throughout this and other chapters, you will be encouraged to look at your own experiences as a group member, and to consider the ways in which these experiences have influenced your assumptions, beliefs and expectations about groups generally.

YOUR OWN EXPERIENCE

You may be currently part of a training group, which is specifically concerned with the study of therapeutic groupwork. If this is the case you are ideally placed to focus on, and discuss, your own experiences and progress within the group, and to transfer what you have learned to other groups outside. Your own experiences in groups is undoubtedly the best way of seeing, hearing, feeling, responding to and ultimately understanding what actually happens when a number of people assemble together for a period of time. This kind of process observation is not something which comes naturally to any of us. It requires discipline and a willingness to learn in a completely different way. Most of us expect to access and absorb information via theoretical input, either through lectures, reading or both. Experiential learning is different, and more effective in relation to groups because it places the emphasis on what is taking place, *as it takes place.* In order to facilitate and complement this method of learning it is a good idea to keep a reflective journal in which to record your impressions and experiences as they unfold. It is also important to link groupwork theory to practice, and throughout this and subsequent chapters you should consider and discuss the theories outlined. If you are not currently part of a training group, you can still develop aware-ness of groups by paying closer attention to those you are already in. All groups, regardless of their composition, type and purpose, have many characteristics in common. It is these gener-al or common elements which we are concerned to initially highlight in this chapter. Later in this first section we shall also look at, and discuss, specific groups and how they have evolved, with particular emphasis on their defining characteristics and applications.

HOW WE KNOW A GROUP IS A GROUP

Think of any group you are currently part of and consider its function and purpose. Was your group set up deliberately with a specific project in mind, or did group members come together in a random fashion with no precise objectives or intentions? What size is your group and how well do members interact? Consider how much members of your group have in common. Do you have shared ideas, goals, tasks or therapeutic aims?

When discussing groups it is usual for writers to offer several defining characteristics which they believe to be necessary before a group can really be called a group. Included in this list of factors are definitions relating to size; quality of interaction; relationship between group members; the existence of common goals and the awareness of all group members that they are, in fact, valued members of that particular group. In his definition of what he calls the 'good group spirit' Bion (1999:25) lists several qualities, including common purpose, recog-nition by members of group boundaries, and a minimum size of three members to describe what he means. Douglas (1995:14) points to a rather more obvious factor in his definition of what a group is. 'The really significant' element is, in his view, that a number of people are together ' in close proximity' for a certain period of time. If we consider this last point first it becomes clear that it poses some questions of its own, the first of which relates to group size. How many people need to come together before they can be called a group? Although most researchers do now tend to be flexible in their definitions of group size, it is worth looking more closely at this particular factor in order to determine its influence on groups generally.

EXERCISE 1

GROUP SIZE
Time: 40 mins.

Working individually, write a list of the groups to which you currently belong. This list might include some of the following:

◆ Social groups

◆ Work groups

◆ Training groups

Consider the size of each group and note the ways in which this factor affects or influences group members and the way they relate to each other. There are, of course, many other elements that affect group communication apart from size, and these will be discussed later. However, in this exercise try to focus on the number of group members in each category and say what effect this has on the group overall. If you are currently part of a training group share your ideas with other members. Since being part of a group is a learning experience in itself, a useful extension to this exercise is to discuss the influence and significance of your training group size, with particular reference to the way in which this factor affected communication when you first came together. Then read the following discussion of group size and compare your actual experiences with the theory outlined.

THE SMALL GROUP

It is usual to define a small group as one whose numbers are three or more and with an upper limit of perhaps ten or twelve. Two people could not be said to constitute a group since their relationship is to each other only. With three or more people, however, there is a change in the structure and nature of communication. Instead of the **personal** quality that exists in the dyadic relationship, a group of three or more will establish what Bion (1999) calls 'interpersonal' relationships. What this means is that the relationship permutations within a group of three or more become more complex, and interactive potential is increased. Small groups have several important advantages over larger groups, including an increased likelihood, which Ettin (1999) highlights, that all members will be directly and actively involved. On the other hand, there may be limited creative potential in a very small group of say three to five, since fewer people are present to generate ideas. The size of a group does, of course, depend on its function and purpose, and a group with a specific complex task might well function at optimum level with a small number of members because in that situation there is less chance of procedural or coordination problems arising. In addition, a therapy group with a small number of people may also prove effective, since vulnerable members especially, may feel less inhibited or constrained about disclosing personal details and interacting generally with others present. In a small group some members may leave, however, and apart from the threat posed to the group's survival when this happens, there is the added disadvantage that group members are likely to be demoralized when they see their numbers dwindle.

THE LARGE GROUP

Any group over twenty could certainly be considered large, and most researchers would agree that anything over thirty begins to resemble a crowd rather than a group. When twenty or more people are present together there is obviously a great deal of creativity and talent available as well. A large group of people can generate numerous and various ideas, and if one or two people leave, the group can continue without too much disruption. Training and seminar groups are often conducted in large numbers, and although closeness among members is possible in these contexts, individual relationships are usually secondary to the agenda set for the group. In very large groups, cliques and sub-groups may form; organizational and coordination problems also tend to increase, and motivation may be difficult to sustain when people perceive themselves as anonymous or insignificant within the group.

On a purely practical level, group members may feel inhibited about contributing verbally in a large group. This is an important point to remember in relation to counselling and therapy groups where there is an emphasis on interaction, sharing of experiences and the kind of intimate communication which is just not possible when members are overwhelmed by sheer numbers. A large therapy group also presents difficulties for leaders or facilitators since it is more difficult to give individual members the support they may need in order to work through problems. However, Yalom (1995) suggests that since one or two members of any therapy group are likely to drop out early on, it is best to start with a group slightly larger than the preferred size in order to redress this attrition. The preferred size for a therapy or counselling group is obviously lower than for a training or seminar group, largely because of the interpersonal interaction the former necessitates.

Many groups do, in fact, of necessity operate with large numbers. Self-help groups are a case in point, and many of these start off with a membership of twenty or more. Equal access is an important principle of self-help groups, and for this reason initial membership may be substantial. Aside from the disadvantages of large group numbers already noted, there is the added factor of the increased communication problem, along with the concomitant difficulty of reaching consensus or agreement. Group members may take much longer to achieve objectives, so the overall efficiency of the group is impaired. The following Case study illustrates this last point.

CASE STUDY: LORRAINE

Lorraine described how she joined a self-help group because she had been addicted to prescribed tranquilizers for a year. There were twenty-two people, many of them drawn from fairly distant surrounding areas, at the first meeting she attended. Most of these people had belonged to the group for months before Lorraine joined. Some members had been off tranquilizers for substantial periods, while others were just beginning the difficult process. One of the meetings was taken up with a lengthy discussion about ways to educate the public about the issue of tranquilizer addiction. Lorraine felts strongly that she did not receive the initial recognition or support that she needed and expected as a new member. In addition, she could see that the discussion was unlikely to be productive for some time, because so many people were involved in it and a consensus was difficult to reach. There were certainly plenty of ideas being voiced, but Lorraine was aware that there were definite communication and linking problems within the group. She was also aware that because of the lack of effective coordination, some members were becoming disillusioned and disempowered. Though decisions were eventually made at a future meeting, it was some time before an informal leader emerged in the group who was able to encourage some structure and organization.

EXERCISE 2

GROUP SIZE

Time: 60 mins (30 mins for each group discussion).

This exercise is intended for use by group trainers or leaders. Its purpose is to consider the effect of group size on the way people participate in group discussion. To begin with, select a topic for discussion. The following is a selection of ideas, though you may be aware of topics that are more suitable for your particular group.

◆ What is the most effective way of encouraging young people to take an interest in the environment?

◆ What is the most effective way of tackling crime in the community?

◆ How can parents help their children to develop emotional intelligence?

◆ How can the work environment be made more family friendly?

Give the whole group the topic that you have chosen for discussion. Observe the group, and afterwards ask each person to complete the following evaluation in writing:

Evaluation

Please underline your response to the following statements

1 I felt involved in the discussion.   Yes / No

2 I was consulted by other group members.   Yes / No

3 My opinions were valued by other group members.   Yes / No

4 I listened carefully to the opinions of other group members.   Yes / No

5 I was happy about any decisions which were taken by the group.   Yes / No

6 Our group worked well together.   Yes / No

When the group has completed the task, divide it into two smaller groups. Ask each small group to discuss a different topic. When they have done this, ask members to evaluate the second group experience. Afterwards, compare the two sets of evaluations and discuss these with the whole group. Were there any significant differences between experiences in the large and small groups?

THE OPEN GROUP

An open group is one that members can join or leave at any time. In fact, membership may be constantly changing in the open group, with some people joining and others leaving on a fairly regular basis. Additionally, the life span of the group itself may be open ended with no specific time limit for its operation or existence. Open groups are commonly used when the purpose is self-help, and in this context the word 'open' often has additional meaning. It may be, for example, that the group is open to everyone in a specific area, regardless of numbers. If the condition or issue that the group is addressing is a rare or uncommon one, the group may even be open to everyone nationwide. As we noted earlier in this chapter, self-help groups are concerned not to exclude anyone on grounds of ethnic background, race or religion. Self-help groups are also open in the sense that not all members will necessarily attend all meetings. This may be because of other commitments such as caring for dependents, or it may hinge on transport or other practical difficulties.

Some difficulties exist when a group is open ended and different members routinely join or leave. In particular, it is obviously harder to nurture and sustain a sense of continuity when participation is as fluid as this. The worker or leader of an ever-changing group has the added task of introducing new members and providing information for them, while simultaneously ensuring that existing members are not subjected to excessive disruption. New members may also experience difficulty in becoming integrated into the group. Predictability, too, tends to diminish in an open group, and this may have an unsettling effect on group members. Discussion may become erratic, less focused and superficial when members are coming and going. Brandler & Roman (1999) suggest that this unpredictability and disruption can be decreased when the leader treats each open group session as a total, discrete experience. In other words, each session is seen as having a beginning, middle and an end, with 'well defined, achievable goals for each session' Brandler & Roman (1999:249).

Groups that are conducted in a hospital, clinic or health centre setting frequently operate a fast turnover. This is because of the pressure to cater for the needs of other clients or patients. A group which is catering for many patients on a long-term basis is likely to be open to new members when they need it. One example is a group for patients recovering from heart surgery. In a group like this patients will recover and leave, while others who have just had surgery will join. A counselling or therapy group with open membership has its own special problems, since self-disclosure is a routine element in this setting. It is obviously more difficult for vulnerable members to feel safe about this, in a context of changing, unpredictable membership.

THE CLOSED GROUP

A closed group is made up of members who start and finish together. In addition, the closed group may last for a specific number of sessions, so that members know exactly when sessions will start and when they will end. Dates are set in advance, though occasionally the time span may be indefinite. In common with open groups, closed groups have some disadvantages. The first and most obvious of these is that the closed group may become stale and conformist, lacking in creativity and new ideas. The intimacy and cohesiveness, which are the strengths of a closed group, can also lead to resistance to change or innovation. On the other hand, the stability and predictability that are also characteristic of the closed group can facilitate group cohesion. The task for the leader is less complicated when the group is closed, since there is less need to prepare and introduce new members on an ongoing basis. When group membership is consistent there is the added advantage that any difficulties, problems or conflicts that arise, can be adequately addressed, resolved and understood. In an open group, such issues are often not dealt with effectively. The following Case study illustrates several of the points just made in relation to closed groups.

CASE STUDY: THE CLOSED GROUP

Six group facilitators, working within a radius of about fifty miles, decided to get together to form their own support group. The idea had first been discussed between two members of the group who were friends. After some consideration they decided to contact the other four, and a first meeting was arranged. At this first meeting, aims and objectives for the group were discussed in some detail. A group contract was agreed and other practical details were considered. One member (Tony) suggested that the group should be kept open to allow other interested members to join. He was also keen to let as many potential members as possible know about the group's existence. Another member felt that the group should remain closed. These differing viewpoints were aired at length, until a final decision was made by the group to allow another two new members to join at the next meeting. During that second meeting it was necessary to reiterate much of what had been said at the previous meeting. The composition of the group had changed because of the new additions, but much of the change was positive, lively and creative. When a final decision was taken to restrict the group to its present membership of eight, there were no dissenting voices. Some time later others applied to join the group, but it remained closed. When, over a period of a year, two members left, both to take up work in different areas, the remaining group members became aware of their reduced creativity, as well as their resistance to change and lack of stimulation. They were also aware that they had become conformist and exclusive. At this stage they decided to re-think their original policy and to invite other members to join. Adding new members meant, of course, that events were less predictable, and some degree of cohesiveness and intimacy was lost. However, these deficits were evened out in the long term once a period of necessary disruption had passed.

HOMOGENEOUS AND HETEROGENEOUS GROUPS

The terms homogeneous and heterogeneous are often used in relation to group composition. When a group is described as homogeneous it implies that members have a common characteristic, or that they share the same difficulties or problems. For example, self-help and support groups are homogeneous in the sense that all members have similar concerns. Groups designed to help people with specific conditions like depression, anxiety, phobias, alcohol dependency or substance abuse are also homogeneous. People who share a particular experience often participate in this type of group. These experiences may include divorce, sexual abuse in childhood, bereavement, illness, bullying, single parenthood and redundancy. Groups are sometimes gender homogeneous: women's groups fit into this category, as do groups which are designed to address men's issues. A group that is assigned a common task can also be described as homogeneous. In addition, there are groups whose members share a particular hobby, interest or purpose.

An advantage of homogeneous groups is that attention can be given to the stated problem, issue or experience members have in common. A strong group bond may be formed when problems, experiences, values or personal traits are the same. Yalom (1995) suggests that homogeneous groups tend to be more cohesive, supportive, well attended and less likely to experience conflict than other groups which are more diverse. On the negative side, however, homogeneous groups may function at a shallow level with less likelihood that members will engage in the kind of challenging work which leads to insight and significant change.

A group described as heterogeneous is one which is diverse in character, composition or membership. The group may be mixed in terms of age, gender, culture and sexual orientation, for example. Counselling and therapy groups are often heterogeneous in membership and composition. This is because they frequently include people with a variety of problems or issues to be addressed. Such groups tend to comprise both men and women, often with differing sexual orientations. The diversity of perspectives, which is an intrinsic strength of the heterogeneous group, mirrors the diversity that exists in society as a whole. On one level

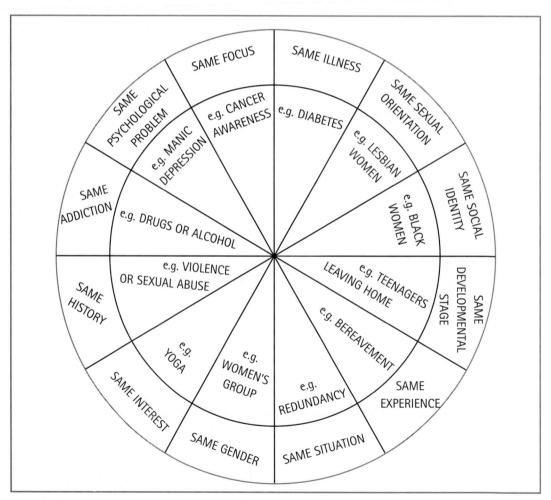

Fig. 1.1 Homogeneous groups

this means that group members are given the opportunity to develop greater awareness of themselves and others through exposure to differing view points and experiences, and through participation in assorted interactional styles. These experiences offer a more comprehensive form of learning to group participants, and the tendency, which is always present in the homogeneous group, to focus exclusively on problems or symptoms is diminished when membership is mixed. On another level, the diversity that exists in the heterogeneous group may work against the development of group cohesion, although this can change if fixed ideas and preconceptions held by individual members are challenged through contact with others in the group. However, if group members are very vulnerable because of either trauma or serious psychological illness, they are unlikely to prosper in a very mixed group. Such a setting might prove too challenging for susceptible clients. In a later chapter we shall discuss the concept of group cohesion, along with the other factors that work for and against it.

DIFFERENT GROUPS: HOW THEY EVOLVED

There are many different kinds of groups, including those that occur naturally in the life cycle of each individual. We know that people have always gravitated towards group inclusion, and it is easy to see how in our distant ancestral past this was a necessary strategy for survival. In a later chapter we shall consider the therapeutic value of groups, and discuss the reasons that people are attracted to them. In this section the objective is to look at different groups, especially those that have been deliberately created for a specific purpose, and to consider how these have evolved.

Aside from the fact that groups occur naturally in the life cycle of each individual, they are also part of the overall social structure. Thus, the family, in all its traditional and changing forms, could be included in this category. Since people have always sought to be included in groups, it seems clear that certain benefits can be gained from group membership. But despite long standing human reliance on groups, systematic interest and research into all aspects of groupwork is, as Baron et al., (1996) point out, fairly recent. At the beginning of the 20th century, however, key areas of interest in groups were beginning to emerge. An example of this interest was shown in the work of Joseph Pratt, a physician who lived and practised in the USA. In 1905 he treated patients who suffered from tuberculosis in groups so that they could share information, personal experiences and support. One of Pratt's most important findings was that group membership was in itself beneficial for his patients. They seemed to derive encouragement from contact with other people whose condition was the same as their own. From 1906 onwards, Pratt published several papers describing his work with patients in groups. The ideas and experiences described in these seminal works are fundamentally important in relation to future developments in therapeutic groupwork.

Another significant milestone in the evolution of groups as a specific area of interest and study was the establishment of Alcoholics Anonymous in Ohio in 1935. Alcoholics Anonymous is perhaps the best known of all the self-help groups. In common with Pratt's patients, its first members found that support and help was most readily available from others with the same problem. Mutual respect and equality were, and still are, fundamental principles of this and other self-help groups. These and other factors will be discussed in more detail later in the chapter.

Moreno

In 1921, Jacob Levy Moreno, a psychiatrist who lived and worked in Vienna, made further important contributions to early groupwork theory and practice. Moreno, who was interested in theatre and strongly influenced by it, was the founder of Psychodrama, a method of group therapy based on the presentation of past traumatic events within a safe and supportive environment. It is widely believed that Moreno coined the term 'group therapy' when he described the work that he was doing. Moreno proposed that people with emotional difficulties were helped most when they were given the opportunity to re-experience or repeat past traumatic events in a way that facilitated greater understanding of them. Once understanding was achieved, group members could then reintegrate these past events in a more positive form. In 1945, Moreno emigrated to the USA where he continued his work and set up the Moreno Institute. He worked at the Mount Sinai hospital in New York, and during the late twenties demonstrated his group methods. Later he practised his method of psychodrama at St. Elizabeth's hospital in Washington DC. In addition to his practical work Moreno wrote numerous articles about groups, edited magazines and contributed a great deal to the terminology, practice and understanding of group therapy. Ettin (1999) highlights Moreno's contribution to the language of groupwork with special reference to the terms group therapy, encounter, interpersonal communication, group psychotherapy and group catharsis.

Freud

Though many of the ideas which are now considered central to groupwork theory and practice (including the theories of unconscious motivation and transference, for example) are based on the work of Sigmund Freud, his name is not always automatically linked with the development of groupwork. However, he is certainly an integral part of its evolution, not least because he contributed, through his writing, many important concepts linking psychoanalytic theory to group phenomena. His paper, *Group Psychology and the Analysis of the Ego*, published in 1922, outlines these ideas and indicates that he was in no doubt about the therapeutic value of groups. Many of these concepts will be discussed in a later chapter, along with other Freudian and psychodynamic ideas relating to groupwork theory and practice.

Adler

Alfred Adler, a contemporary of Freud, was greatly interested in groups, especially the family group. According to Adler, social interest is nurtured within the family and it is in the context of social interest that people learn to relate, in unselfish ways, towards others. Adler used groups for teaching and educative purposes: he also used this medium when he worked in the field of child guidance. His emphasis was always on relationships, since he believed that human behaviour could only be fully understood in a social context. Groups were, in his view, ideally suited to the development of his particular approach; they also proved to be the ideal environment for psychotherapy since they fostered cooperation, established trust and eliminated emotional isolation.

Training groups

During and after the Second World War, a social psychologist called Kurt Lewin was responsible for setting up the first Training Groups (T-groups) in America. These were taken into industry, schools and many other organizations, in order to facilitate, through discussion and role play, the development of social and interpersonal skills among student and working group members. In common with many other groupwork researchers Lewin found that group members derived personal benefits from their participation in groups, especially when constructive feedback was given, even though his original objective had not focused specifically on this area. Lewin's original intention had been to encourage communication, reduce racial tension, and consider issues relating to leadership and change. However, Lewin was also interested in the way in which the group influences individuals, as well as the way in which groups could actually be used to change individual attitudes. Influence processes are, as Arrow et.al., (2000) point out, a continuing source of interest to groupwork researchers, though they add that the early emphasis on majority influence has now been extended to include minority influence processes as well.

Task groups

Groups that are set up specifically to perform tasks are usually in response to a particular need and to address a particular problem. When compared with other areas of groupwork, a substantial amount of research has been conducted into this aspect of group theory, some of it pre-dating research in other areas. One example is the work carried out by Norman Triplett an American psychologist who, in 1898, discovered that social conditions were often a help to task performance. Triplett's research indicated that a group of people, with a specific task, were inclined to complete it with alacrity when they were in the presence of, or in competition with, other groups of people. This effect is known as Social Facilitation and it is frequently observed in many group situations. Later researchers, Zajonc (1965) for example, were concerned to show that social facilitation is not always evident. The nature of the task has some bearing on whether or not it operates, and on easy tasks it is more likely to be evident than on difficult ones. Baron et al, (1996). Thus a group of athletes in a relatively simple running competition might well be encouraged to run faster when observers are present. If the task becomes more complex, a ball game for example, and different responses are needed, social facilitation becomes less marked.

Task groups are often set up to work on specific projects like research, community plans, or development initiatives. Many of these tasks are complex, but when group members are aware of the goals from the outset, a high level of commitment to achieving them is usually present. However, it is interesting to speculate on the concept of social facilitation in relation to such groups, and to look at the progress they are likely to make when onlookers are present, or when competition from other groups is a factor for them. The following Case study highlights some of these points.

CASE STUDY: THE TASK GROUP

A group of sixteen students on a training course were asked to complete a group task. Twelve of the students were given a specific exercise to do, while the other four were asked to observe (with the aid of a video camera) what happened. The actual exercise was quite straightforward: the twelve were told that £100 was available to spend on lecture room equipment. They were also told that they must decide as a group how this money should be allocated. Within the allocated period of time (thirty minutes) the group of twelve came to an agreement about what items should be bought. However, the agreement was not reached without occasional dissent and friction among group members. When the task was finished both groups were asked for feedback on their impressions. Almost unanimously the group of twelve students said they had not been helped by the scrutiny of the other four students. In discussion they expressed the view that their task would have been easier if they had been allowed to get on with it unobserved. The four student observers were also aware that their contribution had not been helpful. Everyone agreed that the task required concentration, though it was not exceptionally difficult. If the task had been very easy though, the twelve students might well have been encouraged by the presence of spectators, especially if they were supportive.

It is important to emphasize that this Case study does not prove or disprove any of the theoretical points discussed in relation to task groups. What it does show is that task groups, like all other groups are different and complex. There are other factors apart from the presence or absence of onlookers, at work in the groups. In the task group just described the members may have been on video camera for the first time. Such an experience is in itself inhibiting. Since video practice is often an integral part of groupwork training, you might have an opportunity to try your own experiment in social facilitation. Why should social facilitation work on some tasks and not on others? As Baron et al. (1996) suggest, nothing is straightforward in this area of research. In some instances people are helped when others are around, while in other instances (the Case study task group, for example) the performance of the group is impaired when others are present.

Contributions in Britain: Bion and Foulkes

In Britain, early contributors to the field of groupwork included W. R. Bion and S. H. Foulkes. Both responded to the needs of World War Two service personnel by providing group therapy for soldiers who had been traumatized in action. Group methods of treating psychological problems proliferated during and after the war, not just in Britain but in America as well.

Experiences in Groups and other Papers (1961/1999) is perhaps Bion's best-known study of groups. Although he had been involved in much earlier research, Bion did not, in fact, publish his work until 1961, as indicated above. His reason for delaying publication concerned the ongoing nature of his work with groups, and his reluctance to publish material that might need to be amended or changed in the light of later experience. In his writing Bion combines elements of psychoanalysis with group dynamics and discusses the unconscious elements which are present in every group. Another important dimension of Bion's work is his focus on the anxiety that is often generated in groups, and the ways in which members respond to this through a variety of strategies including what he described as basic assumptions. These basic assumptions are unconscious ideas which members of the group share, at certain times, about their purpose and aims within the group. In describing these unconscious ideas Bion refers to them as group mentalities, which are, he says, 'the unanimous expression of the will of the group' Bion (1999:65). Although we shall be discussing unconscious aspects of group life in more detail later, it is worth looking more closely at Bion's basic assumption model in this chapter since he was, in fact, one of the first people to record observations of group behaviour.

Basic Assumptions

The first of Bion's observations in relation to basic assumptions is that when two people in a group become involved in a discussion, other members of the group assume that the relationship is intimate. This assumption of intimacy indicates an underlying, unconscious preoccupation with reproduction and group survival. When groups operate in this mode they are not addressing their proper task, which in Bion's case is the study of the group itself and the processes unfolding within it. Study of group process is an intrinsic part of group therapy because it enables people to become aware of how they, and others, interact. However, it is often uncomfortable for individual members to engage in and sustain this kind of work. There is, therefore, an impulse to avoid it and to engage in other activities. The basic assumption (shown in pairing behaviour) is that the purpose of the group is an atavistic one, relating to survival and reproduction. When pairing behaviour occurs members are not consciously thinking about survival and reproduction, however. The mentality and behaviour described by Bion is taking place at an unconscious level. In a group whose members break up into pairs, therapeutic aims are lost, at least temporarily. This kind of innate response is easier to understand when you consider that the group would indeed have been more important than the individual (in terms of survival) to our distant ancestors.

The second basic assumption which Bion refers to is described as fight or flight. When groups resort to this mode of functioning they are, once again, adopting a procedure which is meant to aid survival and self-preservation. When in fight or flight the group acts as if the whole purpose of meeting is to preserve the group. The emotional difficulties of group members are therefore subordinate to the greater task of keeping the group together. This subordination of the individual's psychological needs has significant implications for therapy groups in particular. Some of these points will be taken up in later chapters when we look at therapy and counselling groups in more depth. Once again Bion links the group's fight or flight behaviour to their basic assumption about how groups should really function.

A strong leader is seen as essential, one who would visibly lead the group to fight or flee when necessary. But a leader who encourages people to address their psychological difficulties instead is seen as inadequate. The group response to the new kind of leader can take various forms, including aggression and hostility. A group in flight may also tell jokes or anecdotes, or indeed any other behaviour which will ward off anxiety. Again it is possible to link these responses to those which would have been appropriate at a much earlier stage of human history.

In describing the third basic assumption (dependence) Bion recounts his own experiences with a group to illustrate it. During his early professional practice he was asked to 'take' a therapeutic group. Before long he was aware that the group members expected, or assumed, that he would conduct the group in a formal way, rather like a seminar or lecture. This was in spite of the fact that they knew from the outset their task was to study their own group and the tensions within it. When it became obvious that Bion, as leader, would not act in a formal or didactic way an alternative leader emerged in the group, although later he was discarded too. What the group seemed to be looking for was a strong leader with whom they could feel safe, and on whom they could depend. In this mode of functioning the welfare of the individual (which would be addressed in a therapy group) is once again regarded as secondary to the survival of the group. This particular mentality is often evident in the early stages of group life when tensions are frequently high. An all-powerful leader who will take care of everyone, and who will take all the initiatives, is almost invariably sought when group members first come together. Contributions made by the leader are regarded as almost infallible, and certainly of more weight and value than contributions made by anyone else. Fortunately, this is a transient stage in group life and members gradually gain in confidence and self-responsibility. Later on, however, groups can move back into a dependent mentality, especially when they feel insecure or tense.

Foulkes

Like Bion, Foulkes was a psychoanalyst interested in individuals in the group context. In fact, Foulkes was involved in the foundation of the Group Analytic Society (1950) and later the Institute of Group Analysis (1971) to provide training for others interested in groupwork. Having trained in Germany, Foulkes came to England in 1933. He also introduced ideas derived from psychoanalysis to illuminate group processes, including the concepts of unconscious motivation, transference and free association. When we come to discuss transference later in the book you will see how important this concept is in relation to groups and the way individual members form relationships, not just with the leader, but with each other as well. In Foulkes' view, members of a group form relationships and behave in ways which can only really be understood in the context of the group as a whole intact system. As we shall see later, this approach is at variance with some other approaches to, and models of groupwork which focus on the individual in the group acting in ways which can, in fact, be interpreted from an individual viewpoint.

The Third Force

During the 1960s developments in groupwork were continuing to spread in America. This proliferation of different groups was directly linked to the success of training groups or T-groups that were discussed earlier in this chapter. The encounter, sensitivity and personal growth group movements started in California and then spread to various parts of the USA before coming to Britain. A central focus of these new groups was the potential for personal development and awareness, which they seemed to offer. Those psychologists, including Carl Rogers, who were part of the Humanistic movement, were aware of the therapeutic benefits of group participation. Since Rogers' person centred approach to psychology stressed self-actualization and personal growth, groups seemed to be ideally suited to their achievement. Open and honest expression of feelings within an empathic, non-judgmental environment, was an integral part of this kind of group experience. In addition, release of strong, often pent up feeling was encouraged and facilitated. A point of similarity between the training groups pioneered by Lewin and the Humanistic movement in groupwork is the degree to which both enhanced social and communication skills. This was largely because of the feedback which group members gave one another. It is important to emphasize here that membership of encounter and other related groups was voluntary, and people who joined them would not necessarily have considered themselves to be in need of therapy or counselling. Other well-known names in the Humanistic movement include Abraham Maslow, Fritz Perls, Eric Fromm and Rollo May. Fritz Perls, the founder of Gestalt therapy, was particularly interested in the expression of individual feelings in the group, and the use of verbal and non-verbal language. The experience of the here and now was, and is, of central importance in the Gestalt approach to groupwork, so too is the creation of an environment conducive to experimentation and creativity.

Eric Berne, another important contributor to groupwork theory and practice, founded his own approach called transactional analysis. Although this particular model of therapy is often conducted on an individual basis, it is more commonly used in a group context. Berne, who had gained a great deal of groupwork experience while working as a psychiatrist in the United States Army Corps in the 1940s, believed that most problems could be addressed more effectively in groups. He took the view that the group format lends itself to the identification of communication difficulties and the analysis of faulty *transactions* or interactions between people. Berne had trained as a psychoanalyst, so he was well acquainted with the Freudian perspective when helping people with problems. Such a perspective tells us a lot about the way people develop as individuals, and about the psychological basis of adult difficulties. However, Berne was increasingly aware that information about the difficulties people have is more readily discernible in groups. Transactional analysis is, in itself, a method of communication. Its uniqueness lies in the fact that it teaches group members to become aware of different interactional styles, and concurrently group members can also learn to identify the dynamics underlying their ways of relating to others. Later in the book we shall discuss Berne's contribution more fully.

Other contributions

It would be impossible, within the scope of one chapter, to describe all the groupwork approaches that have evolved since the beginning of the 20th century. There are many prominent names associated with later and continuing developments in this area, and these will be referred to at specific and appropriate stages throughout the book. In addition, contributors who have not been directly involved in groupwork studies, but who have, nonetheless, contributed to our understanding of group theory and practice, will also be discussed in the appropriate context. Included in this last group are psychologists like Bowlby and Winnicott who have introduced various concepts, including theories of human attachment and bonding, which extend our knowledge of how and why people behave as they do in groups.

Self-Help groups

Before we go on to consider the expansion and development of counselling and psychotherapy groups, it is important to discuss the ever increasing use of self-help as a way of coping with a variety of specific problems and illness. We have already seen that self-help groups were in the vanguard of group development generally, and it is because of their position as precursor to other group types, that we need to identify and understand the factors that make them therapeutically effective. Self-help groups, sometimes also referred to as mutual aid groups, are made up of people who share a particular problem, illness, life experience, addiction, injury, adversity, or indeed any other circumstance which is ameliorated through contact and support with others in the same situation. Since self-help groups are run by and for their own members, involvement of professional workers is not necessary for their success. This is not to say that professionals, including social workers, nurses and counsellors, are never associated with self-help initiatives. Many self-help workers are aware that good working relationships with professional people can enhance their efficiency and general profile. A corollary of this is that links with self-help initiatives can be good for professionals too.

However, as Wilson & Myers (1998) point out, developing good links can take a long time, and there may be many difficulties in establishing good relationships between self-help workers and professionals. Some of the difficulties that Wilson & Myres refer to include ignorance (on the part of professionals) about self-help groups generally. In fact, professionals may see these groups as a challenge to their status, expertise or skill. Certain areas of distrust may also exist in relation to the kind of responsibility that self-help workers undertake; some professional workers, may feel that 'amateurs' should not take responsibility for matters of health, publicity or even advice. On the other hand, self-help workers themselves can be suspicious of professional involvement, especially if experience of earlier involvement has not been satisfactory.

One of the factors that make self-help groups particularly effective is the degree to which members feel empowered through association with them. Being an equal player in decision-making processes is, for example, therapeutic in itself. This is especially true when previous experience of illness, trauma or injustice has conditioned group members to feel impotent about dealing with their difficulties. On a much more basic level, contact with people in a similar situation means that self-help members feel, as Pratt's patients mentioned earlier in this chapter felt, less isolated and lonely. Information and experiences can be shared and ways of coping discussed. Communication problems can, of course, arise and this is especially likely when group numbers are large. In the Case study mentioned earlier, we saw that Lorraine didn't feel she received the attention and support she needed in the large group she joined. This example underlines yet another potential difficulty in self-help groups: unless some group members possess good interpersonal skills, there is a possibility that the group culture which develops will not be inclusive and egalitarian in the way that it should be. When some group members have hearing, speech or visual problems, it becomes even more important that effective and inclusive communication is the norm from the outset.

Group counselling and group psychotherapy

Before going on to discuss group counselling, we need to look more closely at the terms often used interchangeably in relation to it. Throughout this chapter, the words *therapy* and *therapeutic* have frequently been used to describe what takes place in groups. The words *counselling* and *psychotherapy* are also applicable to groupwork, and in this (as in many other texts) they are meant to mean the same thing. It is difficult to identify any appreciable differences between these two terms. As Tudor (1999:4) points out, much of the debate seems to centre on 'superficial distinctions' concerning the length of time needed to complete counselling and psychotherapy. According to this distinction, counselling is a short-term approach to helping, while psychotherapy is long term. Another distinction often made is that group counselling tends to be problem solving in nature, while group psychotherapy is directed more towards personality change. This is not a distinction that everyone would agree with, however. After all, the resolution of personal difficulties or problems often leads to an accompanying change in certain aspects of personality. A person with a specific problem like addiction might, for example, experience quite profound changes in disposition and temperament once the addiction has been mastered. The following Case study highlights the kind of long-term change that is possible when problems are tackled and overcome.

CASE STUDY: MARINA

Marina, who had just started a part time job as a clerical assistant at her local hospital, was worried that she would be unable to cope. She had two small children, now at school, but had been at home with them for some years and felt she lacked confidence when working with, and relating to, other adults. Marina had, in fact, been shy all her life, and had always experienced some difficulty in relation to authority figures. Her worry about work, which had started off as a mild preoccupation, grew worse when she was admonished by a senior colleague, for a task incorrectly done. After a while she had difficulty in getting to sleep at night. A knock on effect of the insomnia was anxiety and further worries about her ability to cope at work. Her doctor suggested that she join a local group that had been set up to help people with similar problems. The group was part of a community initiative, and was designed to address the needs of women in particular. The counsellor who led the group was trained in transactional analysis, an approach that we shall look at in more detail in a later chapter. She was able to help Marina identify the underlying cause of her problem in relation to authority figures. She also showed her how her communication with others tended to elicit certain responses from them, which in turn perpetuated Marina's own problems. Over time Marina became more confident and self-assured at work, and in her relationships with people generally.

It can be seen from this Case study that when problems are successfully addressed, overall personality does tend to change in ways that are beneficial and rewarding for the individual. A fundamental component of change is, of course, understanding. In Marina's case, this understanding was achieved when she was encouraged to look at her childhood experience where the source of her communication difficulty was located.

Other distinctions

In addition to the distinctions already mentioned in this section, there are various schools of counselling and psychotherapy, and various lengths of training too. Both terms refer to a form of psychological helping that values, and seeks to identify, each person's innate, and often unrealized, coping abilities and resources. Though both terms refer primarily to work with individuals, they also apply to groupwork. In fact, many models of counselling and psychotherapy, including transactional analysis, for example, appear to work more effectively in groups. Throughout the rest of this text, the terms counselling and psychotherapy will be used interchangeably to describe all therapeutic groupwork, and the inclusive word 'therapy' will be used to denote either.

GROUP THERAPY: THE PEOPLE WHO BENEFIT

People join counselling and psychotherapy groups for many reasons. The problems that prompt them to seek such help often seem intractable, and difficult to understand without support, interaction and communication from other people willing to use the group approach. Though group members are often encouraged, by health personnel, care workers or other professionals, to participate in groupwork, the decision to do so should ultimately belong to the individual member alone. This is because groupwork necessitates a high degree of commitment and some belief in its effectiveness as a way of achieving change. Pressure on reluctant clients or members to participate in groupwork, is likely to have a counter productive effect, leading to alienation, resentment and lack of real involvement. The next Case study highlights this last point.

CASE STUDY: MARK

Mark, who suffered from anorexia nervosa, was admitted to hospital when his weight became dangerously low. Because of the seriousness of his condition he remained as an in-patient for three months. During his stay in hospital Mark put on weight, but the eating regime prescribed for his condition caused him a great deal of stress. He felt that diet was not his real problem, though he did eat the meals provided because there was real pressure on him to do so. In addition to strictly supervised meals, Mark, along with other patients from the eating disorders unit, was involved in group therapy. However, his membership of the group was certainly not voluntary, since all patients were expected to participate as part of their treatment. This mandatory element meant that Mark was never committed to the group, and gained nothing through his association with it. Some time after his discharge from hospital, Mark sought individual counselling. The following is part of an exchange between him and Vince, his counsellor.

Vince: So you spent time in group therapy, but didn't like it?

Mark: I couldn't understand it, or see the point of why I was there.

Vince: You gained nothing from it ...

Mark: Absolutely not a thing.

Vince: But you feel individual counselling will help ...

Mark: Well yes ... I asked to be here. The other thing I felt compelled to join. So I just closed up.

It can be seen from the above example that Mark's group was meant to help a specific group of people. In common with self-help and support groups, therapy groups also address the needs of a very wide spectrum of people. When, in a later chapter, we come to discuss setting up groups, we shall also consider issues relating to composition and purpose in more detail. Meanwhile, the following list includes just some of the therapy or counselling groups that address specific needs. You can probably add others from your own experience of what is available in different areas.

◆ A group for children who have been bereaved
◆ A group for adults suffering from depression
◆ A group for people with alcohol dependence
◆ A group for sexual offenders in prison
◆ A group for men who have been made redundant
◆ A social skills group for itinerant adolescents
◆ A group for refugees who need practical and psychological support
◆ A group for young mothers who experience difficulties in parenting
◆ A group for male prisoners who have problems in relation to anger control
◆ A group for elderly men who have been widowed
◆ A group for young people with learning difficulties
◆ A personal development group for students
◆ A group for carers of mentally ill relatives

◆ A group for people who have been victims of violence

◆ A groups for people with post traumatic stress disorder

In addition to the specific groups referred to in this list, there are, of course, many other groups that are not homogeneous, but are composed of people with many different problems. In fact, as we have noted earlier in this chapter, counselling and therapy groups are often heterogeneous in this way. The relative advantages of both homogeneous and heterogeneous groups have also been highlighted.

One important dimension of group counselling and therapy is the extent members are helped to understand and cope with their own emotional and relationship difficulties. Many of these very common problems stem from early experience, and have their roots within the original group, the family. The therapy group, which in many ways resembles the family, is therefore an ideal forum for exploring and identifying relationship problems. Later in the book we shall consider the unconscious forces at work within groups, and link these to feelings about different family members and their roles.

A significant difference between encounter groups (referred to earlier in the chapter) and psychotherapy and counselling groups, is that the former tends to focus on personal growth and development, while the latter encourages a remedial approach to emotional or relationship problems which are impeding personal growth. We can see the differences, too, which exist between self-help groups, encounter groups and therapy groups. Quite apart from the fact that self-help members set up and run their own groups, very often without any professional involvement, there is also an important difference in terms of aims and objectives. Self-help members share a common bond of experience and seek mutual support, but there is no stated emphasis on personal growth and development as an end in itself, nor is there an intention to engage in remedial therapeutic work. The fact that personal growth and awareness often follow self-help involvement is an added therapeutic bonus. A practical benefit of group counselling and psychotherapy is that many more people can be given attention than is the case with individual therapy. Reduction in cost is another consideration when a number of clients or patients can be helped together. In subsequent chapters, we shall discuss the many other advantages, and some disadvantages of group therapy involvement and membership.

EXERCISE 3

PAST EXPERIENCE
Time: 1 hour.

This is an exercise that trainers or leaders should use with discretion in their own groups. The exercise asks group members to look at aspects of their early life experience, and to consider the effects of these experiences in adulthood. The purpose of the exercise is to highlight the point, made in this chapter, that many of the problems discussed in therapy groups are directly related to childhood events. Members should complete the sentences, and then share what they have written in small groups of

---

SETTING UP A GROUP

Time: 40 mins.

This is an exercise that you should complete as a whole group. You are asked to identify any situation in which groupwork might be relevant or useful. Spend some time initially looking at the different areas where groupwork could be used appropriately. Some ideas include:

◆ A health awareness group for men / women

◆ A group for people with tinnitus or other hearing problems

◆ A group for teenagers who have been bullied at school

◆ A group for carers of elderly relatives

◆ A stress management group

◆ A social skills training group

When you have decided on a particular group decide on a plan of action and preparation for the group. Then discuss the following factors: the need for such a group in your area; the accommodation and resources required; any permission needed; the aims and objectives of the group; whether the group will be closed or open and why; how prospective members will be selected; the kind of leader or facilitator needed; any programmes or methods to be used; the structure of the group including duration; frequency and timing of sessions; recording and evaluation of group purpose; anyone else who needs to be informed or consulted (including professionals, colleagues, relatives, other agencies); preparation of potential group members; and any difficulties likely to be met in any of these or other areas. When you have discussed these factors, ask the question: how much time would be needed realistically to plan for a group in this way?

IS THE GROUP REALLY NEEDED?

In the description given by Marian, the psychiatric nurse, it is clear that she was able to identify the need for groups in certain key areas. This identification of needs was relatively easy in her case, since her professional position gave her special insight into the problems common to a number of people. It may not always be that easy, however, to determine how useful a group might be in serving the needs of people with particular problems or difficulties. In order to evaluate needs successfully it is necessary to have comprehensive general knowledge of the population and its requirements. This is why working within an organization or agency will make identification of needs somewhat easier. On the other hand, since an important consideration in group planning is the amount of support likely to be given by other interested people, it is vital that the organization or agency is in agreement that a need does indeed exist. This is especially true of group planning in a residential context where there may be many different views about the benefits of such an approach for residents. Tudor (1999:147) highlights the point that even when residential managers are supportive of groupwork, they are nevertheless also aware of its potential to disrupt. The need for a group approach should, therefore, be clearly established within the context of the community, and when this is done, agreement about its appropriateness is essential too.

WHAT NEEDS DO GROUP MEMBERS HAVE?

In assessing the need for setting up a group, the needs of prospective members should also be addressed. The suitability of members for group inclusion will be discussed later in the chapter, but in this section we are concerned to clarify any specific practical or personal needs that members might have. Brandler & Roman (1999:115) refer to the cultural needs of ethnic and immigrant groups that should be carefully considered as a part of group planning. There may, for example, be differing cultural views about appropriate body language, self-disclosure, authority and formality, and communication generally. Groupworkers should familiarize themselves with the culture, customs and conventions of the client group they wish to help. Group members may also have needs in relation to disability and access. All client needs should be clearly set out, including those concerning basic practical details like accommodation and the selection of a suitable room for group sessions. Libemann (1991) suggests that a group needs to be conducted in a comfortable, warm and trusting environment if members are to feel sufficiently safe to talk about intimate and confidential matters. Because of this need for an accessible and stable base, consideration during planning should be given to addressing the following points:

◆ Is the room suitable for the number of people? Is it comfortable, heated and adequately furnished?
◆ Are the chairs suitable, and are they the same height? This is important if people are to feel equal in the group.
◆ Can the chairs be placed in a circle so that communication takes place face to face? Once again this is important for reasons of equality in the group.
◆ Is the meeting place located in an area which group members find accessible?
◆ How about accessibility, including toilets and ramps, for people with a physical disability?
◆ Can members find the room in the building, or do they need details of how to get there?
◆ Is privacy assured, and is the area quiet?
◆ Is car parking available, and is it close enough to the entrance for people with disability?
◆ Is the lighting adequate, and are there power points, if needed?
◆ Does the environment meet health and safety standards?
◆ If you have to book the room, can you do so for a series of meetings in advance?
◆ Is privacy assured and is the area quiet and free from interruption?

Finally, in choosing a room for group meetings, Wilson & Myers (1998) suggest that groupworkers need to establish beforehand if there is anything in particular about the chosen location that might cause difficulty or distress for prospective group members.

THE PURPOSE OF THE GROUP

Having established that there is a need for a group, the next aspect of planning concerns its purpose. In the first chapter of this book we looked at different types of groups, including those which are task orientated, those which are social and /or educational, and those with a therapeutic focus. It is the third kind of group that we are concerned with here. Therapy groups also differ a great deal from each other, in terms of their aims and objectives and their individual or specific purpose. However, they do have in common the aim of encouraging personal change in group participants. The degree of personal change that the group hopes to facilitate is another point to be considered, however. In long-term group psychotherapy, significant personal change will be envisaged, whereas in groups of shorter duration relief of particular problems along with some personal change may be the outcome.

If we accept that counselling and therapy groups help people to change, the next point to consider is what it is that people actually wish, or need to change. Often prospective group members are vague, or perplexed about the true nature of their problems, which means that interviewing and selecting members for a group is another essential part of planning. For this reason, it is important to ensure that the counsellor's stated purpose for the group is in accordance with what group members have in mind.

While the purpose of the group should be defined at the outset before the initial meeting takes place, it also needs to be questioned at regular intervals throughout the group's life span. This is because the purpose of the group is never entirely static, but continues to evolve as individual members communicate their needs and provide their own input. Corey (1995:7) suggests that group members should, themselves, decide what their specific goals are. In other words, members should be encouraged to articulate their objectives in terms of what they think they will achieve, contribute or experience as a result of group participation. In addition to difficulties in identifying the nature of personal problems, however, prospective members are also likely to be vague or apprehensive when it comes to articulating objectives or goals. Later in this chapter we shall look at a Case study (Aileen) that emphasizes some of the problems which members might have in this area.

When we look at other characteristics of group counselling we can identify further, more general goals in setting up a group. These characteristics include what Edelwich & Brodsky (1992) refer to as the non-directive, non-didactic, but nevertheless disciplined nature of group counselling. If we consider this description more closely, it becomes clear that the central purpose of any counselling group is the facilitation of personal awareness and empowerment. The development of decision making and problem solving skills are also central to group counselling. Counselling groups may focus on accomplishing tasks too, along with an emphasis on therapeutic work (or homework) that takes place outside the group.

More specific reasons

Many of the reasons given for starting a group, including, for example, the development of personal awareness, are fairly general, and could easily apply to almost any therapy group. Bearing this in mind, it is useful to consider more concrete and specific reasons for initiating such a project. A proposed group for women who had surgery for breast cancer, therefore, might have as its stated purpose some of the following:

◆ To help members express and overcome feelings of fear, apprehension or isolation
◆ To enable members to share information about services and any practical support available
◆ To increase members' knowledge and personal awareness of the condition
◆ To provide an environment in which members can express their experiences of, and feelings about, changed body image

WHAT TYPE OF GROUP WILL IT BE?

In chapter one we looked at several characteristics in relation to groups, including their size, whether they are closed or open, as well as their actual composition (homogeneous or heterogeneous). These characteristics tell us something about group type, and they are also factors that need to be addressed and clarified when a group project is envisaged.

We have already seen that group size has a marked effect on the way members communicate and interact. In large groups there tends to be a greater pool of skills. This increase in skills might work well in a task or problem solving context, but in group counselling there is a danger that some members will be overlooked or unheard. Timid (though needy) group members may effectively conceal themselves if a group consists of more than eight to ten members. On the other hand, dominant group members may seek to control what is happening in the group once numbers exceed the stated eight to ten. In terms of planning, therefore, the optimum number for a counselling group is, ideally, eight. However, those involved in groupwork are too often aware of the pressures exerted on them by agency or organizational demands. Edelwich & Brodsky (1992:6) suggest that in situations like these, one way of coping is to change the focus of the group, so that discussion, education and basic skills training exercises are emphasized in place of group process. Later on in the book we shall look at the subject of group process, and discuss its implications for both leaders and members.

Whether a group is to be homogeneous or heterogeneous in composition depends on the analysis of needs that we referred to earlier. However, since counselling groups often encompass people with a variety of problems, they are also frequently mixed or heterogeneous in terms of membership too. Thus, a counselling group could theoretically include a wide range of men and women: some young; some middle aged; homosexual and heterosexual members; as well as members who differ in terms of race, culture, ethnicity and religious affiliation. A group diverse in composition will obviously produce a richer, more varied, and ultimately more realistic, therapeutic forum. This is because such a group mirrors the diversity in society itself. When ideas, problems, feelings, and styles of interaction are to be explored within the group, it is, as Corey (1995) suggests, a good idea to have a range of interests, backgrounds, ages and concerns, from which to draw.

When we consider the issue of closed versus open groups we can see that the counselling group, if it is to be a true microcosm of society, should be open ended. If members can join and leave in a way that accommodates their individual needs, then this is clearly more representative of the ebb and flow of society as a whole. In addition to the benefits of changeable or mobile membership, open groups have the added advantage of discouraging too much dependence on the group itself. If the group is continually changing, group members are less likely to become reliant on it to fulfill their relationship and interpersonal needs. Another advantage of the open group is that themes of separation, endings and loss, can be facilitated and explored as they arise. The closed group is one in which the same members meet for a specific number of sessions with a predetermined date for closure. This has some clear benefits, in that members are likely to feel safer and more contained, because they are not subjected to disruption and constant change. Once again, the needs of group members should determine the closed versus open structure of the group.

The length, frequency and duration of meetings should also be considered in the initial stages of planning. Group counselling usually takes place on a weekly basis, with sessions lasting one and a half hours on average. Some groups, those that include programmes or activities (art therapy, for example) may be scheduled to last longer, however. There are also certain therapies, including Gestalt, where sessions may be open ended, but these are the exception rather than the rule. In addition, some groups are conducted over a longer continuous period of time, perhaps during a weekend. Conversely, there are groups with shorter sessions to accommodate the needs of specific client groups. Included in this category are some groups for bereaved children. Here, sessions may last an hour, rather than the usual hour and a half. Attention span and fatigue are obviously factors to be considered when conducting groups for children. Play therapy is another specialized area of child groupwork, and here, once again, sessions are kept short, and may even be less than an hour for very young children (West (1992)).

The life span of adult counselling groups may be three months to two years, depending on the theme, purpose, or level of therapeutic work to be achieved. Groups that have a definite theme, self-esteem, for example, tend to be shorter. Regardless of the time scale for the group, however, members need to be told beforehand how long it will last. This last point is especially relevant if group members are paying fees, which they need to budget for in advance.

SELECTION OF MEMBERS

In selecting members for a counselling group, a key consideration is the extent to which they will be able to use, or benefit from, the group. A further consideration is the amount of information that the prospective client has about groups and the way they function. From the point of view of group planning, it is essential for leaders or facilitators to be clear themselves about which members are likely to benefit (and those who are not) from participation in a group. Applicants for group membership should, ideally, be seen on an individual basis in order to assess how much they are likely to gain and contribute to the planned group. Some group therapists devote several individual sessions to seeing group members beforehand, so that a solid relationship is built and preparation for therapy is undertaken. However, this kind of assessment about suitability should not be one sided, but should provide ample opportunity for prospective members to discuss and clarify what it is they themselves need and expect from group participation. The following Case study describes one person's experience of assessment in preparation for group counselling.

CASE STUDY: AILEEN – PRE-GROUP ASSESSMENT

During a particularly stressful time in my life I left my job to move to a different part of the country with my husband. The house move involved several major hitches, and shortly after we settled in our new home I became ill with 'flu. I missed my friends, my job and my former social life. Some time later I began to feel depressed, and my doctor prescribed antidepressants. At first I was reluctant to take them since I didn't believe they were a long-term solution. When, having started the antidepressants, I did feel a little better; I decided to apply for membership to a therapy group, which had been set up by a counselling psychologist working in private practice. The counsellor (Peter) sent me a questionnaire in response to my application. This had to be completed before arranging a first appointment. The questionnaire was quite extensive, and apart from the usual personal details relating to age and family background, I was also asked to say why I thought group membership would help me. When I did have my first interview with Peter, I talked again about my reasons for applying, and described what I thought I would gain from the group. I do remember that he asked me to describe how I usually communicate in groups. This led to further discussion about my (large) family and my place within it. We also talked about my depression, with particular reference to its severity, and any suicidal intentions that I might have experienced. Throughout these discussions I became very emotional and distraught. When I look back on it, I think this was because I was aware that many of my difficulties did indeed stem from family relationships. At the end of this assessment interview, Peter suggested that I should attend for six individual sessions before making a final decision about joining the group. I agreed to this because I felt that I would benefit from individual help. During the discussion I began to think about two family bereavements that had happened years ago. Because of other complications in my life at that time, I had simply put my feelings about these deaths 'on hold.' This meant that I now had to acknowledge the losses, a task that I knew would be better facilitated in individual counselling to begin with.

It can be seen from this account that clients are sometimes discouraged, for various reasons, from joining a group at a particular time. Applicants for group membership are often, as Yalom (1995:243) points out, excluded from this form of therapy if they are in the middle of a life crisis. The life crisis that Aileen described included clinical depression for which antidepressants had been prescribed. It also included unresolved grief, and very high levels of stress associated with the loss of her friends, her job and a complicated house move. In addition to the careful history which Aileen's counsellor obtained, he also asked her permission to communicate with her doctor about her general condition and the medication she was on. Edelwich & Brodsky (1992:18) recommend that, whenever possible, group facilitators should communicate with prescribing physicians in this way.

A general practitioner, who knows, for example, that a group is available and feels sure that it is the right approach for the patient, may refer prospective members. In such a situation it is even more important to establish just how suitable or useful the group might be. Another type of selection, what Brown (1998:59) refers to as 'control by inclusion' is sometimes used as a compulsory measure by certain agencies. In-patients in psychiatric hospitals may, for example, be compelled to accept group membership as a condition of their treatment. As we saw from the Case study (Mark) outlined in chapter one, there are special difficulties intrinsic to compulsory group membership. In Mark's case, he simply closed off from the whole experience and felt he had gained nothing from it. Motivation, which Yalom (1995:235) sees as the most important criterion for group inclusion is less likely to be present when pressure is exerted on people to join.

SUITABILITY OF MEMBERS

When we start to consider membership suitability, it is perhaps easier to identify the factors which point to the way individuals are likely to behave in a group. With the best will (and skill) in the world, however, it is impossible to be one hundred percent accurate about such a nebulous indicator, especially if an assessment is made on a single, individual interview with the applicant. If someone really wants to join a group, s/he may make a very good case for doing so. In addition, the way a person presents in a single interview may have little in common with their communication style in a group. One way of surmounting this problem is to set a questionnaire (as the counsellor in the last Case study did) that asks prospective members to identify what usually happens to them in communication with other people. Other questions designed to elicit prospective members' understanding might include some enquiry about what they hope to contribute and gain from the group. If certain clients do not seem right for a particular group, it may be that another kind of group experience might help. One client was considered unsuitable for a personal development group, but was later invited to join an anger management group, and was accepted.

What other reasons might prospective members have for wanting to be in a therapy group? One answer to this question is that some group applicants may hope to gain social contacts within the group. This kind of hope is often based on a general misunderstanding about the purpose and function of therapy groups, which is another reason for careful selection of members beforehand. Prospective members may have little or no idea about the commitment and hard work needed if group therapy is to be of benefit to them. Identifying and working through personal issues is difficult for most people, but there are certain situations, personal characteristics and types of behaviour that make such work impossible. Included in this category are:

◆ Severe mental illness that might make it impossible for the person to keep in touch with reality, or even to stay for the length of a session

◆ Any history of violence or uncontrollable behaviour in groups

◆ Inability to relate without recourse to drugs or alcohol. Heavy prescribed medication, which interferes with thinking and communication skills

◆ Lack of cognitive and thinking skills

◆ Inability to communicate or speak the same language as other members of the group.

All of the above disqualifying reasons, adapted from factors listed by Edelwich & Brodsky (1992) may seem fairly negative, in the sense that they focus on exclusion, rather than inclusion, in relation to group membership. However, just because a client is not likely to be helped by a particular group approach does not mean that other forms of support, or even another specific kind of group, will not help either. Indeed, both prison and probation services routinely work with groups of people who have a history of extreme violence; this is a specialized area that Cox (1978) refers to often. Many group therapists now tend to emphasize more positive aspects of selection, with a focus on those prospective members *who are suitable*, rather than unsuitable, for inclusion in the group. Barnes et al. (1999:39) take this approach when they describe the attributes that prospective group members should have before they can be considered suitable for group therapy. Included in their criteria for suitability is the ability to identify one's own contribution to personal difficulties, and some motivation towards personal understanding and change. In addition prospective members need to appreciate how they relate to others, and they need to be willing to cooperate with group members in order to achieve personal insight, and ultimately change. A capacity to form and continue relationships is also regarded by Barnes et al. as an important prerequisite for inclusion in groups.

PREPARING MEMBERS FOR THE GROUP

Quite apart from the selection procedure carried out in the planning stage, group members also need some preparation before they join. As far as most new members are concerned, inclusion in a counselling group may produce some feelings of apprehension or even anxiety. It is for this reason that prospective members need to be told what to expect in a group. If members are not fully prepared, there is the risk that they will quit prematurely, once they start to feel any degree of risk or discomfort. The information they are given should include details that are clear and precise, even in relation to the actual setting in which the group takes place. A former group member describes what he was told in this way:

CASE STUDY: WHAT THE GROUP WILL BE LIKE

The group counsellor spent a lot of time talking to me about how groups work, and how they help us to look at the way we communicate. She linked this to families and the problems in communication that often stem from these. She described the size of the room where group sessions would be held, and said that there would be eight of us there together sitting in a circle. She added that we would be talking to one another about issues, difficulties and problems we face. People would give feedback about the various topics people bring up. All of us would be asked to listen attentively when someone else spoke, and to resist talking about the group, or the people in it, between sessions. She said that what we discussed would be confidential and kept to the group, but added that more would be said about this once the group started and a contract was established. An exception to confidentiality, in my case, was progress reports to my doctor, which I agreed could be provided. During this preparation session I was also encouraged to ask questions myself, and to voice any concerns that I might have about groups. Because I had heard some scare stories about confrontation in groups, I asked about this and was told that group members would be protected from harmful attacks, verbal or otherwise. However, the counsellor did talk about differences of opinion and conflict, which, she said, is unavoidable in groups. But she added that this can help us to look at new ideas and different ways of doing things, and this often helps us to change and move forward.

MAKING A CONTRACT

It is usual practice to make a contract with prospective group members, and to support this later on with another general contract among group members, as soon as sessions start. It is important to stress here that contracts are voluntary and may be either written or verbal. Prospective members need to know that they are active, rather than passive, participants in the group experience. The first contract (between the counsellor and the new member) should emphasize those aspects of behaviour and engagement, which each individual in the group is reasonably expected to pledge. Included in this first contract are clear statements about the central importance of regular attendance and commitment. Practical details relating to time, fees (if relevant) and location of meetings are also specified. The actual establishment of a contract serves to clarify any obscure or ambiguous areas that might exist in relation to the purpose and objectives of the group. What prospective members, themselves, expect and want from the group, are also key areas for exploration and agreement in this initial contract. Additionally, individual members need to know what they and other members will be expected to do in the group, which means that the purpose of group tasks should be explained. This also means that programmes and other methods to be used should be discussed. Prospective members also need to know if programmes or activities are voluntary, or whether they will be expected to participate in them. Occasionally prospective members have unreasonable or unrealistic expectations about what is possible in a group.

Pre-group discussion and contracting can address these and other related issues, so that individual members are reassured and informed in advance.

EXERCISE 6

INDIVIDUAL CONTRACTS

Time: 40 mins.

Working individually, design a written contract that could be used with prospective members prior to joining a group. Spend about 20 mins on this first part of the exercise, focusing on the areas that might be of concern to someone who has never been in a group before. What kinds of issues would prospective members and a leader/facilitator need to agree about? When you have finished, discuss your contract with members of your own group. In discussing your contracts, pay particular attention to areas of commonality: what are the factors that seem most important to all members of your group? Having looked at these common areas, identify individual areas of concern that are apparent in the contracts you have designed. Are there marked differences between members of your group here? Some questions to ask in relation to possible differences are:

◆ What prompted individual members to identify certain areas for inclusion in the contract?

◆ Are these identified concerns related to past (and personal) expectations of what happens in groups?

◆ Are these individual areas related to personal experience, either in the past or since joining your present group?

◆ Is it ever possible to have absolute clarity between prospective members and leaders in relation to group purpose and objsectives?

EXERCISE 7

EXPECTATIONS QUESTIONNAIRE

Time: 30 mins

Leaders can use the following questionnaire when a group is starting. The exercise is not specific to counselling groups, but can be used with most groups meeting for the first time. It is meant to examine the importance of group contracts, with particular emphasis on the expectations that members and leaders have of each other. The exercise comprises a list of statements to which members are asked to make true or false responses. Afterwards, discuss with the whole group, the statements and members' responses to them. Right or wrong answers are not the issue here; what is important is the discussion which the statements generate.

1 The leader should tell members what they need from the group. True / False

2 The leader should decide who is suitable for a particular group. True / False

3 The leader should say exactly what would happen in the group. True / False

4 Prospective members need previous group experience before they join. True / False

5 Group members are collectively responsible for running the group. True / False

6 The leader should attend to practical aspects of organization. True / False

7 The issue of confidentiality should be discussed before the group starts. True / False

8 Group members are responsible for stating what they need in the group. True / False

9 Group members should expect and ask for feedback from the group. True / False

10 The leader should protect group members from uncomfortable feelings. True / False

11 Attendance at all group meetings is important. True / False

12 Anxieties and expectations about the group should be discussed. True / False

13 Groups should start and finish on time. True / False

14 Group members should share all their experiences. True / False

15 Group membership should be fun. True / False

16 Group members should have the right to decline involvement. True / False

17 The leader must tell the group in advance if s/he cannot take a session. True / False

18 It is important to establish ground rules before the group starts. True / False

19 The group leader should encourage competition in the group. True / False

20 The leader is responsible for a successful outcome in the group. True / False

THE GROUP CONTRACT

Once group members come together for their first meeting, another contract is usually made to support the first one. However, the group contract is different, precisely because it is an agreement made between all members present and the group counsellor. In contrast, the initial contract, made between counsellor and the individual member did not have the agreement of everyone else. Benson (1987:52) stresses the importance of simplicity when outlining the rights and responsibilities of the members and the person facilitating the group. The group contract should also be clear, and though groups differ in their contractual needs, there are several considerations common to all of them. These include:

◆ All members have agreed to be in the group, so everyone subscribes to the contract

◆ Members and counsellor agree to attend sessions on time and to participate in the group

◆ Members and counsellor come to a decision about confidentiality. This involves stating what can and cannot be discussed outside the group.

In addition to those agreements just described, the are a number of other ground rules that need to be established once the group starts. Tudor (1999:76) makes a distinction between contracts, rules and working agreements, and describes rules as 'non-negotiable' requirements made by the counsellor prior to starting the group. Individual counsellors, and their groups, obviously differ in relation to their non-negotiable requirements. However, a summary of these requirements might include rules about eating, drinking and smoking in the group. In most counselling groups the usual practice is to prohibit these activities, on the grounds that they are often used to divert attention away from the more difficult task of dealing with personal issues. Consumption of drugs or alcohol is prohibited too, and for fairly obvious reasons. Breaks during group sessions are commonly discouraged. One reason for keeping the group intact like this is that member concentration is not disrupted by people coming and going. A therapy group is quite different from a social group in this respect, and group members need to be aware of the difference. In some groups, particularly those whose members may have a history of violent behaviour, rules about overt aggression are common as well.

One of the areas which needs to be addressed at the beginning stage of a group is that concerning social relationships outside the group. Some group counsellors take the view that contact between members outside the group should be discouraged. The main reason for this is that extracurricular social contact tends to have a very real and direct effect on other group members, and on group communication generally. When this happens, it can, of course, be addressed in the group. The significance of the relationship and its effects on the group can, and should, be discussed. If it is not, it is likely to impede all other useful communication within the group. However, it would be impossible (and pointless) to prohibit casual member association outside the group. It could also have the effect of introducing an anti-therapeutic and closed mentality, which some group members might find sinister or even threatening. Either way, the issue of extracurricular social contact needs to be defined and discussed at the start of a group, and when guidelines relating to it are given to members, they need to understand what they mean and why they are necessary.

When meeting for the first time, group members are usually nervous, and unclear about how to behave in relation to the counsellor and other group members. In a later chapter we shall look in some detail at this and other stages of group development, and at the various kinds of behaviour and communication characteristic of them. Even though members are apprehensive to start with, they will be prepared to some extent if individual pre-group contracts have been made giving them some basic information about groups and what is likely to happen in them. Afterwards, the group contract will support and reinforce much of the information imparted on an individual basis. We have considered different aspects of behaviour in the group, and looked at some possible ground rules which counsellors might regard as non-negotiable for all the members. Some additions to these guidelines concern communication within the group, with an emphasis on behaviour that is likely to enhance it. Thus, group members may be encouraged to negotiate firm ground rules in relation to the following:

◆ Listening: everyone agrees to listen carefully when a member is speaking

◆ 'I' statements: group members agree to own their statements by using the personal pronoun 'I'

◆ Respect: group members agree to show respect towards everyone else present. This means not attacking, blaming or gossiping about each other

◆ Confrontation: group members agree that confrontation must be done in a sensitive and straightforward way.

THE GROUP LEADER'S ROLE

The group leader or counsellor has certain obligations in relation to group contracts and ground rules. We have seen that members are often unsure about their own roles and responsibilities in a new group, which means that guidance from the leader is needed to orientate them. In addition to uncertainty about their own roles, however, group members are also frequently in the dark about the leader's role and function. The role of group leader is a subject which we shall look at in more depth later in the book. We shall also discuss member expectations of what a leader should do, or be. In this section, however, we need to consider the basic assurances which group members are entitled to have before and when a group starts. These assurances are often not explicitly stated, but are conveyed in the general demeanour and behaviour of the leader from the outset. Earlier in this chapter we discussed the subject of pre-group contracts, and stressed that members need details about practical issues including payment, length of sessions, holidays, attendance and commitment. In addition to the organization of practical and other details, group leaders should also provide information on an ongoing basis, as and when members ask for it. This means being psychologically, as well as physically, available to the group. It also means fostering a climate conducive to open communication, so that tension, which all new members experience, is never allowed to become a major problem. To ensure that members achieve maximum benefit from group participation, from the outset the leader should establish attitudes of mutual respect, trust and acceptance.

ONE LEADER OR TWO?

Co-leadership of a group has several significant advantages over single leadership. The most obvious advantage is that two leaders share responsibility and support each other, though in order to achieve this kind of united approach, care, once again, should be given to planning. In fact, it is probably true to say that detailed planning is even more important when two leaders are involved. Lack of preparation is, according to Benson (1987:41) a major problem in relation to co-leadership. If group leaders are not adequately prepared beforehand, confusion can arise over individual roles, styles and contributions. Confusion may even arise over the actual purpose of the group. Personal honesty, and a willingness to discuss all points of difference or conflict are also essential prerequisites for leaders who intend to work in partnership. Pre-group planning should provide adequate periods of time between sessions for co-leaders to discuss their joint approach, and any difficulties or inter-personal issues which arise. If co-leaders do not address their differences in this way, group members will sense whatever conflict exists, and may use it in negative or unproductive ways. This kind of response is just one of the aspects of group behaviour which we shall consider more fully in a later chapter.

However, there are other, more positive, benefits to be gained from co-leadership. Included in these benefits is the fact that group members will be given more attention and support when two people are present to facilitate the group. Furthermore, it is obviously easier to keep track of everything that is happening in the group when there are two sets of antenna to monitor it. When co-leaders give each other feedback between sessions, this monitoring or scanning effect is enhanced even further. This also ensures that a much safer environment is provided for members in which to explore personal difficulties and problems.

Another effect of co-leadership is that both leaders represent (at an unconscious level) parental figures in relation to members of the group. This effect is especially pronounced when one leader is male and the other female, and it gives group members the opportunity to explore their relationships with parental and authority figures. Co-leadership can be beneficial for trainee group counsellors too, since a joint approach like this provides opportunities for developing skills in the presence of a more experienced person. Training in a context like this means that group members are less likely to be harmed by an inexperienced person leading the group. Moreover, trainee group leaders are given the chance to become more confident themselves as a result of modelling and learning from a more experienced and competent leader. In referring to 'complementarily' of leaders, Tudor (1999:70) highlights the advantages of co-leadership, not just in terms of gender difference, but also in relation to differences in sexual orientation, and to ethnic or racial differences too. Thus, he suggests, there are clear advantages for the group when, for example, one leader is black and the other white, and when one leader is heterosexual and the other homosexual. Again, these differences serve to mirror those present in a modern society.

Co-leadership has a further advantage in that group members are provided with an obvious example of two people working together in co-operation and harmony, who are able to resolve differences and conflict. This last point is especially important, not least because it is an area which is often problematic for people and causes many relationship difficulties. However, the need for preparation, co-operation and ongoing review of the working partnership between two leaders is an obvious prerequisite for successful modelling of the kind described here. The way in which conflict and difference is resolved is important too. For group members to benefit from any differences of opinion which exists between the leaders, they need to see and hear these expressed in open, non-hostile, non-blaming and respectful ways.

All the advantages referred to in relation to co-leadership may give the impression that few, if any, problems exist in this approach to working with groups. However, any partnership, including co-leadership, is multi-faceted and more complex than what it may seem superficially. The potential for rivalry is always present, and co-leaders may even deceive each other, especially when barriers to authentic and honest communication exist. If, for example, one leader is experienced and the other inexperienced, there is a possibility that the learner may not feel sufficiently confident to confront a co-leader when it might be useful and therapeutic to do so. Co-dependence is another problem which can arise between co-leaders, especially when they are more concerned to support each other, than they are to facilitate the group overall. Issues of power and dominance are other potential hazards in co-leadership, and these may surface when one leader is from a dominant culture and the other is not.

Ideally, co-leaders should like, respect and even select each other in order to establish the most effective partnership for working with a group. But conditions are not, of course, always as straightforward as this, and agency requirements may mean that co-leaders do not have total control or choice when it comes to selecting a partner. Regardless of agency arrangements, however, co-leaders need, for the sake of the group and their relationship, to work towards mutual understanding, while acknowledging and respecting any differences which exist between them. In a later chapter we shall consider the subject of leadership in greater depth, with special reference to the factors which impinge on its style and effectiveness.

EXERCISE 8

CO-LEADERSHIP
Time: 40 mins.

This is an exercise, which is designed to encourage you to look at some of the factors involved in this approach to working with groups. You should work with a partner to complete the exercise, spending about twenty minutes on the first half, and twenty minutes discussing any differences which become apparent between you.

First half:

Select a partner to work with and look at the following list of statements. Complete the questionnaire individually, and then look at the differences, which emerge in your responses. Discuss these together to begin with, then with other members of the whole group.

1 Group members can feel overwhelmed in the presence of two leaders who may represent too much power and authority. Agree / Disagree

2 Co-leaders should meet before and after every group session to discuss their joint approach. Agree / Disagree

3 Co-leaders should express and resolve their differences in the presence of the group. Agree / Disagree

4 Co-leadership is safer in a large group. Agree / Disagree

5 Co-leaders should decide beforehand who would have responsibility for what in the group. Agree / Disagree

6 Two leaders are always superfluous in a small group. Agree / Disagree

7 Unavoidable absence of a leader is less disruptive for the group when a co-worker is present. Agree / Disagree

8 When co-leaders are of opposite gender groups members are likely to become dependent and treat them as parents. Agree / Disagree

9 In a single gender group of women, two male leaders would be inappropriate. Agree / Disagree

10 Problems will arise if co-leadership does not represent and acknowledge the experiences of gay and lesbian group members. Agree / Disagree

11 It is more important for opposite gender co-leaders to communicate about differences than it is for same gender leaders. Agree / Disagree

12 Two female co-leaders will experience special problems in an all male group. Agree / Disagree

13 When one leader is male he will automatically be regarded as a father figure by group members. Agree / Disagree

14 When one leader is female, she will automatically be treated as a mother figure by group members. Agree / Disagree

15 Group members are always more confident when there are two leaders. Agree / Disagree

16 A trainee leader will always learn good practice as a result of co-leadership with an experienced person. Agree / Disagree

17 A trainee leader will be disadvantaged when it comes to expression of conflict or difference with an experienced co-leader. Agree / Disagree

18 Co-leaders from different cultural backgrounds will find it difficult to identify and define their approach to the group. Agree / Disagree

19 Co-leaders will always have problems when their training and experience is markedly different. Agree / Disagree

20 Co-leaders can only be effective when the choice to work together has been theirs. Agree / Disagree

USING PROGRAMMES IN GROUPS

Group therapy is not exclusively confined to observation of group processes, self- disclosure or in-depth analysis of self in relation to others. On the contrary, different forms of activity are often incorporated into group therapy, and short term counselling groups, in particular, frequently use programmes to address specific difficulties which members have. When we look at various theoretical approaches to groupwork, we shall see that procedures, activities and programmes have a central focus in several of them. The underlying assumption of a programmed approach to group counselling, is that members learn and benefit from doing things, especially when these things encourage the development of personal potential, enhance self-esteem and facilitate the acquisition of skills. Additionally there are certain groups whose members would not be able to communicate effectively without alternative ways of expressing their feelings and problems. Children, for example, are encouraged to express themselves through the medium of play, toys and fantasy. This approach to working with children is especially relevant when there is a history of sexual abuse. This is because such abuse often makes direct, verbal expression difficult, threatening or even impossible. Some adult group members may also find direct communication difficult, and may be unable to get the support and feedback, which they need from verbal interaction with other group members. Inhibitions like these can stem from a background that has forbidden the expression of personal concerns and deep emotions in open or public ways. In fact, even group members who do not share these inhibitions, often find it easier to access deeply felt emotions when a suitable medium such as painting, writing or music is provided to help them.

CASE STUDY: GREG

Greg, who is a musician and trained counsellor, described his work with groups of children from the divided communities in Northern Ireland:

My work is part of a peace initiative set up in Northern Ireland to foster understanding between the two communities. The main objective in my work is to encourage school children from both sides of the sectarian divide to come together, to communicate, to talk, and ultimately to recognize the similarities, which exist between us all. In order to do this I (along with a colleague) arrange for groups of children from Protestant and Catholic schools, to meet at regular intervals to get to know each other. These groups are not counselling groups as such, although I do use counselling skills in order to facilitate the development of trust, communication and respect. For example, I show children how to listen, how to respond, and how to respect viewpoints, which are very different from our own. However, suspicion and quite high levels of anxiety are usually apparent when several new groups meet for the first time. On one of these occasions recently, groups of children from Protestant and Catholic schools sat directly, and silently, opposite one another. All my efforts to encourage communication met with minimal results. Then I decided to bring in some of the musical instruments, which we often use in situations like this. My colleague and I placed a selection of these on a table in the centre and invited the children to have a look at them and try them out. Within a short space of time groups of children were trying out various instruments, talking to each other, and clearly enjoying the interaction. After the music session, we discussed what had happened. Several members of both groups said they had felt very threatened by the prospect of direct communication with people they had never talked to before. On the other hand, the introduction of music, and the instruments, which provided a focus for discussion, meant they were able to relax and talk. Following this, some very useful dialogue and sharing of experiences took place in the group.

Programmed use of coping skills

Group programmes may be used to foster coping skills too. An example of such programme use is often seen in anxiety management groups, or in those designed to encourage the development of assertiveness and self-esteem. Stress management groups also include activities, which are meant to replace ineffectual ways of dealing with everyday tension and pressure. When we come to consider cognitive behavioural approaches in groupwork, these activities and coping skills will be highlighted and described.

Other programme approaches

Some groups may engage members through the use of stories, or discussion about films or television characters. This is a way of facilitating fantasy discussion, with the aim of leading to personal introspection, group interaction and the exploration of feelings about deeply felt personal issues. This form of discussion, which Brandler & Roman (1999:139) refer to, means that self-disclosure becomes less threatening and group members are helped to deal more effectively with their problems when they use it.

If they are to be effective, group programmes and activities need to be well planned before the group begins. In fact, most group programmes should be committed to paper so that their order and sequence is clear, meaningful and related to group members' needs and problems as the group progresses. Environmental factors need to be considered too when activities are included in a programme. Role-play and psychodrama, for example, require considerable space if they are to work effectively in the group. Artwork also needs appropriate accommodation if group members are to benefit from it. On the other hand, many other programmes and activities require no special provision but can be incorporated fairly unobtrusively within the group setting. The following are some examples of activities which might be used in different counselling groups:

Group for people with panic attacks – some possible activities:

◆ Regular practice of deep breathing

◆ Panic attacks questionnaires and discussion

◆ Keeping a journal

◆ Negative thought stopping exercises. e.g. teaching members how to anticipate and stop negative thinking

Group for people with phobias – some possible activities:

◆ Visualization. e.g. group members might be taught how to use imagery to modify behaviour

◆ Using tape recorders to aid relaxation

◆ Setting clearly defined goals in writing

◆ Practice in using coping statements

Along with the exercises and programmes mentioned, activities in small groups may also be used to extend, supplement, or elucidate issues which are of concern to the whole group. If you are part of a training group, you will probably have experience already of working in pairs or triads. The advantage of working in these ways is that members are allowed to address specific topics in a more intimate, less exposed and less threatening atmosphere. However, work in small groups is more likely to take place in training or educational pro-grammes, than it is in counselling or therapy groups. A disadvantage of working in small groups is that attention is diverted away from the dynamics of the whole group, for short periods at least. In counselling and therapy groups these short term disruptions would work against total group interaction and cohesion, and could lead to the formation of sub-groups and fragmented discussion. Douglas (2000:43) highlights the possibility that sub-groups may form a base for certain members who might wish to opt out or rebel. This is because

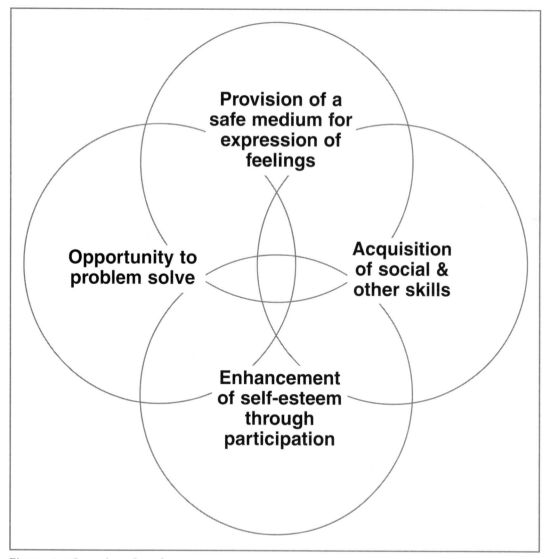

Figure. 2.1 Some benefits of group programmes

some members feel stronger in the smaller group, which offers them a support system from which to challenge the larger group. Sub-groups can, according to Yalom (1995:327), be extremely disruptive in therapy groups, a factor that we shall consider later on in the book.

Some benefits of group programmes

If we consider the overall benefits of group programmes and activities, we can identify several important functions which they serve. These include the provision of a safer alternative medium for the expression of feelings; the acquisition of social and other skills; the opportunity to problem solve, and the enhancement of self-esteem through direct participation in group tasks and activities.

EVALUATION

The planning and setting up of any group requires some consideration of the ways in which the success of the project will be evaluated. It is important to stress that strategies for evaluation should be in place before the group itself actually starts, though the process does continue throughout the life of the group, and on its completion too. It is not enough to assume that a group is successful simply because it exists and members attend sessions. On the other hand, if members do not attend, leaders are provided with a fairly obvious signal that something is seriously wrong. However, this last point refers to a rather extreme example of group failure, while the reality is that dissatisfaction is unlikely to be expressed so explicitly.

Brown (1998:196) suggests that evaluation of a group can be undertaken at both formal and informal levels. Formal evaluation is sometimes used for research purposes, whereas informal evaluation is carried out at regular intervals throughout sessions, and at the end of each session. In fact, informal evaluation should take place at all stages of a group's life span. Group leaders may, as Corey (1995:76) indicates, need to encourage and guide members towards reflection and evaluation in order to appraise their goals and the effectiveness of the group for them. This continuous reflection and evaluation need not be complicated, but can take the form of timed observations and questions, which serve to focus the group's attention on the progress made so far. The following questions and observations from a group leader are examples:

1   Does anyone want to add to what has been said so far?
2   Is this something we need to explore in more depth?
3   What do you think we can do to make our goals clearer?
4   I wonder if we are avoiding something very difficult here.
5   Right now everyone wants to respond to what Bill has just said.
6   Let's just stop there for a minute and think about the feeling in the group.
7   In what way can the group help you at this stage?

8   Perhaps you could consider how satisfied you are with things as they are now.

9   It seems that everyone is clear about what they need to do at this stage.

10 At this stage everyone has talked personally about goals.

Aside from informal evaluation, some form of structured evaluation is also frequently required, and there is often pressure on group counsellors to provide objective evaluative data to support group initiatives within agencies or other organizations. The difficulty of actually doing this kind of objective assessment of outcomes is highlighted by several groupwork researchers, including Corey (1995:125) who refers to the problem of measuring 'subtle changes in attitudes, beliefs, feelings and behaviour.' Brown (1998:197) also points out that evaluation is complicated because so many people with very 'personal agendas' are involved. Perhaps the most important prerequisite for some form of objective evaluation is, therefore, the setting down of clearly stated and specific goals for each individual in the group. Again, this needs to be built into the planning stage when members are asked to state, often verbally and in writing, what their problems are, what they hope to achieve, and how the group can help them. Afterwards, when the group has ended, members need to assess whether or not their goals have been reached. Some form of written evaluation – which may be a questionnaire – should be completed, either at the final group session, or at a follow up session later on. Another structured, though slightly less formal model of written evaluation, can be used when the group has finished. The reference here is to journal entries made by group members, or to descriptive accounts of what the group meant and provided for individual participants. Regardless of which written model is used, however, there are key areas, which should be addressed within the document. These include:

◆ Members' expectations when they joined the group

◆ What members hoped to get from the group

◆ Whether member's hopes and expectations were realized

◆ What members found most helpful about the group

◆ What members found least helpful about the group

◆ Some reference to the way in which individual members used the group to achieve their goals

◆ Some reference to the ways in which the group met, or did not meet, the needs of members

◆ What group members have learned about their ways of communicating with, and relating to others

◆ Any changes which members will make in the context of communicating with, and relating to others

◆ Whether members have put into practice what they have learned in the group

◆ Any destructive or negative experiences which members have had as a result of group participation.

In addition to written evaluations designed to elicit member responses, it is also a good idea to evaluate other factors, which can, in fact, be measured in a more objective way. For group counsellors to be really professional and accountable, it is important to do this kind of evaluation. For one thing, it simplifies future proposals for groupwork, and any problems or deficiencies which come to light can be remedied before a new group starts. In order to do this, records of previous groups can be kept, with special reference to external factors such as resources, number of members attending and completing the group, and any changes to timing, rooms, or use of programmes which may need to be modified in the light of experience. Once this kind of objective evaluation is done, it is then possible to refer to it, if only to check that any recommendations made have been carried out. Additionally, when future problems arise, the evaluation can be used to identify possible causes. When someone else proposes changes (which can happen in an agency setting) evaluations can help to show whether these will work for particular groups. Lastly, objective evaluation will enable group counsellors to identify and celebrate achievements, thus adding to a sense of personal accomplishment.

SUPERVISION

Although we shall look at supervision later in the book, its central importance at the planning stage needs to be emphasized here. Whether group counsellors work individually or in co-leaderships, the requirement for adequate and regular supervision remains the same. Indeed, as Edelwich & Brodsky (1992:164) indicate, the need for regular supervision may be even more important when group leaders work together. This is because supervision acts as a check on the kind of symbiotic dependence and lack of awareness which can easily develop when two people are not receiving feedback from an objective source. Before starting a therapy or counselling group, the leader or leaders should confirm that professional supervision is not only available, but also that it is adequately resourced for their needs.

References

Barnes, B., Ernst, S., & Hyde, K. (1999) *An Introduction to Groupwork: A group Analytic Perspective.* London, Macmillan.

Benson, J. (1987) *Working More Creatively with Groups.* London, Tavistock Publications.

Brandler, S. & Roman, C. P. (1999) *Group Work: Skills and Strategies for Effective Interventions.* New York, The Haworth Press.

Brown, A. (1998) 3rd Ed. *Group Work.* Aldershot, Ashgate Publishing Co.

Corey, G. (1995) 4th Ed. *Group Counselling.* California, Brooks Cole Publishing Co.

Cox, M. (1988) *Coding the Therapeutic Process: Emblems of Encounter.* London, Jessica Kingsley Publishers Ltd.

Douglas, T. (2000) *Basic Group Work.* 2nd Ed. London, Routledge.

Edelwich, J. & Brodsky, A. (1992) *Group Counselling for the Resistant Client*. New York, Lexington Books.

Libemann, M. (1991) *Art Therapy for Groups*. London, Routledge.

Tudor, K. (1999) *Group Counselling*. London, Sage.

West, J. (1992) *Child Centred Play Therapy*. London, Edward Arnold.

Wilson, J. & Myers, J. (1998) 2nd Ed. *Self Help Groups*. Nottingham, R. A. Wilson.

Yalom, I. D. (1995) 4th Ed. *The Theory and Practice of Group Psychotherapy*. New York, Basic Books.

3

Communicating in groups

INTRODUCTION

This chapter is about the way people interact and communicate in groups. The subject of communication, and the skills which it entails, is not always, in my view, given the prominence it deserves in therapeutic groupwork literature and research. There is a tendency to overlook basic communication skills and to stress group participation and experiential learning, both of which are rightly regarded as fundamental to training programmes. Barnes et al (1999), for example, highlight the importance of learning through doing, while Benjamin et al (1997:131) also refer to the "best kind of learning that goes on in groups" which, in their view, takes place at an experiential level.

In discussing the ways people learn about groups, it is useful to start by looking at the various elements, which actually comprise the learning process itself. Johnson & Johnson (1997:50) describe what they term 'Procedural Learning' which is based on experiential learning, and they detail the factors, which should be present for effective study of group dynamics. These factors include a firm grasp of group theory and practice, the translation of this conceptual understanding into a repertoire of group skills, actual practice of group skills, and the refinement and mastery of skills through repetition and systematic elimination of mistakes and errors.

It can be seen from this description that while Johnson & Johnson support the view that experiential learning, practice, and mastery of skills, are of paramount importance in group training, they are nevertheless also concerned to point out that acquisition of knowledge and understanding of group dynamics theory, must underpin practical experience. In this chapter we shall look closely at the repertoire of group skills, which are necessary for effective communication in groups. Throughout the chapter we shall link theory to practice by providing exercises which you can complete at various key stages in order to test and evaluate your own progressive mastery of skills. Before going on to discuss communication skills, however, it is important to define experiential learning as well, and to place in context some of the other terms which are frequently used in relation to group interaction. In addition to experiential learning these include:

◆ Group processes

◆ Group cohesion

◆ Group norms

◆ Group roles

EXPERIENTIAL LEARNING

The term experiential learning is often used to describe the process of learning through experience, or learning through doing. In this sense the term is self explanatory, and refers to the most basic and necessary elements for learning about groups and what happens in them. If you think about it, this is the way we learn many of the important skills, which are essential for survival from infancy onwards. Toddlers learn to walk by trial and error, for example, and even later in life the process of learning through experience is a central part of everyday living for all of us. Those writers and researchers, including Johnson & Johnson (1997), who emphasize the importance of experiential learning, frequently point out that while information and knowledge can make us interested in change, we are unlikely to implement this change unless we gain first hand experience ourselves, and practise the skills thereafter. This learning is not just about memorizing facts, formulas and other aspects of theory. It is also about making connections, achieving insight and using our powers of observation, reflection and evaluation. These are processes which we cannot develop fully unless we are given the opportunity to gain practical experience in the very situation, i.e. groups, which we hope to study.

The value of practice and work based education has traditionally been recognized by other professional organizations, including teaching, nursing and social work. As well as encouraging learners to engage in supervised work, these professional organizations also acknowledge and draw from any previous experience and any other prior learning which their students have. Previous experience and prior learning are important aspects of group education too. This acknowledgment of past influences stems from the fact that all of us, from childhood onward, have in fact, lived and worked in groups. A consequence of this prolonged and early exposure to group influences is that a range of communication and behavioural skills is already in place even before groupwork training starts. The fact that our previous experience in groups may have been problematic or faulty does not preclude the acquisition of new skills, which can be measured against the old, less effective ways of relating to other people.

Through the medium of experiential learning, group participants are given an opportunity to develop and enhance a variety of interpersonal skills, including those of listening, seeing, paying close attention, reflecting on what someone else has said, clarifying areas which are obscure, and confronting others in supportive and sensitive ways. On the face of it, these are skills which many people believe they possess already, but in fact, this is certainly not always the case. All around us there are examples of people not listening, and if you observe carefully and become more self-aware, you will see that poor listening is probably the norm, in both ourselves and others.

These very ordinary skills, of which listening is one example, can be refined and developed through participation in, or by membership of groups. This approach to learning is infinitely more effective than passively learning about groupwork skills through exposure to theoretical concepts alone. Such a truism applies equally to people who hope to facilitate or lead groups, as it does to those who simply wish to gain maximum benefit from group membership. In other words, potential leaders and group facilitators need to spend considerable time as group members before they can hope to understand how skills are used, why they are needed, how feedback can aid learning, and last but not least, in order to practise and assess the group skills they hope to master.

GROUP PROCESSES

The term, group processes, refers to the multitude of interactions which take place between members. Another way of defining the term is to say that it is a general one used to describe the emotional life of a group and its members as developments and stages unfold. An ability to identify and understand group processes is essential for anyone, especially prospective leaders and facilitators, who wish to consider groupwork as part of their professional role. Douglas (1995:47) makes a distinction between what people say in groups (content) and what they actually do (process). This distinction is extended when he defines process as everything that happens between group members, apart from the actual words spoken.

However, the words that are exchanged between group members do not exist in a vacuum, and will inevitably produce some effect at an emotional level. In this sense, content and process, though often described as if they were always separate, are in fact closely linked. In order for group process to evolve, therefore, communication between group members has to take place. To understand group processes, including all the subtle and more obvious patterns of change which are produced at different stages, it is important to note what has been said and the effects which follow from this. The following short Case study considers these two elements.

CASE STUDY: CELINE

Celine, who was a member of a groupwork training programme comprising ten students, initiated the following dialogue ten minutes into the opening of a new session.

Celine: *I almost didn't make it today. My car is in the garage and I had a real hassle getting a lift.*

Peter: (another member): *But you're here anyway, which is good.*

Celine: *It was touch and go ... I felt so stressed* (sighs).

Rene: (another member): *Sounds as if it was a bit of a drag coming.*

Celine: *Well, as I said, it was touch and go.*

After these exchanges a long silence fell in the group. Several members appeared disconcerted by what they had heard, and an atmosphere of irritation was discernible. When conversation resumed among members, several important issues emerged. It became clear that Celine's contribution had produced a marked effect on the group. In analyzing their perceptions, members referred to feeling disconcerted, of not measuring up because Celine had implied reluctance to actually join the group that session. The fact that she had made a considerable effort to attend was less important than her words that it was 'touch and go' whether she was in the group at all. So what seemed on the surface to be a fairly innocuous conversational statement on Celine's part about her difficulty in attending the group, had in fact, generated several significant group processes including resentment among some members, and an extended discussion about what these feelings meant for individuals in the group.

In order to understand what takes place in groups, it is necessary to both hear and see events as they unfold. In addition to observation, however, group participants who wish to learn more about processes also need to monitor their own responses to what has taken place, and afterwards reflect on and assess these experiences. This is why knowledge of, and practice in groupwork skills is vital for a thorough understanding of group processes. In subsequent chapters we shall extend the subject of group processes with further discussion about the feelings, emotions, behaviours and general reactions, which are generated in groups. Before concluding this section on group processes, however, it is relevant here to refer to the work of R. F. Bales who conducted early research into group processes and identified the different contributions which members make to groups. His work entitled *Interaction Process Analysis* (1950) focuses on two main areas of contribution under the headings of Task contributions and Socio-emotional contributions.

In describing these two main types of contribution, Bales found that issues relating to one would prevail at certain times, while issues relating to the other would predominate at other times. In the first stage of group life, for example, members are usually concerned about their positions within the group and how they will relate to others. This concern could be categorized under the socio-emotional heading, which Bales provides. Once interpersonal issues have been settled, however, task related factors are likely to come to the fore. On the other hand, the socio-emotional and task phases do, as Wilson (1995:163) indicates, overlap or interact at times because issues of relationship and task ebb and flow as changes occur within the group.

EXERCISE 9

WHAT MEMBERS CONTRIBUTE TO THE GROUP

Time: 1 hour total.

This exercise is best conducted with the use of a video camera so that group members can view and evaluate their individual contributions afterwards. It is based on Bale's Interaction Process Analysis which identifies two main areas of contribution (task and socio-emotional) that members make in groups. In order to start the exercise members should be given a group assignment to complete. This could take the following form, although almost any group task that requires cooperation among members would be appropriate.

As a group you are asked to read the following statement and then rank your responses to it (from one to twenty) in order of importance, one being the most important and twenty the least.

Children can be helped to develop self-esteem when parents ...

A)	Are always there.	K)	Are reliable.
B)	Differ occasionally.	L)	Show fairness.
C)	Give unconditional love.	M)	Encourage expression of feelings.
D)	Are predictable.	N)	Praise accomplishment.
E)	Are models of good behaviour.	O)	Encourage creativity.
F)	Insist on ground rules.	P)	Stress educational achievement.
G)	Show respect towards each other.	Q)	Forgive mistakes.
H)	Model consistency.	R)	Show interest and listen.
I)	Overlook bad behaviour.	S)	Like fun and recreation.
J)	Show physical affection.	T)	Are financially secure.

When the group has completed the assignment (which should take about 30 minutes) replay the video so that members can view their interactions. Ask members to identify, and write down, their own contributions and to say whether they fall into the 'A' Task category or the 'B' Socio-emotional category. The following is a guide to these categories:

Task:

The contributors in this area are prompted by a need to solve problems and to get the job done. They include:

◆ Getting started.

◆ Identifying the task.

◆ Analyzing the task.

◆ Asking for opinions.

◆ Asking questions.

- ◆ Making suggestions.
- ◆ Checking on progress.
- ◆ Clarifying.
- ◆ Giving information.
- ◆ Providing a summary.

Socio-emotional:

Contributions in this area take note of other group members' emotional needs. They include:

- ◆ Supporting and affirming.
- ◆ Agreeing.
- ◆ Releasing tension through laughter or jokes.
- ◆ Sharing personal experiences.
- ◆ Encouraging.

However, not all contributions in the socio-emotional area are positive. Antagonism, tension and aggression are, for example, sometimes evident when disagreement arises in a group. As group members observe and analyze their contributions they need to realize that these are theoretical categories, which are never static or mutually exclusive. A group member may show preference for contributing to the group task at one stage, whereas later on, that same member may contribute to the socio-emotional area. One of the main points of the exercise is to encourage members to look more closely at their contributions overall, so that any imbalance between these two areas can be addressed.

CASE STUDY: TASK AND SOCIO-EMOTIONAL CONTRIBUTIONS

The following transcript shows contributions from seven members of a training group. The context of the dialogue was an assignment similar to the one just described. When students reviewed their session, which was carried out on video, they were able to identify their own Task or Socio-emotional contributions.

John: *What is the best way to approach this to get it done? We have thirty minutes to rank them.*

John's contribution – Task (Getting started, identifying the task)

Melanie: *Let's read them first. Let's spend some time doing that.*

Melanie's contribution – Task (Making suggestions)

Joe: *Yes, we need to read them first.* (Laughs)

Joe's contribution – Socio-emotional (Supporting, releasing tension)

Ed: *I'll call time. What have we got, half an hour?*

Ed's contribution – Task (Asking questions)

Nuala: *Shall we do this like a straw poll; everyone says what they put at number one?*

Nuala's contribution – Task (Making suggestions, asking questions)

Sandra: *Well I would like to think about it first before we jump into that. What does anyone else think?*

Sandra's contribution – Task (Asking for opinions)

Frank: *I agree with Sandra* (Smiles at her). *I did an exercise like this before and I think it best to ask for everyone's opinion first about how we should do it.*

Frank's contribution – Socio-emotional (Supporting and agreeing, sharing personal experience)

GROUP COHESION

Group cohesion is the term used to describe the joining together and sense of common purpose which binds members to each other and to the group. Cohesion is, therefore, an essential part of group process since it is something which develops over time among members. It is also according to Cathcart et al (1996:179) the 'glue', which causes members to stay in the group, even when there are pressures to leave. When there is a high level of group cohesion member participation and commitment tends to be high. As well as commitment and participation there is also greater trust and support among members, which in turn leads to the possibility of enhanced scope for personal growth and self-awareness. As we shall see when we come to discuss the subject of conflict later in the book, group cohesion does not imply that frustration, disagreement and hostility are never present or experienced in the group. In fact, the opposite is often the case, since groups which avoid uncomfortable feelings tend to leave so much unexpressed that suspicion and distrust are frequently the outcome. The more assiduously a group works towards common goals and needs, the greater the therapeutic potential for individual members too. This is an important point to remember in relation to counselling and therapy groups in particular. Brandler and Roman (1999:6) make the interesting observation that group cohesion can be equated with 'group ego strength.' Another way of expressing this is to say that a group which is cohesive has a strong sense of itself, its needs and resources, and the needs and resources of the individuals within it. Certain skills are conducive to the establishment and maintenance of group cohesion. Brandler and Roman (1996:12) discuss these skills and include the following:

◆ Setting clear boundaries, especially in relation to timekeeping and attendance.

◆ Clarification of structure – 'The group will meet each Monday at 2pm in this room.'

◆ Identification of purpose and goals – 'We talked about why we are here, but lets just look at that again.'

◆ Clarification of group roles – 'You are here to talk about things which are of concern to you. I am here to conduct the group and look after the practical details.'

◆ Use of inclusive language – 'So what is it we are saying now, that we, the group, are losing track of the main issue?'

◆ Including all members – 'Noella, do you want to say something about that?'

◆ Linking contributions – 'It seems like your view has something in common with what Sam said just now.'

Maintaining a 'here and now' focus is another skill which is conducive to group cohesion. This means encouraging members to speak directly to each other about what is actually happening in the present. For example:

◆ 'Vicky, what you said about feeling nervous in the group, I feel that too, especially now.'

A high level of group cohesion is obviously desirable in most groups, but it is especially important in counselling and therapy groups where trust, support and intimacy are valued characteristics. Whitaker (1992:41) suggests that it is possible for a group to become too cohesive, a state of affairs which can arise when, for example, members cling to the group as a means of avoiding ordinary social involvement and personal change. A skilled leader or facilitator should be aware of such a possibility, and avoid it. This can be done by ensuring that the group adheres to its therapeutic goal of enabling members to develop self-reliance and ultimately, independence. The following Case study illustrates this point:

CASE STUDY: THE BEREAVEMENT SUPPORT GROUP

Laura, a social worker, was approached by the vicar of her local church who asked her to help in setting up a bereavement support group in the district. Because she had experience of, and training in groupwork, she agreed to do this. However, she also stressed that members of the new group would be quite capable of running it themselves if they received some initial advice and help, as well as continuing interest and support. These assumptions proved to be correct, and the group, comprised of eight members, met on a regular basis and gradually developed its confidence, skills and self-help. Laura encouraged group members in their efforts to do things for themselves, then gradually, and in consultation with them, lessened her involvement with the group. Over a period of a year and a half, the group continued to meet on a weekly basis, all the while keeping in regular contact with Laura.

Shortly after this they asked if she could help them, since several members now felt 'stuck' and unable to move forward. In discussion with the group, Laura became aware that members had developed a remarkable degree of cohesion during their time together, so much, in fact, that they tended to depend on each other for almost all their social and emotional needs. However, there had been a recent and gradual change, and several group members now felt they were ready to move on and establish new relationships. Their appeal to Laura for help was linked to guilt feelings about abandoning their friends in the group. This was a very difficult thing for them to contemplate doing, and it was almost as if they needed permission to actually try it. Over a period of a year and a half, the group had grown in importance for all the members, and in some cases outside relationships were neglected because of it. Laura's task was to help all the members express, communicate and work through their feelings about ending the group and all the safe contact it provided. She also encouraged them to evaluate and celebrate what the group had achieved, and to view their decision to end it as a positive one, which might lead to other, interesting, developments and possibilities.

The above Case study highlights the point that intense cohesion in a group can prevent members from looking outside it for social involvement and friendship. Too much cohesion may stem from other causes as well, including the fear of disturbance and conflict among members. As we noted earlier in this section, conflict does not preclude the development of cohesion in a group. In fact, avoidance of uncomfortable feelings may produce an inauthentic quality in the group, which might not be discernible to members themselves. The following account by a group facilitator shows how this can happen:

CASE STUDY: AVOIDING CONFLICT

When the subject of cohesion is discussed I think about a particular group who were determined to agree at all costs. The group I refer to was made up of students on a counselling skills course. Attendance and timekeeping were excellent, and members seemed to 'gel' right from the start. The group was clearly attractive to them all, and they looked forward to our weekly meetings. During the course, however, I was increasingly aware that the group appeared to lack vitality and depth. Group members did not see it like this though, and when, at regular intervals, we engaged in process observation, it was clear they were very satisfied with the way things were. It was not until the course finished, that I finally understood what had been happening in the group. There was never any open disagreement or conflict, which went some way to explaining the cosy flatness of the group. On the other hand, nothing of great interest happened either. They were all just too close to take any risks.

NORMS

The word norms is often used in groupwork literature to denote those conscious or sometimes unconscious rules which members are expected to observe. These parameters of behaviour are important in defining what is acceptable or unacceptable for group members. Rules, explicit or implicit, are necessary for any group since they guide members in how to behave in different situations. A group of students on a training programme will, for example, be familiar with norms about a variety of issues, including attendance, completion of the course, submission of work and an expectation that they will contribute to group interaction. These are fairly formal and usually explicitly stated norms and they help to maintain behavioural consistency. Commonly acknowledged norms help to reduce uncertainty, insecurity and any ambivalence which might exist if they were not stated. Implicit norms can be more problematic, however, since they are liable to cause uncertainty especially when members are unclear about what is expected from them. In a therapy or counselling group, the onus is on the leader to guide members towards what Yallom (1995:109) calls 'an unwritten code of behavioural rules or norms' which will ensure that the group is conducive to effective interaction and communication. Included in this unwritten code of behavioural rules or norms is the expectation that group members will be honest and spontaneous in relation to their feelings about the group and others in it. Thus, from an early stage, group members are encouraged by the leader to interact freely, to be non-judgmental and accepting of others, and to trust the group sufficiently to engage in self-disclosure which will lead to new understanding and change. Some of the rules or norms referred to here may have, in fact, been explicitly stated by the leader even before the group started, and individual members are often aware of the kind of behaviour which is expected from participants. Pre-group assessment procedures and selection of members (referred to in chapter two) will have gone some way in teaching prospective members about ways to proceed. However, in shaping group norms, it is the example of the leader, which has more impact than anything expressed verbally or explicitly. The term 'modelling' is used by Yallom (1995:116) to describe this kind of example setting whereby the leader demonstrates a range of behaviours conducive to therapeutic outcomes. Attitudes of active listening, sensitive responding, respect for and non-judgmental acceptance of others, are all behavioural norms which group leaders should seek to exemplify in therapy and counselling groups.

Regrettably, groups are not always therapeutic in the way just described. Sometimes a culture develops in groups which values norms that are antipathetic to helpful or therapeutic outcomes for members. Such a situation can occur when, for example, the leader does not have sufficient experience or confidence to model attitudes of openness, honesty, and a willingness to use self-disclosure when appropriate. A consequence of this kind of inhibition is that group members become inhibited in turn: conversation becomes shallow, and connections between members is reduced to a superficial level which precludes real involvement and communication.

Norms develop early in a group which means that the kind of behaviour valued from the outset will help shape their development. Group members are concerned to establish from the beginning what is acceptable behaviour, and they are more likely to conform to standards of acceptable behaviour when the quality of interpersonal relationships is perceived to be positive from the start.

⟨ EXERCISE 10 ⟩

GROUP NORMS
Time: 30 mins.

This is an exercise which you can complete regardless of the type of group you are in. It is meant to encourage you to think carefully about the implicit norms of your group, and to identify, through completion of the following questionnaire, the unstated rules and standards which you and other group members have consistently and tacitly observed. Working individually, complete the questionnaire, and then compare your answers with those in the rest of the group.

1 I can use any kind of language I choose in this group. Agree / Disagree

2 I can wear whatever I like in the group. Agree / Disagree.

3 Addressing the leader informally is usual in the group. Agree / Disagree.

4 Addressing other members by their first name is usual in the group. Agree / Disagree.

5 Members don't mind if someone arrives late for a group meeting. Agree / Disagree.

6 Members don't mind if someone leaves before a meeting is over. Agree / Disagree.

7 It is all right to disagree openly with anyone in the group. Agree / Disagree.

8 It is all right to make jokes in the group. Agree / Disagree.

9 It is all right to say so when you are confused in the group. Agree / Disagree.

10 It is acceptable to talk about how you feel in the group. Agree / Disagree.

EXERCISE 11

BREAKING THE RULES

Time: As follows.

This is another exercise which is meant to encourage discussion about implicit group norms. It should be organized by leaders or facilitators in a way which will actively demonstrate to the group what happens when some members violate certain group norms. In order to do this, the leader or facilitator should ask several members of the group to agree to an experiential exercise, which will be carried out at the following group meeting. It is probably best to ask two to three members (out of a group of say ten to twelve) to participate in the exercise, but the number depends on the size of the group overall. The exercise should be conducted in the following way:

Ask selected group members to come to the next meeting prepared to break one, or more, of the group's implicit norms. They can do this by **(A)** Wearing a style of dress which differs from the group's usual style. If, for example, group members tend to dress informally, ask those taking part in the exercise to dress as formally as possible for the next meeting. **(B)** Arriving late for the next meeting and leaving early. **(C)** Addressing the leader in an unaccustomed way. If the usual way of addressing the leader is an informal one, those taking part in the exercise should switch to a formal style. **(D)** Using inappropriately timed humour or jokes in the group. **(E)** Engaging in a combination of some or all of these behaviours.

In order to conduct the experiential exercise successfully, the leader needs to observe and monitor the reactions of group members to the behaviour of those taking part in it. Those taking part should also monitor their own perceptions of what is happening in the group when they break implicit rules. Afterwards, the subject of group norms needs to be discussed by the whole group, along with an analysis of all the responses generated by the exercise.

GROUP ROLES

In the section entitled Group Processes we looked at some of the ways people interact in groups, and at the various contributions they make. The word roles is used to describe the different parts which members play in a group. These different roles are taken on by individual members and are based on their past experiences in groups, as well as on their current perceptions of how they should behave in the present one. Within organizations people may, of course, be assigned specific roles in groups, in which case each individual's role is clearly defined from the start. However, even when this formal definition is absent, roles evolve anyway and when they are not based on each person's past experience and current perceptions of how to behave, they may be prompted by what Baron et al. (1996:5) call 'psychological needs within the group'. It may be, for example, that the group needs a joker to relieve tension and anxiety, or even to draw attention to issues within the group, which are deliberately avoided in more serious discussion. At other times, the persistent questioner or critic may be needed by the group to clarify or elucidate certain subjects which are too threatening for the other members to address themselves. Obviously, when a member assumes a group role in this way, it has much more to do with the collective needs of the group than with a particular member's own requirements. Ettin (1999:162) suggests that a member selected in this way may be the only person allowed to express certain views or demonstrate certain attitudes. In this kind of situation, where roles are prescribed and handed to one person, other group members need to be encouraged to consider why this is happening. The following Case study highlights this point:

CASE STUDY: LARRY

A therapy group had been set up in an area which had a high incidence of depression among young men. The response to the initiative was immediate, and the group facilitator (John) had ten members in the group when it started. However, at an early stage he became aware that most of the group members were very anxious, and obviously nervous at the prospect of sharing and communicating in the group. It was also apparent that many of the members were reluctant to address or question him directly, preferring instead that a particular member (Allen) should speak indirectly for them. At the second meeting of the group Allen asked several questions:

Allen: *What happens if someone else wants to join? How will they know what is confidential or not?*

John: *The group is complete now. This is the complete group. Remember we talked about it being a closed group?*

Allen: *Yes I know we did, but I was just thinking about confidentiality and wondering what would happen if there were changes?*

John: *Changes ...*

Allen: *What if someone left early?*

Martin: (another member) *All these questions.* (Laughs) *We did talk about all that at the start.*

John: *Perhaps Allen is asking about things that concern everyone, things you might not want to ask yourselves. Confidentiality, for example, that's something everyone wants to be sure about.*

Martin: *Well that's for sure. Yes, I agree with that.*

In the Case study above, Allen was clearly asking questions on behalf of the group, and although Martin expressed some impatience with the persistent questioning, he did concede that he, and other group members, needed answers too. The group facilitator was concerned to highlight the group's preoccupation with the issue of confidentiality, and to bring questions relating to it into the open. If he had not addressed the group's concerns in this way, anxieties about confidentiality would not have disappeared. Instead, these anxieties may have re-surfaced, probably at regular intervals, and perhaps in a disguised form, effectively hampering the work of the group and any therapeutic outcomes it might hope to have. In the next Case study, joking rather than questioning, serves to mask the concerns of the whole group. Again, one member of the group takes on the role of joker.

CASE STUDY: PAULA

In a training group of fourteen students, Paula acted as the group joker from the beginning. The other students in the group appeared to enjoy and encourage her humour, especially when she focused on the shortcomings of Richard, one of the group trainers. Richard was often late for group meetings, though the reasons he gave for his behaviour were always, superficially at least, legitimate and hard to challenge. When he appeared late, yet again, for a group session, Paula was the first to greet him.

Paula: *We were beginning to wonder if we should send out a search party!*

Richard: *I do appreciate your concern; all your concern* (looks around as everyone laughs).

Paula: *Well, aren't you going to tell us ...*

Richard: *Tell you what?*

Paula: *What it was that happened this time.*

Angela: *Paula!*

Paula: *Come on ... you know we would all like to know. Everyone is just as curious as I am.*

In fact, everyone was indeed just as curious as Paula about the meaning of Richard's behaviour. But since they were dependent on him for good grades on the course, members were unwilling to challenge him openly. Paula's joking served a purpose, because it routinely highlighted Richard's habitual lateness. This was not an adequate solution in the long term though. A more effective, open and direct course of action was needed to challenge Richard's behaviour. At a much later stage in the life of the group, another member (Zoe) did voice her anger about his time keeping, and then asked openly for an explanation. As a result of this challenge, other group members became sufficiently confident to voice their resentment too. It goes without saying that Richard's cavalier attitude to time keeping, his casual disrespect for students, as well as his lack of self-awareness, were all reprehensible for someone in such a position. It is very difficult for students, who are aware of the power imbalance in their relationship with a teacher, to question behaviour, even when it is clearly unprofessional.

The role of scapegoat is another role which is often assigned to (or taken on by) one particular member of the group. The dynamics underlying this phenomenon are fairly complex in psychological terms, and usually represent the projection of unacceptable feelings by various group members onto one person. A victim, who is designated to carry unacknowledged or unwanted personal attributes for others, often invites the role, though not, of course, consciously. However, the group scapegoat is frequently a person who is used to the role, which may have first been assigned to them within their own family. Because of this early identification with the role, the scapegoat is likely to exhibit habitual ways of behaving which, in fact, invite hostility from other group members. An anxious, apologetic person, might, for example, tacitly invite others to dump their faults and negative feelings onto him. On the other hand, the scapegoat in a group may simply be different in more obvious ways. Someone from another cultural background, race or ethnic origin, may be singled out, quite simply, because of their distinction. Any member of a group, who is dissimilar in some way, may become a scapegoat victim to be blamed when things go wrong. One effect of this transference of negative attributes to one person is that other group members can avoid looking more closely at themselves and their own unacceptable characteristics. A central task for the group leader / facilitator is to encourage members to address and own all the difficult issues which they avoid by means of scapegoating. This explicit focus is essential, not only to enable group members to confront their own negative feelings, but also to protect the scapegoat who is likely to leave if the situation is not addressed. In the next Case study we can see how the group counsellor deals with scapegoating:

CASE STUDY: RONAN

In a group made up of young adults with a history of substance abuse, one member, Ronan, was singled out and scapegoated at quite an early stage. Ronan had lived as an itinerant for many years, and, largely because of ill health, had a poor employment record as well. However, nearly all the other members of the group had been in and out of work too, though this was not openly acknowledged in the group until the leader encouraged them to look closely at their attitude and behaviour towards Ronan who seemed to epitomize all the difficulties they denied in themselves. There were indirect references to 'spongers,' and more direct comments made to Ronan about his New Age lifestyle:

Wayne: *What did you live on when you were roaming around the country?*

Ronan: *It wasn't like that ... I had T.B.*

Lynda: *Yes, but not all the time you didn't.*

Wayne: *Didn't you ever think, sod it, I'll get a job and settle down?*

Colin: (Group counsellor) *I wonder what's happening in the group right now.*

Liz: *Everyone seems to be attacking Ronan.*

Colin: *Yes, that's right. Maybe attacking one person for a particular thing is a way of not looking at ourselves.*

Liz: *Well, I for one have been on benefits for yonks. Why should I be ashamed of that? What I mean is, why should we have a go at Ronan when we're all in the same boat?*

In this instance, the counsellor's intervention was minimal, but sufficient to direct the group's attention to their scapegoating behaviour and what it implied. By focusing on group process, Colin was able to offer some protection to Ronan, who was clearly being used by the group as a target for their own unacceptable feelings. Liz, who had closely observed what was happening, was able to pick up on Colin's comment and then identify straight away what was happening. Later in the book we shall look again at the subject of scapegoating, and at the meaning of other types of behaviour, which individuals exhibit in groups.

GROUPWORK SKILLS

At the beginning of this chapter we noted that the actual communication skills used in groupwork are sometimes not emphasized in research and literature. This is because other forms of learning about groups, including experience and participation, tend to be seen as the best kind of education in this context. However, it is difficult to see how participation and experience can be truly beneficial in the absence of skills practice and theory. In this section, we shall discuss those interpersonal skills which form a basis for effective communication when people come together in groups. Included in this category are the central skills of active listening, observing, paraphrasing and summarizing.

Hargie et al. (1994:310) discuss a further range of groupwork skills, with particular reference to those essential for effective leadership. These encompass both task and maintenance skills and include: initiating / focusing, clarifying / elaborating, promoting contributions, and supporting or encouraging. Therapy and counselling groups also require a range of affective skills, especially those that encourage the exploration of feelings, and those which acknowledge and validate feelings. Skills of sensitive confrontation and interpretation are two such skills; so too are the skills of reflecting feelings and giving feedback.

Listening

It is probably true to say that most people over-estimate the quality of their own listening. Students often assume that good listening skills are somehow acquired over time, without too much attention to the process. However, effective listening is never passive, but requires practice and awareness of all the factors which work against it. Active listening, a term commonly used in relation to individual counselling, is just as relevant in group therapy, but is seldom developed without effort, and a willingness to listen to oneself as well as to others. Throughout our daily interactions with others, whether at work, with the family or socially, most of us listen in a casual or perfunctory way. The fact that our relationships may suffer as a result of this superficial approach is unlikely to occur to many people. Occasionally a deficit in listening ability is identified when someone in crisis who needs, and expects, the kind of emotional support we find ourselves unable to give, confronts us. At times like these we may 'hear' the words spoken, without making or establishing any real connection with the person in distress. In this context, it is important to stress that hearing and listening are not synonymous. It is, for example, possible to hear what a person is saying without ever being aware of the total communication, and all its emotional implications. In fact people are often afraid to listen in an active way, because to do so might encourage the speaker to get in touch with emotions which could alarm the listener. Poorly developed listening skills are due to a variety of factors, many of which stem from experiences in early life. For example:

◆ Although children may listen to their parents, their parents frequently do not listen carefully to them. One reason for this is that even the most enlightened adults often (and sometimes without thinking) subscribe to the view that children should be seen and not heard. This inattention from adults may persist into teenage years. One of the often-repeated complaints of teenagers is that parents do not listen to them.

◆ When children go to school they are, once again, required to listen, this time as they are being taught. However, because of the numbers of children present in any class, each child is unlikely to experience sustained quality listening from teachers. In any case, teachers do not have the time, or training, to listen with empathy to each child's emotional concerns.

◆ Being able to express oneself verbally is a skill highly valued at all levels of work and society. There is no corresponding emphasis on listening and observing skills.

Active listening means actually hearing the meaning behind what is being said. One student in a group of trainee counsellors described her growing awareness of this when her teenage son approached her tentatively on several occasions to talk about problems he was having.

Because I'm so busy as a single mum, and so stressed at work, I found myself getting irritated each time he said he was fed up. I couldn't understand what he was on about, especially since I work so hard and he gets most things that he asks for, within reason. Then recently, after our two sessions here in the group talking about active listening, it became clear to me that I wasn't remotely listening to him. So the next evening, when I knew we would have time together, I set aside everything

*else and brought up the subject of how he felt. I made sure I gave him all my atten-
tion, and I know he was aware of this too, and we talked about loads of things I
didn't even dream he'd be concerned about. One result of this was that I discovered he was quite depressed. This gave me a shock, but I was able to persuade him
to let me make an appointment with our GP to see him. Another outcome was that
I agreed to let him have a dog. This was something he wanted for a very long time,
but I had never really listened to him before, so I didn't know just how important
it was to him. Now when I see him with the dog I can't believe the change in him.
I make sure we talk on a regular basis now. More than anything, I make sure I listen
to him.*

In addition to the reasons for poor listening already discussed, a number of other factors can
impede our capacity to actively hear what another person is trying to convey. To test your
own listening skills, complete the following exercise and then discuss the points raised in it
with other members of your group.

EXERCISE 12

ACTIVE LISTENING
Time: 15 mins. to complete the questionnaire. 15 mins. for group discussion.

1 When someone needs to talk I sit down and give them time. True / False

2 Sometimes I wish people would hurry up when they talk. True / False

3 I often spend time alone so that I can listen to myself. True / False

4 It doesn't matter if I have lots of things on my mind, I still listen well. True / False

5 When I am tired I don't listen well. True / False

6 When someone doesn't listen to me I feel humiliated and discounted. True / False

7 If I feel angry I can't hear a thing anyone is saying to me. True / False

8 When I listen to others I find myself making judgments about them. True / False

9 When someone talks to me I think of my own, similar experiences. True / False

10 When I'm listening I keep thinking about what I should say in reply. True / False

11 If I'm busy I don't listen well. True / False

12 I get resentful if the person I'm listening to won't listen to me. True / False

13 Learning to listen takes time and practice. True / False

14 Good listening means noting voice tone and body language too. True / False

15 I always listen to others because I want people to like me. True / False

16 When someone tells me something I don't like, I tend to switch off. True / False

17 Adults tended to listen to me when I was a child. True / False

18 I can listen well to facts, but not to strong emotions. True / False

19 To listen well there should be no interruptions. True / False

20 To listen well you need to hear what is not being said too. True / False

The exercise you have just completed should generate some discussion about various aspects of listening and the factors which work against it. The next exercise is more experiential, since it asks you to participate in a group listening exercise, and to note any difficulties you, and other members of the group encounter.

⟨ **EXERCISE 13** ⟩

LISTENING IN TURNS
Time: 40 mins.

This is an exercise which needs to be organized by a group leader or facilitator. Participants are asked to work in groups of 4–6, each taking it in turn to speak for several minutes on a specific topic. The other members of the group should listen in silence, without asking questions or offering any comment. Possible subjects for discussion include the following:

◆ A very happy experience in my life

◆ My most heroic failure

◆ The biggest surprise I ever got

◆ What I would love most in the world

◆ My greatest achievement

◆ The best holiday I ever had

◆ The thing I regret most

In order to do this exercise, participants will have some preparation time to choose, and think about, a topic for discussion. When each person has contributed, ask him or her to discuss the exercise, with particular reference to:

1 Any difficulties they experienced in listening when each person spoke.

2 How each individual perceived the group's listening when speaking.

Afterwards, in the whole group, discuss and share experiences. This is important if several groups were involved in the exercise.

Observing

In addition to listening as an aural activity, it is also important to develop habits of observation and seeing. These habits are essential if we are really concerned to communicate effectively. In order to refine our listening skills we need to learn to look at people as they speak, not just to show that we are interested, but also to comprehend and appreciate the totality and essence of what they communicate. Observation is especially relevant in the group context. This is because each person speaking will have some effect on everyone else present. To work effectively with groups, therefore, it is essential to learn how to observe each speaker in turn, while simultaneously observing the reaction of group members to what is being said. This kind of observation is something which group participants, as well as group leaders, need to be able to do. Earlier in this chapter we discussed group process, and made a distinction between what people say in groups (content) and what they do (process). If we look again at this distinction we can see that content refers to what a group says, while process refers to how a group talks about something. Observing group members, and monitoring one's own responses, means looking, listening and tuning in to the overall feeling or atmosphere in the group at all stages. Barnes et al. (1999:5) define observation as 'the best starting point for what happens in a group.' In addition, they link this kind of observation to the tradition of mother–baby studies in which an observer records not just what is seen, but also his own emotional response to the interaction he has witnessed.

Non-verbal clues

The most obvious way of observing others in a group is to notice all non-verbal indicators, including gestures, voice tone, facial expression, body posture, responses when others are speaking, as well as frequency and order of individual contributions. Hope & Timmel (1999:54) describe the kind of observation which they find useful in monitoring group process. Included in their description are the following considerations:

◆ Who is speaking?
◆ For how long does that person speak?
◆ How often does that person speak?
◆ Who does that person look at when speaking?

In relation to this last point, further observation is useful. For example, does the speaker address one individual (possibly the leader) more often than she addresses others? Is he / she looking at certain individuals for possible support, or is he / she glancing at everyone in the group in turn? Perhaps the speaker is unable to give eye contact to anyone, or maybe he / she keeps her eyes fixed on an inanimate object like the floor or window? When one person finishes speaking, who agrees or disagrees, and who speaks next? Do people interrupt when someone is speaking, or do other group members listen with respect and patience, even to views very different from their own? Are there people in the group who seldom interact, and if so how do they look? Video recording is one way of observing what happens in groups. When participants are given the opportunity to observe themselves in this way, they are often surprised by what they see. One member of a training group described her experience of watching a video recording of herself and other members.

> We were all horrified when we saw ourselves on video. First of all, we could hardly believe how we cut across each other and interrupted at times. I was able to see that I frequently dominated the group, that I talked a lot, and that I gave people advice, even when they didn't ask for it! I know I have been accused of this in the past, especially at work, but I always resented the suggestion that I was bossy or domineering. I simply didn't see myself in that way. When I saw myself on video though, I knew it was true. It was a very hard lesson to accept, but the reality of it was there to see.

RECORDING INTERACTIONS
Time: 45 mins.

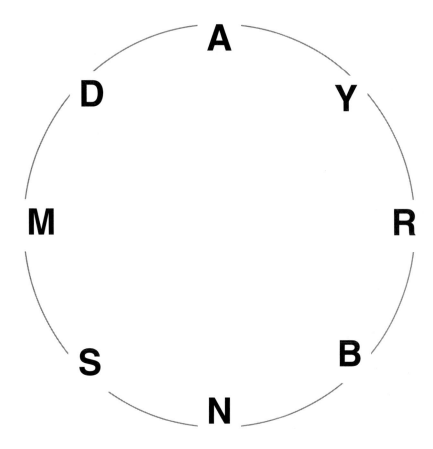

Figure 3.1. Drawing the group.

A – Aoife **B** – Brenda **D** – Dylan **M** – Meera
N – Nick **R** – Ross **S** – Suhail **Y** – Yasmin

There are other ways, besides video, of observing and recording group interactions. One method of observation is to draw a circle, indicating each member along with his or her seating position in the group. Fig. 3.1. is an example of how this can be done. It is a chart which shows who speaks to whom in a group, and is based on the work of Jacob Moreno (1943). It also shows how often each person speaks to other members, and to the leader as well. In chapter one, we referred to Moreno's influence on groups, and to his interest in theatre. Another important innovation from Moreno was his development of the sociogram or 'social compass', which he used to map the inter-personal dynamics of a group. By noting non-verbal signs, spatial relations and physical proximity, Moreno was able to see the exact order of social interactions within a group.

In order to complete the exercise, it is necessary to appoint an observer (or observers) who should record interactions as they occur. It is best if the group leader or facilitator appoints the observers for the exercise, bearing in mind that the exercise can be repeated at other sessions using different observers each time. The group may be given a specific topic for discussion, or they may simply be encouraged to interact in a more spontaneous, less structured way. The observers should chart interactions between members, using arrows to show who speaks to whom. See Fig. 3.2.

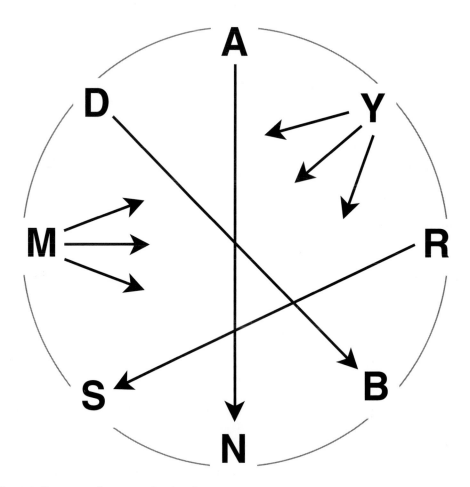

Fig. 3.2. Patterns of communication in a group.

When the exercise is complete, the sociogram should show a series of lines connecting group members. An arrow pointing to the person addressed indicates one person speaking to another. Remarks made to the group as a whole are indicated by shorter arrows from the person making the remark. It should be possible to see a pattern of interactions which can then be discussed by the group as a whole.

Paraphrasing and Summarizing

Paraphrasing (or rephrasing) and summarizing are skills used by both leaders and participants in groupwork. The word paraphrasing describes the process of re-wording what
another person says, while the word summarizing describes the skill of summing up the
main elements of that communication. The phrase 'reflecting back' is also sometimes used
to describe the process of re-wording, but it has added meaning because it tends to encompass feeling as well as content. When responding to another person in the group it is important to show that you understand what is said, and what is felt. For example:

You felt unjustly treated by the examining board when they rejected your appeal.

The above response could be summarized to make it briefer. Thus:

You felt unjustly treated ...

Even though the second response is shorter, it still picks up and acknowledges the speaker's
feelings about what happened, and indicates that he has been heard. Summarization is also
sometimes used by group leaders to coordinate or bring together various themes or ideas
expressed by group members. For example:

*So, there are several views here about conflict and what it means. Let's just look at
these ...*

This kind of summary enables group members to look again at all the ideas and issues discussed so far.

Focusing

The skill of focusing is used, as the term suggests, to keep track of group discussion, and to
draw members' attention back to this:

*We seem to have wandered off from the point we were discussing earlier about
group attendance ...*

Focusing is a skill that is often used by group leaders, but can, in fact, be used by group
members too. In fact, members of both counselling and psychotherapy groups often learn,
through observation of the leader, to use many of the skills described in this section.

Clarifying and Elaboration

The word clarifying is also self-explanatory. It refers to the skill of seeking to make things
clearer, and again group leaders often use it in particular. For example:

Though I did understand your first point, I'm not sure about your last ...

In seeking to clarify what the last speaker said, the leader starts by showing that she / he
is, in fact, listening, but needs some help. She also invites the speaker to elaborate on what
she has said.

Asking questions

Most people have a tendency to ask too many questions in their day-to-day interactions with others. Often questions predominate when people should be listening, and therapy groups are no less susceptible to this propensity than other gatherings. In fact, one danger that can arise when members decide to 'help' a particular individual in the group (who may or may not have solicited this support) is that assistance may take the form of persistent questioning or advice giving. Once again, the leader needs to model a much different approach, relying less on questions and more on active listening, paraphrasing, reflecting back, and clarifying. When questions need to be asked, they should be open ended rather than closed. Open questions give members the opportunity to reply at their own pace, to expand on and clarify specific areas if they wish. For example:

Is there something you would like to say about your present relationships?

Can you say what that past experience means to you now?

And the feelings associated with that?

Active listening and competent questioning go together in groupwork; indeed it is probably true to say that when group participants listen well, they are less likely to ask frequent questions.

Initiating

The skill of initiating is essential in groups, and is especially useful when members appear to be stuck or unable to move forward. Thus:

Perhaps we could start by saying how it feels to be here …

The above opening remark might be made when, for example, group members have gathered together for the first meeting.

Promoting contributions

To promote contributions, the leader needs to be constantly aware of each member's participation in group discussion. She also needs to know when certain members want to speak, but have not been given the opportunity to do so. For example:

Louise, I can see you want to come in on this …

The group leader was aware that Louise was trying to make eye contact with her, and that she had, on several occasions, started to speak.

Supporting and Encouraging

In any group it is important to support and encourage group members, especially those who appear shy or tentative. In counselling and therapy groups there may be many such members, so the leader may need to support and encourage at regular intervals. The following is one example:

> That was obviously difficult for you to say Justin, but you showed great courage in doing so.

The group member referred to here (Justin) was quiet and withdrawn in the group until a discussion about bullying arose. Then he recounted some of his own experiences.

Interpretation

When using the skill of interpretation the group leader seeks to give meaning to what is taking place in the group. Thus:

> It seems to me the group is now saying that control is the issue, not slimming.

Through the use of this interpretation the leader gives voice to several indirect comments made by group members concerning their eating problems.

Confrontation

Confrontation is a word with strong connotations, but the skill it describes is one which should be used sensitively and with care. In the next example the leader confronts a group member who is argumentative and disruptive:

> Jo, it seems to me you argue with people when they describe their own experiences of becoming addicted.

In this instance the leader had to confront Jo because she refused to listen to other people's experiences without imposing her own view about what they should have done.

Feedback

Group members need feedback from the leader at regular intervals throughout their time together. Edelwich & Brodsky (1992:133) suggest that feedback, to be successful, should be 'solicited, not imposed.' In order to give feedback in an appropriate way, therefore, 'I' statements should be used by the person giving it. Group members may also be asked to give feedback, and when this is the case the leader should offer some directives on how it is done. For example:

> Garrett has asked for feedback from the group about his fear of applying for the job. He's not really looking for advice because he's said so, but he would like to hear how others coped in the same situation. If you feel you have something that would

help, just start by saying what it was. Be specific and keep to the point. Talk direct-ly to Garrett, and try to give definite examples. Then we need to confirm with Garrett that this is what he needs.

In the example given, the leader clarifies what Garrett says he wants from the group. The leader is also concerned to discourage advice giving. This is because advice tends to 'impose' solutions belonging to someone else, and is therefore seldom helpful. It also has the effect of putting people on the defensive. Judgmental statements should also be discouraged in feedback. Giving constructive feedback is obviously a skill which group leaders need to pos-sess themselves before they can teach group members about it. When they do possess it though, they can then model it for the benefit of the whole group.

References

Bales, R. (1950) *Interaction Process Analysis: A method for the study of small groups.* Reading, M.A., Addison Wesley.

Barnes, B., Ernst, S. & Hyde, K. (1999) *An Introduction to Groupwork: A group analytic per-spective.* London, Macmillan.

Baron, R. S., Kerr, N. L., & Miller, N. (1996) *Group Process, Group Decision, Group Action.* Buckingham, O.U. Press.

Benjamin, J., Bessant, J., & Watts, R. (1997) *Making Groups Work: rethinking practice.* New South Wales, Allen & Unwin.

Brandler, S. & Roman, C. (1999) 2nd Ed. *Groupwork: Skills and Strategies for Effective Interventions.* New York, The Haworth Press.

Cathcart, R., Samovar, L., & Henman, L. (1996) 7th Ed. *Small Group Communication: Theory and Practice.* U.S.A., Brown & Benchmark.

Douglas, T. (1995) *Survival in Groups.* Buckingham, O.U. Press.

Ettin, M. F. (1999) *Foundations and Applications of Group Psychotherapy.* London, Jessica Kingsley Publishers.

Hargie, O., Saunders, C., & Dickson, D. (1994) 3rd Ed. *Social Skills in Interpersonal Communication.* London, Routledge.

Hope, A., & Timmell, S. (1999) Book 2 *Training for Transformation.* London, Intermediate Technology Publications.

Johnson, D. W., & Johnson, F. P. (1997) 6th Ed. *Joining Together: Group Theory and Group Skills.* U.S.A., Allyn & Bacon.

Moreno, J. L. (1943) *Who shall survive? Foundations of Sociometry, Group Psychotherapy and Sociodrama.* New York, Beacon House.

Whitaker, D. S. (1992) *Using Groups to help People.* London, Routledge.

Wilson, G. I. (1995) 4th Ed. *Groups in Context.* U.S.A., McGraw Hill Inc.

Yallom, I. D. (1995) 4th Ed. *The Theory and Practice of Group Psychotherapy.* New York, Basic Books.

4

How groups develop

A group experience, like any good story, has a beginning, a middle and an end. Like stories, groups also have stages in between, all of which have been described by researchers, practitioners and writers in the field. In this chapter we shall consider the various stages of group development, with special reference to some of the theories proposed. Well-known models of group life, including those suggested by Tuckman (1965), Benson (1997) and Yallom (1995) will be discussed.

In addition to theories of group development, however, it is important that you consider your personal participation in groups generally. If you are currently part of a training group you should look closely at your experiences in it, and then examine these in the light of the theoretical concepts described. For these reasons, theory will be linked to practice at key points throughout the chapter, with exercises designed to highlight and consolidate these links. The various phases of group development, which have been outlined by theorists and practitioners, approximate in many ways, to stages in the life cycle of the individual. Because of these similarities, this chapter will also focus on links between theories of group development and the life stages through which we all have to pass to achieve maturity and growth.

It is important to state at this point that not all groups conform to an exact pattern or sequence of events throughout. On the other hand, it is useful to consider models of group life, since they offer some guidance about what is likely to happen at key stages. They also provide useful information about the possible thoughts, feelings, fears and inhibitions which participants experience over time. These factors have special significance for leaders and facilitators, since they need to appraise and monitor group stages and process if they are to fulfill their leadership tasks effectively. The following Case study illustrates this last point:

CASE STUDY: STUART

Stuart, who worked as a teacher in Further Education, and was trained in groupwork skills, was asked to stand in for a colleague who was unable to teach his evening class because of illness. The twelve students attending the class were all adults on a basic skills counselling course, and they were aware that there had been a last minute change of group leader.

When Stuart arrived for the first session he found that group members who arrived shortly after he did, were quiet at first, though judging from their expressions, body language and demeanor, they were obviously anxious as well. Almost as soon as the session began several students expressed concern about the absent teacher. One member of the class asked Stuart, indirectly, about his qualifications to teach, a concern which was clearly meant to ascertain just how safe or reliable this group and its leader were going to be.

At this stage, two other group members talked about their difficulty in locating the room in which sessions were to take place. They also wondered if they would be able to stay in the group, since they had identified other pressing work and domestic commitments which had surfaced after their registration. Stuart was aware that group members were expressing a high level of dependency and anxiety, both directly and indirectly. He was also mindful of the fact that members were already establishing their degree of commitment to the group. This concern about commitment is characteristic of the initial stage of group development. Other concerns include issues of trust and mistrust.

These preoccupations may be compared to certain theories of human development. According to Erikson (1995), for example, the first year of life is marked by feelings of anxiety, estrangement and mistrust. At this fundamental stage the quality of the child/carer relationship is crucial since it is through this relationship that a sense of trust and confidence develops. In new situations, especially those where issues of inclusion and exclusion predominate, unconscious memories of the earliest and most vulnerable period of life are re-activated. Later in the book, when we come to discuss psychodynamic theories, we shall look more closely at the unconscious motivating factors in the life of a group.

Participating in a new venture with a number of strangers represents a novel and quite threatening experience, which tends to trigger the kind of responses which Stuart observed in the group. In this instance the response was heightened because the original facilitator 'failed' to turn up. During this explorative stage, therefore, Stuart's task was to encourage and facilitate the expression of individual feelings and concerns. Other tasks which he needed to address included the development of ground rules, setting norms, the establishment of trust, dealing openly with problems and modelling open and non-defensive behaviour.

An important point here is the degree to which Stuart as group leader was able to anticipate, contain and deal appropriately with the anxieties and concerns expressed by group members. Without adequate training and theoretical knowledge he would have been unable to do this. In the absence of a structure or framework to guide him, his task would have been impossible.

EXERCISE 15

BEGINNINGS

Time: 40 minutes.

Working in pairs, discuss your experiences of joining your present group. Look at these experiences under the following headings:

◆ Anticipatory feelings.

◆ Feelings on first meeting other group members.

◆ Your own behaviour during the first meeting.

◆ The behaviour of the group as a whole.

◆ Your expectations about the role of the group leader.

When you have finished your discussion, join the other members of the whole group to share your ideas and findings. Which experiences, if any, were common to all of you?

CONCERNS AT THE BEGINNING

At each stage of development, groups are faced with different problems and issues which leaders need to understand and address if they are to help participants benefit from the group experience. When the beginning stage of a group is marked by attitudes of consistency, safety, trust and support, members are encouraged to express their private feelings, fears and anxieties. Not all group members will, of course, feel the same degree of anxiety and concern about their present and forthcoming experiences. Some members may lack experience of groups, while others may have participated in a variety of groups. Other factors, including the nature and purpose of the current group, will also have a bearing on the expectations and behaviour of members at the initial stage. A therapy group in which participants are expected to disclose personal information will, for example, tend to generate a high level of tension and concern. When the group does not require this level of self-disclosure, members are less likely to feel the same degree of anxiety.

Regardless of group types and purpose, however, any new situation where a number of people meet for the first time is sure to provoke apprehension about personal performance, acceptability and the degree to which others can be trusted. Benson (1997) refers to what he describes as 'inclusion' issues arising during the beginning stage of group life. These inclusion issues are common to all groups, and point to a basic ambivalence or conflict which members experience in relation to the group itself. Another way of stating this is to say that each individual in a new group has to make an important decision about how much personal involvement s/he wishes to have. The desire to be part of the group is finely balanced against a need for autonomy and separateness. Fears of rejection are a common experience also in the early stage; the impulse to reject the group before we are rejected by it is another, often unconscious fear. Tuckman (1965), who proposed that groups progress through several developmental stages, including forming, storming, norming and performing, described the first of these (forming), as a time characterized by anxiety, uncertainty and dependence on the person leading the group. At this stage, members of the group often want to be told what to do and how to behave. Ettin (1999:407) refers to a developmental sequence, the first phase of which is marked by what he describes as an 'inherent regression' to a much earlier stage of experience in life. In her discussion about integration in groups, Long (1992:54) points to the way in which group members usually expect to *join* a group, rather than to *create* or *form* one. To create or form a group implies an active approach from the beginning, whereas the act of joining a group seems more passive, and by extension, more dependent by comparison. Yallom (1995: 294) suggests that all groups follow a broad developmental progression, a knowledge of which should help group therapists understand what is likely to happen at various stages. In his description of the initial, or orientation phase of group development, Yallom defines it as one in which group members search for guidance, structure, goals and clear boundaries. Dependence on the leader is another characteristic of Yallom's definition, as it is with so many other researchers and groupworkers.

From these descriptions and definitions we can identify a remarkable degree of consistency about the general attitudes and behaviour of members on first joining a group. However, as indicated at the beginning of this chapter, not all groups conform to an exact linear sequence of events and much of what happens in different groups is unique and unpredictable. In fact, it is probably true to say that there is a current trend opposed to the notion of definite sequential stages in groups. In its place, Barnes et al. (1999:52) refer to the 'developmental tasks', which, in their view, need not necessarily be resolved once in the life of a group, but may recur at various intervals thereafter. Moreover, these developmental tasks, issues and themes need to be highlighted and discussed as they emerge in the group. When they are addressed in this way group members have a better chance of understanding what is happening for them individually and for the group as a whole. In any group there is a tendency to return repeatedly to different issues, especially those that are problematic for many people. One example of such an issue is conflict in the group. This is a subject which we shall consider in some detail later in the book. However, it is important to highlight it here, since it represents a recurring theme in groups, and serves to illustrate just how cyclical group issues and phases are. Awareness of this and other aspects of group dynamics can help facilitators (and members) to become more effective, not just in the present situation, but in the various groups they belong to thereafter. On the other hand, a rigid sequential interpretation of group development is unhelpful, especially when it is used (either by group members or leaders) to impose a predetermined picture of what *should* happen at different stages. Yallom (1995:306) emphasizes the detrimental effects of rigid definitions in relation to group development, and sums this up by saying that 'each group is, at the same time, like all groups, some groups, and no other group.'

EXERCISE 16

MEMBER CONCERNS

Time: 30 minutes.

In this exercise you are asked to consider the many concerns which group members have to address when they first join a group. Working individually, look at the following list of preoccupations, which participants often experience in the forming stage of a group's life.

◆ Do I belong, or can I belong to this group?

◆ Will I be accepted or rejected in this group?

◆ How dependable is the person leading the group?

◆ Will I make a fool of myself if I speak?

◆ If I reveal something about myself will it be confidential?

◆ Will I understand what is happening in the group?

◆ Will I get what I want from the group?

◆ Can I trust the other people in the group?

◆ How much commitment can I make to this group?

In the first instance, consider how many of these concerns are familiar to you. Then, as a group, discuss the ways in which these anxieties and concerns can be contained and dealt with by group leaders.

Fig. 4.1. Group members' concerns.

PROBLEMS AT THE EARLY STAGE

Because of the range of anxieties which group members experience at the beginning, certain problems have a tendency to surface. We have already mentioned dependence on the leader as being common at this stage. In counselling and therapy groups, however, dependence is not regarded as a problem *unless* the group leader encourages it in a way which fosters certain expectations among members. These expectations include a belief that someone else (the group leader) can be relied on to solve everyone's problems and provide answers to them. The group therapist's task, therefore, is to help members identify and use their own coping and problem solving abilities, though this cannot obviously be accomplished at once. The realization and acceptance of personal, and group resources is something which tends to evolve gradually over time, and should not be forced didactically upon members, especially at the vulnerable early stage of group life. However, these considerations do not cancel the therapist's responsibility to ensure that member's anxieties and concerns are anticipated and identified when the group starts. In addition, group members should be encouraged to express these concerns in appropriate ways, so that they can be processed and understood. In the next chapter we shall discuss leadership function at this (and other) stages in more detail. Meanwhile, the following is a brief summary of the leadership tasks needed to create an environment which is therapeutic, open, and accepting for all group members at the initial stage. Some points in this summary have already been highlighted in chapter two.

◆ Careful planning before the group starts.

◆ Encouraging discussion about expectations and concerns.

◆ Being clear about the intention and purpose of the group.

◆ Being clear about confidentiality and how it applies to the group.

◆ Negotiating a group contract with members.

◆ Being clear about procedures, programmes, methods, and dates of meeting.

◆ Encouraging group cohesion and trust.

◆ Modelling attitudes of respect, openness and receptiveness to other people's views.

◆ Identifying the leader or therapist's role in the group.

◆ Defining and clarifying the distribution of responsibility in the group.

The difficulties which people experience when first joining a group are not, of course, always expressed in an explicit, verbal way. Often behaviour is much more indicative of this orientation phase, as the next Case study shows.

CASE STUDY: THE NEW GROUP

Nine members of a new counselling group met for the first session. They all arrived on time, except one woman who came fifteen minutes late. Before her arrival the other group members had begun to chat to one another in a social way, about various subjects, including the weather, and any difficulties they experienced in finding the room. Five minutes after her late arrival, the newcomer (Lorna) got a call on her mobile phone. Looking flustered, she excused herself and was about to leave the room to speak to her caller, when she changed her mind and switched the phone off. Several members of the group showed signs of disapproval at these proceedings. One member of the group (Hal) positioned his chair slightly outside the group circle, and looked nervously round the room. The group counsellor began by stating briefly why they were all there. She then referred to some basic ground rules which members already knew about through pre-group preparation. She gave her name and suggested to the members that they also introduce themselves by name, which they did. Afterwards, there was a long period of silence and some awkwardness. Attention was directed towards the group counsellor who was clearly expected to signal a beginning. Eventually she said:

> Would anyone like to make a start? I know it's difficult to get started. I feel that myself in a new group. Are there any concerns you would like to begin with?

After this Lorna spoke up and apologized for her phone call and, laughing nervously, added that she wouldn't bring it again. In response to this, other group members nodded in approval and Hal moved his seat more firmly into the circle.

EXERCISE 17

THE NEW GROUP
Time: 20 minutes.

Working in twos, discuss the Case study outlined above, with special reference to the following points:

1 Since all behaviour in a group has some meaning, we can assume that the behaviour shown by both Lorna and Hal has meaning for them and for the group as a whole. Bearing these considerations in mind, can you identify the reasons that (A) Lorna brought her mobile phone with her to the first meeting of the group, and (B) Hal moved his chair out of the group when the phone rang.

2 The awkwardness and silence in the group was broken when the group counsellor spoke and referred to the difficulties people experience in new situations. Why, in your view, did she not refer directly to Lorna's phone call? In what way did this acknowledgment of difficulty prompt Lorna to apologize for the phone call?

The Case study just described highlights some interesting aspects of behaviour among members at the start of a group. The ringing of a phone at this vulnerable early stage was bound to cause more ringing (of alarm bells) for the group members who would have been concerned about confidentiality anyway. A caller might well have been perceived as an intruder who had not enrolled, and should not be present, even by phone, in the new group. Hal's movement out of the group signaled his discomfort when the phone rang. In one way he was saying that he now had doubts about belonging to a group which might be invaded in this way. The disapproving looks of the other members also indicated a similar concern. The group counsellor made a decision not to address the subject of the phone call immediately, since to do so would have focused attention on Lorna who was clearly anxious to begin with. When the matter was discussed later in the group, Lorna spoke of her phone as a link with home. Instead of referring directly to the phone call, the counsellor used what she regarded as appropriate self-disclosure when she spoke of her own difficulties of getting started in a new group. This level of disclosure was sufficient to encourage members, specifically Lorna to begin with, to interact with others in the group.

EXERCISE 18

SILENCE

Time: 5 minutes silence followed by group discussion.

The previous Case study describes the awkwardness and silence which is often present at the start of a new group. These silences seem interminable when they occur, and group members sometimes feel that they will never end. Silence at the beginning phase of a group can be seen as an indication that members are waiting for the leader to do something. More specifically, silence often indicates dependence and an expectation that the leader should tell everyone what to do. But the task for the leader is to encourage members to use their own resources, and the resources of the group. When group members are struggling to do this, silence is often the result.

This exercise is an experiential one, which should be organized by group trainers or leaders beforehand. The aim of the exercise is to explore silence and its effects on individual members of the group. At the start of a group session, ask members to sit in total silence for a period of five minutes. Afterwards, discuss the experience with the group as a whole. Encourage individual members to say how they experienced the silence, with special reference to its perceived length and their thoughts during it. Ask members to say in turn what they found most uncomfortable / comfortable about the experience. To complete the exercise you should describe your own feelings, as leader or facilitator, about silence in a group.

OTHER PROBLEMS

Other problems which may occur in the early stages of a group's life include poor attendance, and time keeping. Group members who habitually come late to, or miss, sessions usually give perfectly valid reasons for doing so. However, in addition to the reasons given, there are often underlying difficulties for members who cannot commit themselves to consistent and total involvement in the group. The importance of regular attendance and timekeeping are, as indicated in chapter two, usually emphasized in pre-group preparation with all potential new members. Once a group has started, however, the anxieties and fears which are characteristic of this stage, may be more pronounced for some people than for others. There may be members who, for example, experience great difficulties in relation to commitment itself, while others may start to doubt the benefits of group counselling generally.

In addition, worries about confidentiality can, as indicated in the last Case study present special problems for some group members. Persistent lateness and poor attendance are issues that should be addressed in the group as part of process observation. However, process observation, if it is to be helpful and not destructive in this context, must take place when all members are present to participate. Talking about absent or tardy members *in their absence* will only encourage gossip in the group. On the other hand, if a member leaves the group for good, it will need to focus on this with special reference to, for example, their feelings about people leaving. An example of the way in which a group counsellor or therapist could address the issues of poor timekeeping or attendance is as follows:

> *Maybe the group could help me identify what's happening when people come late. I am aware that people were late last week and today. I think we need to look at that.*

REPEATED NEW BEGINNINGS

An important consideration in relation to the initial phase of counselling and therapy groups, is that although they have just one actual beginning, they may also have what Rutan & Stone (1999:116) call repeated 'modified new beginnings'. This means that as the group progresses, new members join, thus recreating some of the early difficulties, themes and styles of group interaction which existed at the initial phase. If we consider Tuckman's model of group development, therefore, we can see that his sequence of stages is not, strictly speaking, applicable to open ended counselling and therapy groups in which beginnings may recur at frequent intervals. As noted in chapter one, the challenge for group therapists in these situations is to facilitate the re-working of themes and issues which emerge when new members enter a group and others leave.

MOVING FORWARD

Once the initial phase of group development has been negotiated, members are faced with several more important issues and tasks. Conflict in the group, and feelings of rebellion against the leader are characteristic of this stage. Brandler & Roman (1999:15) refer to this as the 'middle' or 'work' phase of the group. They also point out that it is never entirely separate from the first or last stages of group development. As we noted earlier in this chapter, issues from different developmental phases often recur in a group. This is especially true when no successful resolution of such issues has been achieved at an earlier stage. When, for example, trust has not been firmly established within the group in its initial phase, cohesion and intimacy are less likely to be present later on.

If we consider Tuckman's storming stage of development, we can see that it describes the beginning of a group's middle phase. This is the point during which residual issues from the past stage are likely to become manifest. Group members are still cautious, anxious and

others in aggressive and destructive ways that do not conform to established guidelines set out by the leader early on. These guidelines include not blaming or accusing others, but accepting personal responsibility instead. One example of scapegoating may occur when one member is seen as not participating in the group like everyone else. This non-participation may elicit verbal attacks from others, as the next Case study shows.

CASE STUDY: BLAME SOMEONE ELSE

In a counselling group of ten people, one member (Colin) did not participate in a discussion about gender roles that had arisen in the group. This prompted the following exchanges.

Gina: (looking in Colin's direction) *You've been sitting there ... not saying a word. It really gets up my nose. Have you no views about the way Jack's girlfriend reacted?*

Colin: (Looking very uncomfortable) *No.*

Raj: *You've not said a word about much so far. You must have some ideas worth hearing.*

Counsellor: *Let's look at what's happening here for a moment. I can see that Colin is being made the focus of attention, and I think we should consider why that should be. Are people angry with Colin because he isn't behaving the way we feel he should behave? If I worry about my own commitment to the group, then I might start blaming someone else for not being committed. That means I'm not looking at myself ... it gets me off the hook when I focus my anger in that way.*

In this exchange, the counsellor's intervention served to focus attention on the people who were inappropriately attacking Colin. This meant that they were encouraged to look close-ly at their reasons for confronting one person in this way. In making her responses the coun-sellor was careful to use 'I' statements to draw attention to the scapegoating, and to invite all group members to consider its meaning.

Giving advice
Occasionally group members slip into a form of interaction which relies heavily on giving advice, though this is more likely in the early stages of a group than later on. Direct advice giving of the following kind is never useful in groups:

Have you tried losing weight with the food combining method?

Why don't you try talking to your partner about it?

I think you should ask your daughter-in-law for more support.

These examples of advice show that the speaker is failing to listen properly to the person being advised. Advice says more about the giver than the receiver, and is delivered without taking into account the uniqueness of another person's experience. In other words, what might work for one person will not necessarily work for another, whose circumstances are likely to be quite different. On the other hand, feedback is certainly helpful, if appropriately given in groups. Thus one group member might usefully say to another:

> *I had real difficulty with my weight too, especially when we moved house and I felt really stressed.*

> *When I talked to my partner about my debts it was a load off my mind.*

> *During my cancer treatment I didn't want to ask anyone for help. When I did, it was a real relief.*

However, in addition to discouraging advice giving, group leaders should also highlight it in the group, so that members are encouraged to interact in more therapeutic ways. The following is an example:

> *The group seems to have slipped into giving advice. I personally don't like to be told what to do, and I'm sure other people have doubts about it too. A better way is to listen and then give some feedback about things that worked for you.*

As we noted earlier, although advice is more common in the early stages of a group, it can nevertheless surface at any time. This is especially true when a group is open ended, and new members join at various stages after the group's initial start. During these mini new beginnings, there is often a repetition of earlier developmental themes, issues and ways of relating among group members. When group members do slip into advice giving as a form of communication, it should be treated as a problem by the therapist or leader, and highlighted accordingly. The group therapist's task is to show members that it is much more productive to listen to a wide range of attitudes and responses to common difficulties, than it is to give, or receive glib advice. Through this kind of productive participation, members are helped to reconsider, and perhaps reject, their own, often dysfunctional ways of dealing with relationships or other life issues. Later in the book we shall discuss other forms of behaviour that can be problematic at any stage of group development.

Completion

Rutan & Stone (1999:118) describe group members' fulfilment of emotional needs, and attainment of goals, as evolving in three phases throughout the life of the group. These three phases include the beginning, when people react to joining and participating in a group. The second phase is one in which members react to feelings of belonging to the group, while the third consists of the 'stabilization of the mature working group.' Group development occurs, therefore, as a result of the interactions among group members, and with the leader / therapist, over a period of time. When groups are coming to an end, however, interactions among members also occur in response to the separation about to take place. Tuckman & Jensen (1977) added a stage which they described as adjourning to the model first proposed by Tuckman (1965). This final stage was seen by them as just as significant in its effects on group members as the other stages that preceded it.

Like most other aspects of groupwork, the ending phase is something that group leaders / therapists need to consider before the group starts. In addition, group members should be prepared in advance for this important stage of their experience in the group. This preparation is part of the pre-group assessment and discussion, which we considered in chapter

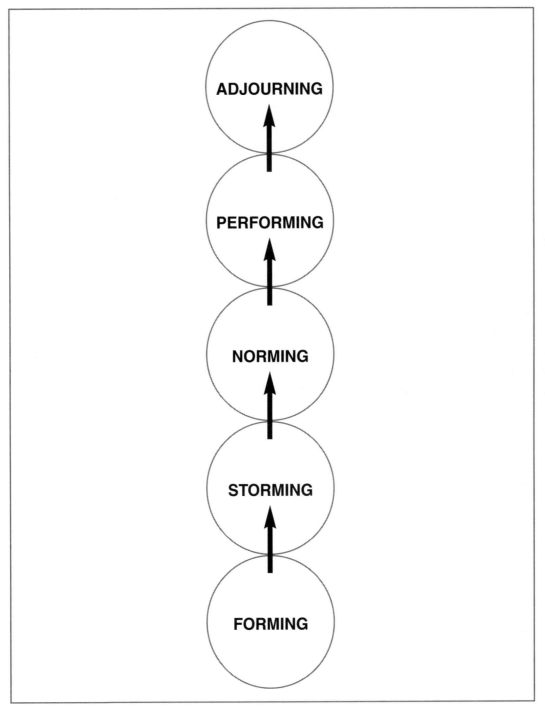

Figure 4.2. The Stages of Group Development

two. We noted that people joining a group need exact details relating to length, frequency and duration of meetings. Moreover, if members are to integrate and consolidate their experiences in the group, the subject of endings needs to be addressed at key points in the life of the group. This is especially relevant when the end of the group is approaching or imminent.

Endings in open and closed groups

When considering the ending phase in groups it is essential to make a distinction between those groups that are open ended and have no fixed termination date, and those that are closed with the end date determined in advance. If a counselling group is limited and problem focused, it is quite likely that it will take place for a specific number of weeks or months, and participants will have a pre-determined date for ending. In a group like this, individual members will obviously know when they will quit the group, as a group. Knowing when the group ends does not imply that separation and endings are made easy for members, however. On the contrary, feelings of sadness and loss are usual at this stage of disengagement. In fact, many of the reactions to leaving a group are similar to those experienced by people contemplating any significant loss. It may be, for example, that members experience denial, depression, anger and finally acceptance when the group is about to end. In an earlier chapter, reference was made to the parallels between developmental phases in groups, and those that occur throughout an individual's life span. If we consider group members' emotional responses to group termination, we can, in fact, see that they have a great deal in common with emotional reactions to impending death. According to Arrow et al. (2000:244) these responses may show themselves in attempts to save the group, plans to revive the group in a new form, and a decline in commitment and effectiveness, especially when depression is the dominant mood. Such reactions vary according to the length of time the group has been together; they also depend on the strength of interpersonal ties established among members and the intensity of their work together. In their review of research on this termination phase, Arrow et al. (2000:244) also note that a definite emphasis was placed on the 'emotional aspect of termination.' A secondary, cognitive, emphasis was also noted in these studies, an emphasis that was demonstrated in the way group members tended to review, evaluate and reflect on the life of the group as a whole.

A salient point in relation to all these findings, is that members of a group do, indeed, go through a period of mourning which needs to be recognized by facilitators / leaders. Members should be helped to come to terms with their loss, prepare for the future and then move on. Ettin (1999:274) highlights the importance of preparing members for termination of the group, and stresses that this preparation is crucial for those members who are especially sensitive to loss. Such members may begin to worry about separation long before the actual end of the group. In extreme cases, group participants may contemplate leaving the group, before the group (and its constituent members) has a chance to leave them. In situations like these, sensitive members need to be reassured about the importance of the remaining time in the group, and the value of the therapeutic work that they can still do.

Not all group members will, of course, experience the same degree of separation anxiety, and many will have derived enough insight and support from the group experience to help them deal with its closure. Most group members fall somewhere in between, however, and are likely to experience some anxiety and sense of loss when the group is about to terminate. An important point to remember here is that in referring to feelings of sadness and loss, it would be a mistake to imply that these are negative responses. On the contrary, emotional responses like these should be viewed as positive, since they indicate commitment to the group, involvement in its work and awareness of the many benefits derived from it. In addition, group termination is as Yallom (1995:261) indicates, an 'integral part of the process of therapy' and should, therefore, be viewed as a process to be understood and dealt with accordingly. Leaving a group is also the beginning of something new for members, something for which they are better prepared and more confident about than they were in the past. The following are some of the changes that members should have experienced on successful completion of counselling group participation:

◆ Acquisition of social skills
◆ Increased self-awareness
◆ Fulfillment of personal goals
◆ Insight into emotional functioning
◆ Greater awareness sof the needs and feelings of others
◆ Enhanced ability to communicate in close, personal relationships
◆ The capacity to transfer learning into everyday living

It should be emphasized that not all group members will attain the same level of gains as those outlined above. This does not mean that participants who fall short of the maximum benefits have failed in some way. It may be that the progress made by certain members is right for them at that particular time. Expectations that all group members achieve the same level of personal progress is just as unrealistic as the idea that everyone is identical in other areas of life. The leader or counsellor's task is to help all members understand that what they have achieved in the group can be held permanently by them, and will be transferred beyond the group to other areas of their lives.

When a group is open ended, termination obviously varies for different members, and is therefore less predictable for the group as a whole. Members may experience a particular kind of disturbance in such groups which is linked to lack of continuity and the challenge of assimilating new members and saying goodbye to those who leave. However, there are also benefits for members when turnover occurs in this way. In the first place, there are constant reminders in the open group of people achieving their goals, and then moving on with enhanced self-awareness and esteem. Goodbyes take place on a regular basis, and established members assimilate incoming members into the group with the help of the therapist or leader. Therefore, issues of separation and loss can be processed as they occur. This movement and change approximates to the shifts which are always present in society as a whole, so in this sense the open group is a much more authentic experience than the closed and possibly insular group could ever be. Regardless of the type of group, however, endings have the potential to activate feelings associated with past unresolved endings, and the experiences of loss that these elicit. So when one member leaves an open group, the counsellor should help other participants identify and acknowledge their own feelings about this, and other significant losses. When an ending is abrupt or unplanned, that is when a member leaves prematurely, the group may experience reactions similar to those caused by unexpected or sudden loss in other areas of life. In a situation like this, it is particularly important that group members are given ample time and opportunity to acknowledge, and work through, their feelings of abandonment or loss.

Behaviour characteristics of the last phase

During the ending period, members of a group may behave in ways that have come to be seen as characteristic of this stage. Brandler & Roman (1999:84) identify certain aspects of behaviour that they link to the ending period of a group's life. These aspects of behaviour include lateness, repeated absences, and increased 'frenzied activity.' Both lateness and absence can be seen as attempts to disengage gradually from the group, before the last or final disengagement. This gradual leave-taking is possibly the only way that some members can cope with the prospect of ending their contact with the group. Expressions of indifference may also be evident among some members. Denial of the group's importance often betrays the depth of loss which certain people feel, but cannot express in other ways. The manner in which individual members deal with endings will, of course, depend largely on their previous experiences in life. Some people will express sadness openly, while others will appear more upbeat and optimistic. Plans may be made by certain members to meet again socially. Such plans can be seen as an attempt to recreate the group in another setting, a strategy which is, of course, never wholly successful, since nothing can replace the composition and ethos of the original group. Regression to earlier patterns of behaviour (including dependence) may be apparent among certain members. In order to help participants deal with these varied responses to separation and leave-taking, the group leader / counsellor needs to understand the underlying meaning of the behaviour, as well as the issues being addressed, however indirectly, by group members. The following Case study highlights some of the points raised in this section.

CASE STUDY: ENDINGS

A closed counselling group of seven participants with severe anxiety had been together for six months, and were now meeting for their weekly session. Since there were just two further meetings to go before the group ended, the counsellor (Marco) decided to raise the subject with members. Earlier in this section we noted the importance of giving group members sufficient time to prepare for leaving. As he was aware of this need for preparation, Marco had also raised the subject of ending in the previous group meeting.

Marco: *As I mentioned to you last week, we have limited time left ... two weeks from now, in fact, we finish. What I'd like to think about now is what we have achieved in this year, your feelings about that, and any thoughts you'd like to share at the moment.*

Zeta: *What we achieved? I looked forward to these days together. I know now I feel better and I can even get here without taking a taxi! That's a real achievement for me.*

Martina: *I don't know if I could say I looked forward to it at the beginning like Zeta did. For me it was torture making it here ... I hadn't even left my own house for a year. To get this far is my big achievement I can tell you.*

Zeta: *I didn't really mean I looked forward to it at the start ... it just feels like that now ... now that we are almost over.* (Looks sad)

Robbie: *I feel sad too. When my wife died I felt sad ... more than sad. Now something is over again. No matter how good things are, it's always going to be over.*

Aoife: (Turning to Marco) *I really appreciate what you did. I'm going to miss you and the group. It turned my life around in many ways. Now at least I can talk to people in a normal way ... without feeling churned up inside.*

Marco: *I shall miss you too Aoife, and the group. What Robbie said about feeling sad ... that is true when something good ends.*

Guido: *I think we should all be glad of what we got out of this ... not labour the point about leaving. I don't know how many times I've had to leave ... my home ... my country, you name it.*

Marco: *You have had many experiences of leaving ... so one more might seem like too much to dwell on?*

Guido: *Yeah. Move on, I say. I got over the attacks I was having. For that I'm really grateful to everyone. Now I want to get on with things.* (Glares at Aoife who still looks sad)

Robbie: *Guido, you can't just pretend it's not happening by being angry ...*

Guido: *Who's angry?*

Robbie: *That's the way you seem to me anyway.*

Guido: *Well could I be forgiven? I am angry if you must know ... to be put through these feelings again..*

Marco: *The feelings of sadness and loss?*

Guido: *Yes. And who will there be to help me with that when the group ends?*

Marco: *I sense a mixture of feelings in the group. The sense of achievement, the sadness and loss ... then the anger that Guido feels, and the feeling of how will I cope without the group?*

One of the difficulties about using dialogue like this to illustrate certain points is that tone of voice, demeanour, body language and timing of interventions can never be adequately conveyed. However, the exchanges do highlight certain attitudes and behaviours character- istic of the ending phase in groups. The exchanges also show how the group counsellor helped members express their feelings, including sadness, gratitude, anger and loss, about leaving the group.

Marco (the group counsellor) opened the session by encouraging members to recall their achievements over the period of time they had been together. Several members responded to this by talking about their personal difficulties and how these had been ameliorated through participation in the group. Marco had also defined the group ending at the previ- ous meeting, thus giving participants time to evaluate the work they had done, as well as the remaining tasks yet to be accomplished. In response to Aoife's statement of apprecia- tion, and sentiments of regret about missing him and the group, Marco expresses his own feelings of sadness about endings too. This open expression of feelings serves to help others become more open and reflective in turn.

Guido's anger could be seen as a disguised attack on Marco who, after all, was the person responsible for setting time limits to the group experience. Intimations of dependency are also discernible in Guido's question about the fate of members once the group experience is over. Regression to dependency is not uncommon at this stage, and often takes the form of a plea for additional support from the group leader. A task for Marco at this stage is to help members explore all their feelings about separation, loss and abandonment. Afterwards, group members need additional encouragement to identify their, now strengthened, coping abilities and to connect these to the achievements derived from group participation. The attention of members needs to be directed back to the goals they set themselves at the beginning, to subsequent progress made, both in the group and outside, and to the significance of these gains for the future.

In making responses to the group, the counsellor should use 'I' statements and encourage members to do the same. This modelling works much better than a more didactic approach. The group counsellor's modelling should also extend (as it did in Marco's case) to open and honest expression of feelings. His self-disclosure was not excessive, but it was sufficient to show him as a real person who, like the members, experienced a range of feelings, includ- ing sadness and loss, as the group neared the end. By owning and expressing his feelings, Marco facilitated the same open and truthful approach from group members.

EXERCISE 20

ENDINGS

Time: 40 mins–20 mins. In small groups, 20 mins. In the whole group, 40 mins.

Working in groups of 3–4 discuss your experiences of group endings. Start with your earliest memory or experiences of coming to the final stage of group participation. Look at the following list for some inspiration to start with:

- ◆ Leaving friends at the end of a school year
- ◆ Leaving school
- ◆ Leaving home and the family group for the first time
- ◆ Leaving the district and a group of friends
- ◆ Leaving a job and your colleagues

Leaving school, friends, family or colleagues is obviously not the same as leaving a therapy or counselling group. However, in discussing your experiences of coming to the end of various groups, you should be able to identify a range of feelings and responses, some of which will be similar to those experienced by members of a therapy group. When you have completed your small group discussion, join the whole group and share your ideas with other members.

EXERCISE 21

THE GROUP STORY
Time: 1–2 hrs.

This is an experiential exercise that should be organized by the group facilitator or leader. It should be used when the group is ending. Its purpose is to encourage group members to reminisce about the life of the group and to evaluate the work achieved by it. Ask participants to recall, in turns, any significant moments in the life of the group. Members should be encouraged to express their feelings about their recollections; they should also be asked to say how they now feel as the group ends. As group leader or facilitator, you could start by indicating your own reactions at this time, remembering to use 'I' statements to describe what you feel.

An alternative way of conducting the exercise is to ask members to write down their recollections of the group-beginning phase. Collect these and set them aside. Next, ask for responses to the middle phase, and then set these aside. Finally, ask for written impressions of the last phase. When these are completed, collect the first pile of recollections and read these to the group. Do the same with the next set of responses, and the next. Finally, discuss any important points that emerge as a result of completing the exercise, with special reference to themes that emerge, feelings expressed, and any discrepancies in relation to how members define the different stages.

EXERCISE 22

THE MEMORY STONE
Time: 1–2 hrs.

This exercise is similar to the previous one, but in this case a stone is used as a repository into which each member of the group deposits sections of the group story. To organize the exercise you will need to find a hand sized (preferably polished) stone which can be easily passed around the group circle. Start by placing the stone on the floor in the middle of the circle, and ask group members to think about the history of the group, and any significant aspects of it that individuals remember. The first person to start should lift the stone, recount his / her memory, and then pass the stone to the next person on the right. When the circle of the group's life is complete, replace the stone in the centre. Group members should then decide for themselves what should happen to the stone. One option is to locate it in an unobtrusive spot in the room used for group meetings. In this way, the group memory is preserved in the very place where the story unfolded. During discussion, however, you should emphasize that the group experience is also preserved in each person's memory. The gains and achievements of the group are therefore carried outside by all participants, and are transferred to new situations, as and when they are needed.

EXERCISE 23

KNITTING THE GROUP TOGETHER
Time: 1–2 hrs.

Again, this is an exercise similar to those just outlined. In this case, however, you will need a large ball of brightly coloured wool. Begin by describing the exercise to group members. Sitting in a circle, start by holding the ball of wool, and saying how you personally feel at this ending stage of the group. Remember to focus on gains and achievements, as well as on any feelings of sadness, relief, or regret which you may experience. Afterwards, throw the ball to someone else in the circle, inviting that person to say what he or she now feels about the end of the group. This continues, with each person throwing the ball of wool to someone else, until a web linking all members is complete. When the exercise is finished, ask members what they would like to do with the web they have created. One suggestion is for each member to cut off his or her own section of the web to keep.

Adequate time should be given to all these exercises on endings. Group members often experience quite strong emotions when experiential exercises like this are being done. However, if the group has been a cohesive one in which members worked well together and communicated openly, expression of a range of feelings should be possible without risk of undue distress. The important point is that members need time to process and understand their experiences in the group. This is as true for training groups as it is for therapy and counselling groups.

References

Arrow, H., McGrath, J. E. & Berdahl, J. L. (2000) *Small Groups as Complex Systems.* London, Sage Publications Inc.

Barnes, B., Ernst, S. & Hyde, K. (1999) *An Introduction to Groupwork: A group analytic perspective.* London, Macmillan

Benson, J. (1987) *Working More Creatively With Groups.* London, Tavistock Publications.

Brandler, S. & Roman, C. (1999) 2nd Ed. *Groupwork: Skills and Strategies for Effective Interventions.* New York, The Haworth Press.

Edelwich, J. & Brodsky, A. (1992) *Group Counselling for the Resistant Client.* New York, Lexington Books.

Erikson, E. (1995) *Childhood and Society.* Vintage, London.

Ettin, M. F. (1999) *Foundations and Applications of Group Psychotherapy.* London, Jessica Kingsley Publishers.

Long, S. (1992) *A Structural Analysis of Small Groups.* London, Routledge.

Rutan, J. S. & Stone, W. N. (1999) 'Psychodynamic Group Psychotherapy' in Price, J. R., Hescheles, D. R. & Price, A. R. (eds.) *A Guide to Starting Psychotherapy Groups*, San Diego, Academic Press.

Tuckman, B. (1965) 'Developmental Sequences in Small groups', *Psychological Bulletin,* 63: 384–99.

Tuckman, B. & Jensen, M. (1977) 'Stages of small group development revisited' in *Group Organizational Studies 2*, 419–427.

Yallom, I. D. (1995) 4th Ed. *The Theory and Practice of Group Psychotherapy.* New York, Basic Books.

5

The leader and the group

INTRODUCTION

In previous chapters we considered several aspects of group leadership, including the leader's role in planning the group, the use of communication skills, the advantages and disadvantages of co-leadership and, more specifically, the leader's role in the establishment of a safe and therapeutic environment for clients in counselling groups. This chapter will focus on other important aspects of leadership, including different styles; definitions of the term leader; group members' responses to the leader; the leader's own countertransference responses; leadership and equality; and the leader's role in promoting anti-oppressive behaviour in the group. In the first instance, it is probably a good idea to look more closely at the term 'leader' and to identify other related terms now commonly used to describe this role.

THE LEADER'S TITLE

If you consult a random selection of books on the subject of groupwork, you will see that different writers have their preferred and individual choice of terms to characterize the person or persons responsible for guiding the group. For example, Yalom (1995) who writes almost exclusively about therapy groups, refers to the group leader as a 'therapist', though he does occasionally use the word leader when referring to certain specific aspects of groupwork. Corey (1995) on the other hand, favours the generic term leader, though he too is writing specifically about working with clients in a therapeutic context.

In their discussion about the group-analytic approach to groupwork, Barnes et al. (1999) use the designation 'group conductor' to refer to the therapist responsible for the group. Their choice is meant to reflect the way in which the therapist integrates both individual and group perspectives by giving 'free-floating attention' to each person in the group *and* to the group itself. Ettin (1999), though also writing from a psychotherapy viewpoint, refers to both leader and facilitator in a way which suggests he regards these titles as inter-change-able, while Douglas (2000), writing about groups in general, describes the role of a 'central person' who is also the leader, and around whom everything revolves in the group. In the context of planning and running a group, Tudor (1999) discusses various aspects of 'leader-ship' while stressing the point that he uses the term in a generic way to refer to the group counsellor, the conductor, the facilitator and any of the other titles commonly given.

We can see from these examples that it is possible to choose from a fairly wide number of terms to describe the person responsible for setting up and leading a group. In addition, it seems clear that a central concern for many practitioners and writers currently involved in groupwork is to distance themselves from the notion of a leader as an 'expert' or authority figure. This preoccupation with suggesting new titles implies a real desire to be precise about roles and responsibilities, but it can also be confusing, especially when you first start learning about groups and people's positions in them. The following exercise should encour-age you to think about the differences implicit in some of the titles suggested so far.

◁ EXERCISE 24 ▷

WHAT'S IN A TITLE?
Time: 20 mins.

Working in small groups of three to four, look at the following list of terms used to describe the person responsible for planning, setting up and running a group. Try to identify any differences that might be implicit in the various titles.

◆ Coordinator

◆ Facilitator

◆ Conductor

◆ Group counsellor

◆ Group therapist

◆ Leader

◆ Animator

◆ Groupworker

◆ Link person

Discuss your ideas with other members of the group, with special reference to any out-standing differences you may identify. Afterwards, consider some of the following dis-tinctions and say whether or not you agree with them.

Coordinator
This title suggests someone with organizational ability who also seeks to harmonize or integrate contributions made by all members of the group.

Facilitator

The term facilitator suggests a person who wishes to help, or promote the efforts of other people. It also seems to denote a role that encourages efficiency and focus among group members.

Conductor

The conductor of an orchestra must direct attention to the group as a whole, and to the performances of individual members. The 'conductor' of a group also addresses this dual task.

Group counsellor

This title has the advantage of clarity, since it denotes a person trained in counselling skills and theory who is responsible for setting up and running a group.

Group therapist

At first glance, this term also seems to describe an obvious role in relation to a group. However, the word 'therapist' may cover a wide variety of occupations, including, of course, counselling.

Leader

The title 'leader' is fairly unequivocal, and suggests a person who is prepared to be directive, who will take overall responsibility for setting up the group, *and* for events thereafter.

Animator

This is a word used by Hope & Timmel (1999) to describe the person responsible for setting up and guiding the group. The title has lively connotations, and suggests someone who is concerned to encourage movement and exploration.

Groupworker

This is a generic term that is often used in relation to different types of groups. It could, for example, be used in a counselling group context, although it could also be used to describe a focus group role, or someone who works with youth or team building groups, to name just a few.

Link Person

Although the term link person is sometimes used in relation to groups, it tends to imply a role that is partly outside, rather than wholly inside, the group. Support and self-help groups often 'link' with a professional person who may not attend all the meetings, but is nevertheless there when needed.

LEADER AS A GENERIC TITLE

Although the terms we have just considered do differ in many respects, the fact remains that all of them imply some degree of leadership at key points in the life of a group. Although the objective in group counselling, for example, is to help clients move towards independence and autonomy, this can only be achieved when a safe structure is provided by a person (or persons) with overall responsibility for leading the group. A group counsellor has, by definition, this kind of responsibility, so the designation 'leader' is appropriate, at least as a generic term that we can use to describe the role. To illustrate the 'leadership' functions intrinsic to the group counsellor's role, let us consider some of the tasks that a person in that position needs to address.

In the first instance, the group counsellor must take responsibility for preparing group members beforehand. He/she must also bring group members together as a physical reality, and afterwards foster the development of what Yalom (1995:109) calls a 'therapeutic social system' that will encourage interaction among members. The term 'primary unifying force' is also used by Yalom (1995:107) to describe the therapist's role at this early stage of the group's life. In addition to these tasks, other related functions are required early on. Included here are responsibilities for helping group members understand what is happening in the group at different stages, interpreting events as they unfold, and using self-disclosure when it is useful and appropriate to do so. The term 'leader' is appropriate to the role and tasks of a group counsellor, therefore, because a group counsellor acts (or should act) in the best interests of a group, with the cooperation of that group. When we look at it this way we can see an emerging definition of 'leader' as someone who does indeed have power, but this power is shared with, and assigned to, the group.

This description of the group counsellor's tasks and responsibilities is a summarized one that we shall further extend and consider later in this chapter. The purpose of outlining it now is to show that leadership functions are central to the group counsellor's role at crucial stages of the group's existence. A problem arises if we deny that group counsellors and therapists do have leadership functions, since this denial serves to obscure or mask many of the misunderstandings, even abuses, which leaders often unwittingly cause. A group counsellor who is oblivious to personal power (either actual or potential) within the group is quite likely to cause some confusion, not to mention damage, among vulnerable clients whose transference responses may see him/her in quite a different light. To understand this particular dynamic it is important to look more closely at the twin concepts of transference and countertransference and to discuss how these responses affect relationships in a general sense. More specifically, we need to consider their particular significance in relation to clients in group counselling or therapy.

TRANSFERENCE RESPONSES TO THE LEADER

In psychological terms the word 'transference' refers to the way we rely on past experience to deal with, or interpret, events and other people in the present. To put it this way, we could say that early childhood relationships act as a blueprint or guide, which we 'transfer' to the present, to help us establish and understand, later relationships. It is clear that we all need guidelines established early on to help us make sense of ourselves, and our relationships with other people. These emotional attitudes and ways of relating were initially felt towards our parents or caregivers, since these were the people on whom we were dependent for everything at a very early stage. When, in later life, we become ill or need help, we tend to regress emotionally to this early stage. As a result, we also tend to invest a lot of power, authority and expertise in the people we approach for help.

Our vulnerability during illness, emotional upheaval, trauma or loss, makes us transfer our early helplessness to the person who is helping us in the present. This usually works well, especially in the initial stage when we really need help, support, treatment or care. However, it can work against us if the people we transfer parental qualities onto are inept, unscrupulous, abusive, unaware of their own power, or very needy themselves. It may be, for example, that the person who is helping actually needs to feel in control of others. She/he may even need to hold on to patients or clients as 'friends' because of an inability to establish real friendships in private life. In addition, the helper, counsellor or group leader might simply need to feel needed. This is why self-awareness is such an important component of counsellor and groupwork training. We all transfer feelings from the past to the present, so we need to be aware of this in ourselves as well as in clients. The following are some examples of transference responses.

CASE STUDY: TRANSFERENCE – KAREN

Karen, who was in her fifties, visited her doctor because of joint pains and recurrent headaches. The doctor (Helen) listened carefully to her, did the required tests and examined Karen. During subsequent visits Helen took time to talk to Karen about other matters that might be causing her patient stress or anxiety. Test results had shown no sign of physical illness. Karen, whose mother had died six months previously, had moved to the area from abroad. As a result of the move, she left behind her friends of many years standing. She was now in a new job, and in the process of buying a house. It was shortly after the move that Karen's symptoms began. Helen explained to Karen that the stress of recent events could cause the joint pains and headaches she described. Over a period of time Karen began to feel much better and her symptoms gradually disappeared. She visited the doctor once more for a check up and left feeling that she had been listened to, cared for and understood.

When Karen first visited her doctor she was in a vulnerable state. She had just undertaken a series of major changes in her life, and desperately needed someone to help and support her at this very stressful time. She had not been in the area long enough to make friends or confidants, and because she was unable to talk to anyone her symptoms of stress took on a physical form. This translation of stress into physical symptoms is not uncommon, and is sometimes evident in people who find it difficult to acknowledge, or verbalize, psychological problems or distress. Karen was fortunate in her choice of doctor, since Helen proved to be supportive and took the time necessary to listen to her patient. Karen sensed this support and understanding, which was similar to the kind of response a loving mother would extend to a child. At an unconscious level Karen probably perceived the doctor in this way, and in doing so transferred early emotional feelings of trust and dependence to the relationship with her.

CASE STUDY: TRANSFERENCE – PHIL

Phil, who was suffering from a long-standing phobia about dogs, made an appointment to see a counsellor. At the first session he felt immediately that he liked the counsellor whose name was John. As an initial assessment, the counsellor suggested that Phil would need to attend for at least ten sessions. Since Phil was paying for his own therapy he had set aside a certain amount of money to cover his costs. However, he had not anticipated so many sessions, and became anxious about the prospect of paying for them. Instead of raising the issue for discussion with the counsellor, Phil decided to say nothing. In any case, he reasoned that John, as the counsellor, must know best.

Although Phil felt at ease with the counsellor and liked him, he also transferred to him emotional attitudes from early childhood, which effectively set John up as an authority figure whose decisions should not be questioned. By responding in this way, Phil placed himself in a dependent, unquestioning position in relation to the counsellor. This kind of response is not uncommon, and of course, professionally trained counsellors are aware of it. Any person working in a helping role is liable to be seen as an 'authority' or 'expert' in that particular field. This is why it is important to understand the dynamics of transference, with its ability to distort or cloud the 'here and now' relationship between helper and client. It should be added that in Phil's case the problem of fees was resolved on the second occasion he met the counsellor. Before the session began John referred to the number of meetings again and asked if the schedule was all right for his client. This gave Phil the opportunity to voice his concerns about the money, and future sessions were planned to accommodate his financial status.

CASE STUDY: TRANSFERENCE – BRETT

Brett, who was twenty-five, joined a training group just six weeks after his mother died. At the start of each group meeting he positioned himself next to the leader, an older woman, of about his mother's age. Brett was unaware of any special significance in his choice of seat, until a discussion about transference arose in the group. It was during this discussion that he made the connection between his decision to sit near the leader (who gave him a sense of security in the group) and feelings of vulnerability about the loss of his mother.

The group leader was aware all along that Brett had chosen to sit by her at each session, though she did not refer to this until he did. Since he identified the transference response himself, Brett gained a great deal, because the realization was experienced at both cognitive and emotional levels. Insights achieved in this way, tend to be more immediate and meaningful, than interpretations made for us by someone else. For the first time since his mother's death, Brett allowed himself to think about her and the loss he had suffered. He was then able to talk about his experiences to the group, and in doing so began the process of mourning the death of his mother.

EXERCISE 25

LOOKING AT TRANSFERENCE

Time: As required.

This is an exercise that should be organized by group leaders who wish to introduce and discuss the subject of transference responses among student participants. It is an experiential exercise, so you need to plan it beforehand and understand that it may elicit strong reactions from group members. Select a particular group meeting to complete the exercise, and on that occasion arrive late for the meeting. The duration of absence is something that you need to calculate for yourself, and will depend on your knowledge of the group, their level of training and their particular needs. Twenty to thirty minutes seems a reasonable length of time, and is not long enough for group members to start leaving the group. On the other hand, it is sufficiently long enough to cause some concern about what is happening and what should be done about it.

When you join the group, do so without offering any initial explanation. Listen carefully to what is said, and observe the general responses to you. Afterwards discuss your lateness with group members, and explain the purpose of the exercise. Ask participants to describe their feelings about being left alone in this way, with particular reference to the following questions:

◆ When did group members first start to express concern about the leader's absence?

◆ What form did the concern take? Were there expressions of annoyance, impatience, or even anger?

◆ Were there any differences among group members in their responses? If so, encourage members to say what these were and discuss them.

◆ Is anyone in the group able to link personal feelings about being kept waiting to earlier experiences of having to wait?

◆ Did any leader emerge in the group, and were any decisions made about what should be done?

These questions should form the basis of an extended discussion about the ways we respond in different situations. These ideas can then be linked to the subject of transference, emphasizing our tendency to transfer emotions, beliefs and attitudes from the past to present situations. Feelings about being ignored, discounted, neglected or even abandoned are often elicited when people keep us waiting.

In completing this exercise you should allocate plenty of time for feedback from students, and discussion. As stated earlier, it is also important to remember that the experience itself, and the discussion, may produce strong emotional responses in some members, which means you need to exercise discretion in using it.

⟨ **EXERCISE 26** ⟩

CHOOSING PICTURES

Time: 40 mins.

The group leader or trainer should organize this exercise. It is meant to stimulate discussion about our immediate responses to people, and where these responses come from. To conduct the exercise you will need to cut out a selection of pictures or photographs from papers and magazines. Each picture should be of one person only, and the general selection should represent a broad spectrum of people from as many ethnic and social groups as possible. Try to choose pictures which are expressive and clear, but without too much extraneous detail.

Spread the pictures out on a large table (or the floor) so that they are clearly visible. Ask students to spend some time looking at them, and then to select one each that they like, and one that they dislike. The group should then spend about 30 mins discussing the pictures chosen, saying why they like or dislike them, and with special reference to the following points:

◆ What each picture represents to the person who selected it.

◆ What each picture is associated with.

◆ What the choice of pictures says about the person who selected them.

The selection of pictures, and the discussion, is useful in helping group members to identify personal bias, especially in their immediate responses to people. It should also help members see that our likes and dislikes often stem from relationships in the past, which we then transfer to people and situations in the present. Another important effect of the exercise is that it sometimes helps us to identify traits or characteristics that we dislike in ourselves. When we meet someone with these same traits or characteristics, we may therefore respond in negative ways to them.

WHAT THE LEADER REPRESENTS TO THE GROUP

A central purpose of exercise 25 is to show that the person with overall responsibility for a group actually symbolizes or represents many other people who are not present in the group at all. These people include relatives and friends of all the individual members, including, and especially, those from childhood. Parents are usually the most important people in a young child's life, and emotional attitudes developed during these early relationships affect all later responses to other authority figures. Each member of a group has a range of feelings about parents and people in authority. However, many of these feelings concerning authority figures operate at an unconscious level. This means that group members are often unaware of them until they surface in some other way. The Case study about Brett shows how this can happen. This Case study also illustrates how the experience of group participation can help us examine our relationships (both past and present) and in doing so identify problems or difficulties intrinsic to them. The next exercise is meant to highlight the significance of early experience and its effects on current relationships.

<EXERCISE 27 >

TRANSFERENCE AND GROUP MEMBER RESPONSES.
Time: 30 mins.

The following are summarized descriptions of childhood experiences as outlined by several group members. Working in pairs, discuss the descriptions given. Can you say what attitudes these members are likely to show in relation to A – Two group leaders, a man and a woman. B – One male leader. C – One female leader.

◆ When he was four years of age, Mark's father died. His mother and her two sisters then brought him up in a loving and supportive environment.

◆ Alice is the only child of older, very protective, parents. They worry about her constantly, even now that she is an adult.

◆ Corinna's parents split up when she was ten. After that she spent some time with each of them, though they argued constantly about access and her education.

◆ Ravi lost both parents at a very early age. He was cared for by members of his extended family, but was especially attached to his uncle whom he admired a great deal.

◆ Seth had a very disrupted education, having being sent to various boarding schools from the age of seven. He was never close to his parents, as both were constantly engaged with travel and work.

◆ Beth's parents were alcoholic and neglectful. As a child she always felt responsible for them. She also took care of herself and her younger siblings.

In completing the exercises it is not, of course, possible to say exactly how any individual has been affected by past experience. Other factors, besides those outlined in the summarized accounts, will have a bearing on each person's coping strategies. In addition, personality factors can affect the way people perceive, and deal with, their own environmental influences. However, children do learn their roles from the influential models, especially parents, which they observe around them. It is possible, therefore, to suggest some anticipated transference responses from those people described, in a group situation.

For example, Beth who was used to taking care of adults, may find herself anxious about the group leader or leaders as well. She might also want to defend other group members, as she defended her siblings, against feelings of discomfort or threat. Alice, whose parents were overly protective, might fear being controlled or taken over by the group leaders. On the other hand, her transference response might take the form of anxiety about herself (as her parents would have been anxious about her) in the group, which is, after all, a new and unfamiliar situation.

Corinna, whose parents argued constantly, might anticipate or expect habitual disagreements between two group leaders. This, in turn, could make her vigilant and watchful in her relationship with them. Ironically, group leaders who disagree openly and without acrimony, and who are seen to resolve their differences in constructive ways, are good role models for members who may witness this kind of positive conflict resolution for the first time. Seth, whose parents travelled a great deal so that he hardly saw them, may not expect too much attention from a group leader or leaders. Alternatively, he may harbour resentment against them, especially if they seem to ignore or neglect him.

Ravi, whose parents died when he was very young, might perceive the group as his extended family, with whom he has a more secure relationship than with either leader. This highlights the point that group members often form transference relationships with each other, as well as with the leader. Since he was especially close to his uncle, however, Ravi might feel more drawn to a male group leader. Another possibility exists which is that he might idealize both leaders, who at an unconscious level, represent the parents he never knew. Finally, Mark, whose father died when he was four, formed close attachments to his mother and aunts. Because of these early experiences, he might feel more at ease with a woman as group leader, though it is also possible that he could resent her prominent position as well.

It can be seen from analysis of these hypothetical transference responses that definite predictions can never be made about them. As we saw earlier, this is because a myriad of considerations influence our responses to other people. As a learning exercise, though, it is useful to discuss some of the factors that might predispose group members to relate to each other in different ways. It is especially important to look closely at the significance of the leader's role in a group, and to link this to the many unconscious connections members make to it.

Although we are concerned in this section with transference feelings directed towards the leader, such feelings can (as we noted earlier) also be directed towards other group members. Transference reactions can take positive or negative forms, including anger, hostility, anxiety, idealization, dependence, love and envy. In a counselling group, the leader can help members understand and gain insight into past and current relationships. Helping members in this way means encouraging them to explore the significance of the attributes and characteristics that they project onto others. Unless group members are helped to see how they respond to others as parents, brothers, sisters or other family members, they are unlikely to understand the difficulties they experience in relationships outside the group. This principle of identification and analysis of transference responses applies, of course, to feelings projected onto the leader as well.

COUNTER-TRANSFERENCE AND THE LEADER

The word counter-transference describes the group counsellor's responses to members of the group. Like transference, it is a 'felt' emotional response, and is also sometimes referred to as Projective identification. In a later chapter we shall look in more detail at psychodynamic concepts, including projective identification, which stem from the psychoanalytic tradition. However, in this section it is important to consider the group significance of counter-transference or projective identification, and its usefulness in helping the leader monitor the group's processes.

We know from our earlier discussion about transference that much of the communication taking place in groups does so at an unconscious level. Group members and the leader communicate at an open and transparent level for some of the time, but at another, and deeper level, transactions continue which are often outside conscious awareness. By using his/her own internal responses, the group counsellor can access and identify previously concealed material, and in doing so help group members understand what is happening in the group. This monitoring and use of counter-transference feelings is in addition to the usual skills of observation, which all group counsellors need to have. However, it is possible to observe processes which on the surface seem quite straightforward, but which are, in fact, complex and covert. The following is an example:

CASE STUDY: WHAT'S THE JOKE?

A leader of a training group described how a particular session developed. There were five men in the group and five women, and the level of group cohesion had developed over time and was high. On this occasion, the session had barely started when two of the men exchanged remarks about an evening out the night before. These remarks led to laughter and some flippant comments about their girlfriends and partners. While listening to this the group leader felt slightly uncomfortable. She also felt she was being criticized indirectly through the remarks made by the men. However, she noticed that the female group members seemed unconcerned about what was happening, and, in fact, some of them joined in the laughter and joking.

The group leader (Irene) decided to share her personal responses to the group by referring openly to what was taking place.

Irene: *I'm not exactly sure what's going on in the group at present, but I have a particular feeling I'd like to share with you. It's something I feel quite strongly now ... uncomfortable with the banter from Eric and Paul.*

Marsella: *What ... You are offended by a few jokes?*

Irene: *No, not offended, but interested to know what is behind the joking. I wonder if there is some criticism in it.*

Larry: *Surely you're not that politically correct?*

Cathy: *I think you can carry political correctness too far.*

Irene: *It seems to me it's not a case of political correctness here, but something else that perhaps we should look at. There was certainly criticism of women outside the group, but I wonder if it applies to some situations in the group as well.*

Larry: *In what way?*

Irene: *Something that's not being said that needs to be said. I go back to my own feeling again ... uncomfortable ... criticized.*

Larry: (laughs) *Well, the only criticism I can think of off the top of my head ... the extensions you gave Sue and Megan for their assignments. That does bug me. I have home commitments too.*

Megan: *Oh come on ... so somehow we are the ones to blame ... what next?*

Irene: *OK ... let's look at what's happening now. Larry is unhappy with the assignment extensions ... anyone else?*

Tony: *I'll stick my neck out on this one ... I don't think it's fair ... there seems to be one system for the women, and another for us.*

After these exchanges between the leader / trainer and group members, another more fruitful discussion took place. This concerned the sense of grievance felt by the men at what they perceived to be preferential treatment shown to the women. The group leader promised to discuss deadlines at the end of the session. More significantly, however, the exchanges highlighted the importance of looking at latent as well as manifest content in the group. In this particular training group there was an underlying conflict, brought to light when the group leader focused on her own responses to the behaviour and verbal exchanges manifest in the group.

In addition to the covert concerns about assignments, and the learning that took place once these were uncovered, another important issue is highlighted in this particular Case study. When the men in the group made flippant and sexist remarks about their girlfriends and partners, the women members joined in, and appeared, on the surface at least, to enjoy this, seemingly, light hearted mood. However, when the session was processed and analyzed, they admitted that they too felt uncomfortable when such attitudes were expressed in this, or any other group. Cathy remembered how she felt during staff meetings at work when male colleagues made similar remarks. She disliked these occasions, but never objected in case she was seen as a 'strident feminist', a description she once heard applied to a female colleague who was consistently assertive. Larry volunteered that he too felt undermined when sexist remarks were made about men. He had experienced this on more than one occasion when he attended work related courses. Ronnie, who used a wheelchair, confided that he disliked the way other group members failed to confront him, even when there was conflict in the group. It was his belief that others saw him as an invalid who could not protect himself, an attitude that he found deeply offensive.

The session proved to be a valuable learning experience for all the group members, since it triggered a multi-faceted discussion, touching on many issues, including the importance of showing respect, understanding and sensitivity towards all members of the group, whatever their differences. In addition, the members learned, through experience, that what is said in a group is not always what is intended.

Sexism, racism and other
oppressive behaviour – the leader's role

In describing the importance of anti-oppressive principles in groupwork, Mistry & Brown (1997:19) point to the need for adequate preparation of members before the group starts. This preparation includes the setting of ground rules, which incorporate anti-oppressive guidelines about general behaviour and relationships in the group. However, even when these are explicitly stated, they are often not regarded as meaningful until someone infringes them. Thus group members need to have theoretical understanding of the nature of sexism and racism in groups, but this theoretical understanding needs to be 'integrated' with experiential learning as well. Benjamin et al. (1997:18) use the word Normalism to describe a widespread belief that all of us should conform to certain 'norms' within society. Such a belief system can lead to descrimination against people who are different in any way, either because of their race, sexual orientation, looks or disability, for example. Group members need to be acquainted with this belief system as well, and with the many ways we all subscribe to and exploit it for our own purposes, and at the expense of anyone who is different, as, in fact, we all are.

In addition to guidelines on anti-oppressive behaviour, group leaders should know how to respond when sexism, racism or any other oppressive manifestations occur among members. An active, interventionist approach is essential in dealing with oppressive behaviour, though as Mistry and Brown also indicate, it is not always easy to identify covert racist, sexist or other oppressive attitudes when they are present in the group. In the Case study described earlier we saw how Ronnie experienced oppressive behaviour in the group. He perceived the behaviour of others towards him as dismissive and condescending. Ronnie explained that since he had not always used a wheelchair, but had needed to do so only in the past two years since an accident, he was well aware of the differences in attitude towards him now. Thus, he was in a unique position to give group members a comparative account of how those with disability and those without, are often treated differently.

Other members of the group were unaware of their attitudes until he highlighted these. These disclosures caused surprise, then reflection, and finally acknowledgment that oppressive attitudes towards Ronnie (and other people with disabilities) were prevalent in the group. The group leader, through her intervention which was based on her own counter-transference responses, was able to help the group examine their attitudes and behaviour in this experiential setting. The experience, along with the underpinning theory and discussion was a valuable learning input for everyone in the group.

Figure 5.1 Groupwork

CO-LEADERSHIP AND EQUALITY

In chapter two we looked briefly at the subject of co-leadership and some of the advantages it offers. We also noted that two people leading a group represent, at an unconscious level, parental figures; an effect more marked when one leader is male and the other female. This is just one of the more obvious advantages of co-leadership. Others include the advantages for the group (which, as we noted earlier, is a microcosm of society) when one leader is heterosexual and the other homosexual. The same principle applies when one leader is disabled while the other is not, or when one leader is from a dominant culture and the other a minority. These advantages can only exist, however, when both leaders communicate with one another in totally open and transparent ways. In a situation where one leader is from a dominant culture, and the other a minority, for example, it is vitally important that the latter feels valued as an equal in relation to his/her colleague. Even before the group starts, and as an integral part of the preparation phase, these factors need to be discussed, and the possibility of difficulties openly stated. The composition of co-leadership matters a great deal. One way of highlighting this point is to consider the issues raised in the following exercise.

WORKING TOGETHER
Time: 30 mins.

This exercise is meant to help you identify ways in which particular kinds of co-leadership could reflect, and reinforce, social attitudes and expectations. Working in pairs, look at the leadership combinations below, and say what impact they might have on group members. Afterwards, discuss your views with members of the whole group.

◆ Two male leaders in a group of all women members.

◆ One black female leader / one white male leader in a mixed gender group.

◆ Two leaders, one with a physical disability, the other without, in a group for people with physical disabilities.

◆ Two leaders, both from the settled community, working with a group of people from a travelling culture.

◆ Two female leaders, both gay, leading an awareness raising group with a predominantly heterosexual membership.

This represents a selection of ways in which co-leadership might be composed. It is possible to identify many others, especially among very diverse societies and cultures. Issues relating to the effects of leader characteristics are sometimes neglected in discussion or research. Perhaps one reason for this neglect is that we may be reluctant to acknowledge or explore our own prejudice or bias in relation to others. Open discussion about the effects of different types of leadership on members, and conversely, the effects on leaders of group composition, serves to encourage transparency among participants. It is not always possible, of course, to say exactly what effects group leaders and members will have on each other. Much of this will depend on each person's experience, degrees of self-awareness, knowledge of cultural, social and individual diversity, and a willingness to remain open to the experiences and differences of others.

In exercise 27 we looked at the effects on certain group members of different types of leadership, and identified some of the possible ways they might respond. It is possible to offer some suggestions here about the ways in which leadership composition can reflect and reinforce social attitudes and expectations. If we consider the first example in the present exercise (two male leaders in an all woman group) we can see at once that the composition seems to support a patriarchal frame of reference which dictates that men are in positions of authority while women are not. It is not difficult to pinpoint the difficulties for members (who may feel disempowered to say the least) in a group composed like this. In a group where both leaders are women and the member's men, the women may be expected to excel at what they are doing, whereas male leaders in the same group might be excused for any perceived failings they show. However, in writing about women and men as leaders, Forsyth (1999:369) suggests that group member's 'perceptual biases' are minimized when the leader, whether male or female, has a good track record. In other words, women are as accepted as men in group leadership roles, providing they can prove they are effective beforehand.

When one leader is a black woman and the other a white man in a group of mixed membership, the assumption of superior status, on the part of the male co-leader and white group members may mean that the female co-leader is disadvantaged in group interaction. Brown & Mistry (1997:21) in a reference to group membership, point to the 'subtler forms of oppression' including 'gradual domination, often unconsciously' by white people and men in mixed groups. This unconscious propensity by white group members to dominate may not be so marked towards a leader, but the possibility exists nevertheless. A leader with a physical disability may also be disadvantaged if group members wish to protect (and marginalize) him as they did with the group member Ronnie whose experiences we discussed earlier. However, when group membership is composed of people with a similar disability, the dynamic may be somewhat different. In this case it could be that members will identify closely with the disabled leader, since they may perceive him to be more empathic and aware than his co-leader.

Group members from a travelling culture may find it difficult to communicate with, or trust, a leader or leaders from the settled community who have no direct experience of their lifestyle or culture. The following Case study highlights this point.

CASE STUDY: CULTURAL DIFFERENCES

Caroline, whose professional background was in adult education and groupwork, was asked to work with a number of women travellers. A central purpose of the initiative was to encourage the women to develop their communication and assertiveness skills so that, in the future, they would be in a better position to influence legislation which directly affected them.

From the outset it was clear to Caroline that she had much to learn about the lifestyle, experiences and cultural values of the members. One of the first things she learned was that the women had very little experience of being heard, or listened to. Thus it was difficult for them to believe that she, a leader and a person from the dominant settled community, could really be interested in them and want to help. Building trust with the women was a lengthy, and at times very difficult, undertaking. Because of their experiences of not being heard, the women were reluctant to express themselves verbally, so communication was a problem initially. Later on, however, one group member suggested telling stories through art. This was a medium which appealed to other members too, and it worked very well for all of them. With Caroline's encouragement the women drew pictures of their life experiences, and afterwards talked together about themselves, the problems they faced and the difficulties they encountered daily as a marginalized community. The women's ability to speak visually through art was linked to their background and culture. It was also a safer way to communicate in the new, and initially quite threatening environment of the awareness raising group.

THE MEANING OF PREJUDICE

The last example given in exercise 28 (two gay women as leaders in an awareness raising group) highlights several important points. In the first instance, it seems clear that group members enrolling for such a course would do so as a matter of choice. It is tempting to assume, therefore, that prejudice and bias would be absent in this context. However, as we noted earlier, such attitudes are often unconscious or outside awareness, hence the need for awareness raising groups to uncover them. In discussing the roots of prejudice, Goleman (1996:159) refers to it as 'a kind of emotional learning that occurs early in life' thus making it difficult for people to eradicate it, even when, as adults, they know it is wrong. So even when people have a genuine desire to change, it is difficult for them to alter the deep-seated emotional responses which were learnt in childhood within the family unit. Intellectual commitment to equality is not sufficient on its own to deal with prejudice. When people understand the roots of prejudice the next step for them is to become proactive in ensuring that discrimination and harassment do not go unchallenged. Group leaders are in a unique position in this respect, since they can help members identify both covert as well as overt prejudice as it is manifested in the group. This applies just as much in counselling groups as it does in any other kind. In order to give participants effective feedback in groups, it is important for the leader to do so in a way that encourages receptivity rather than defensiveness. This means delivering feedback directly, but with sensitivity, so that the expression of prejudice or bias is seen as unacceptable and demeaning for everyone. Even more effective, however, is the establishment of clear ground rules at the outset stating that diversity among members is the basis of creativity, and therefore must be respected and celebrated.

LEADERSHIP STYLE AND ITS IMPACT ON GROUP MEMBERS

In describing group leader characteristics, groupwork literature often refers to individual styles, which, it is believed, certain people in that role may possess or acquire. It goes without saying that no two leaders are the same in their approach to facilitating groups, and that each person brings a completely individual style (informed by training, knowledge of theory and experience of group participation) to the task of leading a group. One of the best known studies in leadership style Lewin, Lippitt & White (1939) identifies three distinct categories which merit special consideration. These include the autocratic or authoritarian leader, the democratic leader and the laissez-faire leader.

The authoritarian leader

In their research, Lewin arranged for groups of boys to meet after school to pursue their hobbies with the help of a leader who adopted different styles. In his role as an authoritarian leader this man decided what should be done and how the boys should do it. As far as decision-making was concerned, there was no input from group members, nor were the goals of the group discussed with them. Group members were directed to work in pairs, and the leader dictated who should work on specific projects.

The authoritarian style is one in which the leader assumes the role of an expert. Contributions from the group are not expected and often not welcomed. Giving directions or orders is a characteristic feature of the authoritarian style.

The democratic leader

In Lewin's experiment, the democratic leader encouraged group members to reach their own decisions. The entire group discussed activities beforehand, and members were allowed to choose their own work partners and individual projects.

The democratic style ensures that participants are included at all levels of decision making in the group. The leader is concerned to help members understand the processes they engage in, and to make decisions that take account of everyone's needs. Experiential learning is regarded as an integral component of groupwork, and though the leader may offer suggestions or opinions, group members are ultimately responsible for their own work.

The laissez-faire leader

In his laissez-faire role, Lewin's group leader intervened as little as possible in the work of the group. There was no participation from the leader in the youth group's decision-making process.

The laissez-faire style ensures total freedom for group members to reach their own decisions. The leader may offer some suggestions at the outset in order to initiate group activity. Thereafter, however, there is minimal leader participation. Participants are responsible for monitoring and appraising their own progress. The underlying philosophy of this style is that leader intervention is unnecessary, and might even inhibit creativity and initiative.

Appraising leadership styles

The three types of leadership yielded very different results in terms of group efficiency and satisfaction among members. The authoritarian and democratic groups spent roughly the same amount of time working on their tasks, while the laissez-faire group proved to be less industrious and efficient. In relation to the effects of leader supervision, however, other differences in performance also emerged. Left unsupervised, the authoritarian group tended to lose motivation, so that work levels dropped, while in the democratically led groupwork continued as before. Perhaps the most surprising finding in the laissez-faire group was the *increased* level of activity that occurred in the group leader's absence.

Attitudes to the three styles of leadership also varied, with the authoritarian group showing more hostility and criticism towards, and paradoxically more dependence on, the leader. In contrast, the democratic group seemed happier, were friendlier and certainly more industrious.

LEADERSHIP STYLES IN
COUNSELLING AND THERAPY GROUPS

The results of this study seem to indicate that a democratic style of leadership facilitates member participation, commitment, motivation and general morale in the group. In an authoritarian group, members tend to become dependent on the leader who is viewed as an expert. In the absence of supervision, members of an authoritarian group may lose motivation and harbour resentment. Individual group members do not feel free to express their feelings, and contributions are ignored. However, when feelings are repressed in a group they do not disappear. On the contrary, they are liable to become manifest in some indirect form. Examples of indirect expression of feelings include absenteeism, poor time keeping, gossiping, scape goating and sub-grouping. In counselling groups in particular, it is essential that members are free to express their feelings in open and unambiguous ways. On the other hand, the authoritarian style does have some advantages. These include clarity, structure and firm direction. There is never any doubt about who is the leader, since all power is located in one person. When a specific task needs to be accomplished, it is usually done efficiently and in the minimum amount of time. The question arises as to whether the authoritarian style is ever appropriate in therapy groups where individual contributions are valued highly. Certain aspects of the authoritarian style are probably useful at the start of a therapeutic group, when members clearly need guidelines about contracts and ground rules. Thereafter, however, an authoritarian approach would work against the basic principles of therapeutic groupwork, which seeks to encourage autonomy and independence among members.

The laissez style of leadership is in direct contrast to the authoritarian, but may cause similar frustration among group members. In this instance, though, confusion is often linked to a sense of aimlessness and lack of direction. An essential pre-requisite for working in counselling groups is clarity about goals, scrupulous planning and a clear sense of purpose and direction in helping clients, all of which seem at odds with the laissez-faire style. There is an important point to be made here, though, which is that individual therapists and counsellors come with their own particular personality traits. In other words, one individual may be more laissez-faire by inclination than another. While it is obviously important to know the advantages and disadvantages of various styles, and to be familiar with theory and research, group counsellors have to be true to their own personality and style. What is important here is awareness that on some occasions firm leadership is appropriate, while at other times a more democratic or laissez-faire approach might benefit group members most. Trained counsellors should be aware that participants in the group have innate potential to help themselves, and that this innate potential is best served when a collaborative, flexible, and more democratic style of leadership is there to facilitate it.

IDENTIFYING THE EFFECTIVE STYLE

Time: 1 hour.

This is an exercise that is meant to help you identify your individual leadership style in different contexts. You should complete the first part of the exercise on your own, and then discuss your responses with members of the whole group. Below are some examples of groups that might require different leadership styles: can you say which approach might work best in each case?

◆ A first meeting with a group of teenage boys with behavioural difficulties

◆ A well established group of new mothers with post-natal depression

◆ A group of elderly people with mild dementia

◆ An established mixed group of people suffering from anxiety

◆ A first meeting of an assertiveness training group

◆ A bereavement support group for adults

◆ A bereavement support group for children

◆ An empowerment group for unemployed people

◆ A counselling group for patients recovering from addictive problems

◆ A support group for asylum seekers

It should be emphasized that there are no right or wrong responses in this exercise. What it should do is encourage group discussion about the various approaches that might work best for different groups, and at different stages.

LEADERSHIP SKILLS AND RESPONSES

In chapter three we considered a range of communication skills used by both leaders and members in the group. The leadership skills referred to included those that are necessary for task achievement (task leadership) and those that are necessary for group maintenance (maintenance leadership). Task skills include giving directions and information; asking for opinions and information; coordinating contributions; paraphrasing; clarifying and summarizing; initiating and energizing, and evaluating and giving feedback. Maintenance skills are those concerned with the emotional life of the group and its members, and include being open and transparent; communicating empathy and respect; observing group processes; encouraging participation; monitoring the emotional climate of the group; modelling active listening; dealing with interpersonal conflict; promoting trust and helping members to understand their own behaviour and the behaviour of others.

No two leaders are exactly alike in the skills they use at different stages in a group's life. Most leaders use a combination of task and maintenance skills, as and when they are needed. We noted earlier in this section that different styles of leadership might be appropriate for different groups, and at different stages. The same could be said about communication skills and responses, all of which are appropriate in specific contexts. However, there are some general points about counsellor responses in groups which Haney & Leibsohn (2001:2) describe as the 'three intents.' In looking at three possible intentions behind their interventions, counsellors are encouraged to think clearly about their reasons for responding in a particular way.

The first intention is acknowledgement of both verbal and non-verbal contributions from group members. This intervention demonstrates respect and interest. It also models good interpersonal skills and encourages communication among group members. The second intention in responding to the group is to explore and clarify what has been said so that members gain insight and new information. The third intention is to challenge the group in order to help members change their behaviour or reassess a particular situation or belief. In addition, Hanley & Leibsohm stress that group counsellors may choose to respond, at any time, to the whole group, a sub-group, or an individual member. The following are some examples:

To an individual member:

Kate, I can see you would like to reply to Mark's comments.

(Acknowledging)

To the whole group:

So the group has now reached an agreement about not interrupting.

(Clarifying)

To a small group within the group:

Some members of the group seem reluctant to come in on this.

(Challenging)

Self-disclosure

Self-disclosure by the group leader is a skill that can be used to encourage members to examine their own responses to what is happening in the group at specific times. According to Yalom (1995:205) judicious use of self-disclosure by the leader 'increases the therapeutic power of the group.' Since members are required to self-disclose in counselling and therapy groups, leaders should model this particular behaviour, but it must be done to help the group and not the leader. In other words, the leader is not, as Haney & Leibsohn (2001:54) point out, a member and should not, therefore, participate as one. The true purpose of self-disclosure is to focus on the here and now of the group's experience, and not on the leader's personal life or problems. The past may be referred to, but only in as much as it has a bearing on the present. The following is an example:

I feel anxious coming into a new group too ...

In disclosing feelings about past experiences, the group counsellor acknowledges group members feelings in the present. The following is another example:

When I talk about personal things in a group, I think about the importance of confidentiality.

In this last example, the counsellor picks up a theme already touched on in the group, and in doing so, invites further discussion of it. It should be added, however, that self-disclosure should be used judiciously, since too much or too little can be counterproductive. When a leader self-discloses too much, the balance of attention is shifted in the group, and members may become anxious about this. On the other hand, too little self-disclosure from the leader, may make him/her seem aloof and detached from the group. Ultimately, the most important guiding principle in relation to self-disclosure is that it should be related to what is happening in the group.

Reasons for using responses in groups

Other examples of skills used by group leaders are given in chapter three, and others will be discussed in various contexts in subsequent chapters. It is useful at this point, however, to focus on the reasons for using specific responses and interventions in group counselling. These are:

◆ To open and close group sessions
◆ To give information
◆ To encourage member participation
◆ To give and receive feedback
◆ To model empathy, respect and transparency
◆ To identify and highlight group processes
◆ To self-disclose when appropriate
◆ To clarify statements and acknowledge behaviour
◆ To ask questions and confront when appropriate
◆ To help group members understand their experiences in the group
◆ To encourage the transfer of learning to other situations outside the group
◆ To facilitate the development of insight among group members
◆ To facilitate the development of confidence and self-reliance among members

---

<EXERCISE 30>

THE LEADERLESS GROUP
Time: 15 mins. Group experience. 15 mins. Discussion.

Sometimes the leader's role in a group is best highlighted when no leader is, in fact, present. This exercise should help you experience and explore a leaderless group. It is an exercise for the whole group and can be carried out by members who are keen to consider the effects of such a group on member participation. There is no specific task or topic of conversation for the group. Members are told to sit together in a circle, and to say what they are thinking and feeling, as and when they wish. Participants can respond to one another, or they may choose to remain silent. At the end of the fifteen minutes, discuss your feelings about the experience, with special reference to what you liked or disliked about the activity.

References

Barnes, B., Ernst, S. and Hyde, K. (1999) *An Introduction to Groupwork.* London. Routledge.

Benjamin, J., Bessant, J. and Watts, R. (1997) *Making groups work.* Australia. Allen & Unwin.

Corey, G. (1995) *Group counselling* (4th ed.) California. Brooks / Cole Publishing Co.

Douglas, T. (2000) *Basic Groupwork* (2nd ed.) London. Routledge.

Ettin, M. F. (1999) *Foundations and Applications of Group psychotherapy.* London. Jessica Kingsley Publishers.

Forsyth, D. R. (1999) *Group Dynamics* (3rd ed.) California. Wadsworth Publishing Co.

Goleman, D. (1996) *Emotional Intelligence.* London. Bloomsbury.

Haney, H. and Leibsohn, J. (2001) *Basic counselling responses in groups.* U.S.A. Wadsworth / Thompson Learning.

Hope, A. and Timmel., S. (1999) *Training for transformation* (book 2) London. Intermediate Technology Publications.

Lewin, K., Lippitt, R. and White, R. K. (1939) *Patterns of aggressive behaviour in experimentally created social climates.* Journal of Social Psychology, 10, 271–99.

Mistry, T. and Brown, A. (1997) *Race and Groupwork.* London. Whiting & Birch Ltd.

Tudor, K. (1999) *Group Counselling.* London. Sage Publications.

Yalom, I. D. (1995) *The theory and practice of group psychotherapy.* (4th Ed.) New York. Basic Books.

6

Individuals and their conduct in groups

INTRODUCTION

A group of people gathered together, for whatever purpose, is bound to include a broad spectrum of personalities, capable of generating and engaging in a variety of behaviours. Counselling and therapy groups are certainly no exception in this respect. Indeed, in these, as in all other groups, individuals tend to adopt their own interpersonal styles that have been learned early in life. These ways of communicating are seldom questioned, and are usually transferred unconsciously to the group setting. The fact that certain behaviours are often problematic, not just for the individuals themselves, but for others as well, means that the group is an ideal context in which people can examine their habitual styles of communication, and change them when necessary.

Many groupwork researchers, including Yalom (1995), Edelwich & Brodsky (1992), Brown (1998), Baron et al. (1996), Barnes et al. (1999) and Douglas (2000) have written extensively about problem behaviour as it occurs in groups. In this chapter we shall look again at some of the difficulties which people experience in groups, with special reference to the kinds of responses which generate problems, not just for the group as a whole, but more specifically for individuals themselves. The emphasis throughout will be on looking at the meaning behind each type of behaviour, the reasons for relating to others in particular ways, and the benefits derived from identifying and changing dysfunctional modes of communication. The following Case study serves as a useful starting point for picking up on these central themes.

CASE STUDY: THE DOMINANT GROUP MEMBER

In a counselling group of eight clients, Stephen showed signs of wanting to dominate or monopolize proceedings from the outset. He sat next to the group counsellor at the first meeting, and interjected at frequent intervals to describe the problems he was having at home, and the many treatments and therapies he had tried over the years. The group counsellor was familiar with Stephen's background, and was aware that he encountered difficulties in his relationships generally. A major problem for Stephen was his inability to identify how others might feel when he talked almost incessantly, without ever really waiting for responses from them.

In this situation the counsellor was concerned to check Stephen's monopoly of the group, but she wanted to do it in a way which was not just effective, but therapeutic as well. Yalom (1995:371) stresses the importance of interrupting a dominant group member's behaviour pattern before it becomes obstructive to the group (and its effective functioning) as a whole. However, the counsellor in this instance was also aware that any intervention made would have to be sensitive and skilful, and should not alienate or threaten other members of the group. This point is especially important, since the group was a new one and members did not know each other well. How each group leader or counsellor deals with the difficulties presented by a monopolizing or dominant member will, of course, vary according to the specific circumstances at the time. An important point to remember, however, is that it is a group problem as much as it is a problem for a particular individual, and it is for this reason that the group as a whole must be included in addressing it. In this Case study example, the group counsellor used a process statement to enlist the attention and involvement of the other members.

>**Counsellor:** *It seems to me that Stephen is doing a lot of work for the group and most people are content to keep quiet and listen.*

>**Stephen:** (nodding) *I do feel as if I've been saying a lot ... I hate it when there are silences.*

>**Babs:** *If someone else is talking ... well it's hard to cut in ... to know if I can offer anything useful, especially when I don't know anyone ... or hardly.*

>**Counsellor:** *So, it's hard for you Babs, and maybe for others here, to speak out in a group when you've just met. I wonder if anyone else would like to say how they feel about it.*

>**Mike:** *I'm usually glad when someone else does all the talking ...*

After these initial exchanges, other members of the group were able to contribute and say how they felt in new situations where they had to interact with people they had only just met. The group counsellor then asked Stephen what he felt about the feedback from the group. His response was that he valued what people said, and he now felt less responsibility for 'keeping things going.' What Stephen did in the group initially, was to communicate in a style that he was used to. The counsellor could have challenged him directly, but this would risk alienating him from the group, or perhaps even losing him altogether, as he might have quit membership.

WHY PEOPLE MONOPOLIZE GROUPS

In this chapter, and indeed throughout the book, we shall concentrate on avoiding any suggestion that certain people are inherently 'difficult' because they behave in particular ways in relation to others. It is true that conduct and behaviour often presents problems for individuals, and for the people they communicate with. People are seldom aware that their own individual style of communication may be inappropriate or alienating to other group members. Part of the reason for being in a group is to learn more about the way we communicate, to understand why we favour a particular approach and to change to a more effective interpersonal style which will improve our relationships overall. If we look at some of the reasons which prompt people to dominate or monopolize in groups, it helps us to understand the behaviour and its meaning. Consider the following:

◆ Anxiety

◆ Lack of confidence

◆ Fear of true self-disclosure

◆ A need to be in control

◆ A fear of intimacy

◆ An inability to empathize with others

It may be surprising to learn that a person whose monopolistic behaviour in a group causes so much annoyance to others is, in fact, probably anxious, lacking in self confidence, afraid of intimacy and unable to experience empathy. The need to be in control is a much more obvious characteristic, though its underlying cause is perhaps less clear. Yalom (1995:373) suggests that the cause of monopolistic behaviour is not always easy to understand, especially at the beginning of therapy, though it may become clearer later on. In addition, he stresses the importance of concentrating on the monopolist's manifest behaviour (and the way others respond to it) rather than seeking to interpret the cause. So, for example, it would *not* be helpful to interpret a dominant member's behaviour in the following way:

It seems to me Sam that you interrupt a lot because you are anxious and need others to pay attention to you.

However, it would be appropriate to focus on Sam's behaviour as follows:

When you interrupt in that way Sam I feel discounted and unable to get my viewpoint heard.

In this second example, the speaker is saying how she feels when Sam cuts across or interrupts. She refrains from *accusing* him in a way that might make him defensive and unresponsive to what she is saying. On the other hand, she *is* telling him how his behaviour affects her in particular. With this kind of feedback from group members (and from the leader) Sam is in a better position to understand what happens in his relationships with other people, not just in this group, but beyond the group as well. The group counsellor can help a dominant member to relate what he learns in the group to his relationships outside it, though this usually takes time and can only be accomplished by degrees, and with great sensitivity.

THE UNINVOLVED MEMBER

We have seen that it is unwise to confront a dominant group member directly about his/her behaviour, and this same principle applies to helping group members who appear to lack involvement with others in the group. At the start of any group, different members may remain silent, often because they are nervous, waiting for others to speak, testing the environment, or simply lacking the confidence to speak out at this initial stage. Later on, however, group members start to participate, some more readily than others. In a well established and cohesive group, all members will, ideally, contribute with increasing confidence, skill and enhanced interpersonal effectiveness. For some group members though, this ideal sequence of increasing confidence and skill does not follow automatically. The group member who is withdrawn or silent, may, for example, have special difficulties to overcome, not just initially but later on as well. In discussing group members who remain silent, Brown (1998:128) describes his own reactions to them, and suggests that it is often difficult to judge why people are quiet in groups, and how much they need or want help to overcome their non-participation.

In counselling and therapy groups, though, silent group members do need to be helped to understand their reasons for relating to others in this particular way. If we assume that participants in such groups generally wish to improve the quality of their lives, and their relationships, then it follows that a focus on faulty or dysfunctional interpersonal communication is very much part of the group's task. On the other hand, it is possible for some reticent members to gain much from simply observing the group, its processes and the behaviour and interactions taking place in it. Such lack of involvement may present difficulties for other group members, however, since it may be interpreted as disinterest or even contempt. Yalom (1995) indicates that though some members do learn through 'vicarious' engagement with the group, other evidence suggests that active involvement in the group is more likely to lead to lasting benefits for participants.

In common with the monopolizing group member, the silent or non-contributing member is often unaware that a communications problem does indeed exist for them. Vague intimations of something wrong may prompt a process of self-exploration, but the exact nature of the difficulty is seldom clear. Possible causes of member reticence in a group include the following:

◆ Fear of exposure
◆ Lack of assertiveness
◆ Fear of saying the wrong thing

◆ Feelings of superiority in relation to other group members

◆ Fear of conflict

◆ Fear of becoming emotional

◆ Lack of verbal skills

◆ To punish others or draw attention to self.

It can be seen from this list of causes that fear plays a significant role in many of them. If we consider once again how people behave when a group first starts, we can see that silence and reticence are the rule rather than the exception. People often fear exposure in new situations, and lack of assertiveness and worries about saying the wrong thing are commonplace too. But for those group members who are habitually silent, their behaviour *is* a mode of communication, however dysfunctional which they have probably used in the past, and will continue to use unless they receive feedback encouraging them to change.

In helping the reticent or silent member, the group counsellor can offer encouragement by valuing and acknowledging any contributions, including non-verbal cues, which the person chooses to make. Helping silent members is obviously easier in groups that incorporate work carried out in pairs or triads, because in these less threatening contexts a shy or reticent person may open up and contribute without too much difficulty. In the absence of this kind of arrangement, however, the group leader must rely on observing the silent member's non-verbal behaviour and highlighting this, though this should be done without making him/her the sole object of attention and comment. The following Case study suggests some strategies for looking at non-participatory behaviour in groups.

CASE STUDY: TREVOR

Trevor joined a men's personal development group to find out why he was unable to sustain a long-term relationship. He contributed little in the first and second meetings, responding only to direct questions, and then only in a perfunctory or indifferent manner. This behaviour continued into the third session, but instead of maintaining a direct focus on Trevor, the therapist (Duncan) decided to enlist the help of the group to understand what was happening. As stated earlier in this section it is important to remember that a person may behave in a certain way in a group *because of something that is happening in the group.* In view of this, the behaviour in question is a group issue, and not just an issue for the individual concerned. In this example the group therapist addressed the matter, first by speaking to Trevor and then by including the group.

Duncan: *Trevor, is there something you could add to what we've been saying?*

Trevor: *Not really ... it's all been said.*

Duncan: *You don't want to interact on this one ...*

Trevor: *I'm fine ... just listening.*

Duncan: *I wonder how the group can come in on this and give some feedback. For myself I feel I want to include Trevor more ... to hear his viewpoint too.*

Casey: *I don't feel comfortable with someone not contributing ... it just seems like we are all uninteresting here ...*

Joe: *Yeah ... I feel uncomfortable with it too.*

Trevor: *It's not meant like that. It's just I don't think I have anything interesting to say ... or anything that you would find interesting. It's not that the group is uninteresting ... by no means.*

Joe: *But with everyone joining in it could be more interesting ...*

Following these exchanges, group members (including Trevor) discussed what it meant to lack confidence with other people, especially when meeting for the first time. Trevor did not become a totally involved group member all at once, but he did make the connection (with the therapist's help) between his behaviour in the group and his difficulty in establishing intimate relationships outside it. Gradually he came to participate more, to have confidence in himself and to trust other group members to engage with him without feeling threatened by their interest and concern.

EXERCISE 31

GROUP BEHAVIOUR QUESTIONNAIRE
Time: 40 mins.

Read the following statements and say whether you agree / disagree with them in relation to your own, and other people's behaviour in groups. When you have completed the questionnaire, share your views and discuss with members of the whole group.

1   I tend to keep quiet and listen when I meet a group of people for the first time. Agree / Disagree

2   My style is to become immediately involved when I am in a new group situation. Agree / Disagree

3   People often talk too much in groups just to hide their anxiety. Agree / Disagree

4   Using humour in groups helps everyone to relax. Agree / Disagree

5   Keeping quiet in the group is one way of showing disapproval. Agree / Disagree

6   When someone dominates the group I tend to switch off. Agree / Disagree

7   When someone shows boredom in a group it means other members are to blame. Agree / Disagree

8   I feel bored when one group member is allowed to monopolize. Agree / Disagree

9   The best way to deal with a noisy group member is to ignore him/her. Agree / Disagree

10 The best way to deal with a quiet group member is to check out occasionally that she is content to stay quiet. Agree / Disagree

11 A silent group member has nothing of interest to say. Agree / Disagree

12 One way of dealing with a dominant member is to avoid eye contact with her. Agree / Disagree

13 The most talkative group member is usually the least confident in the group. Agree / Disagree

14 It is important to praise or affirm timid group members. Agree / Disagree

15 I tend to avoid interacting with angry group members. Agree / Disagree

16 When I am angry in a group I tend to show it. Agree / Disagree.

17 Feedback from the leader is the best response to problem behaviour. Agree / Disagree

18 Feedback from other group members is the best response to problem behaviour. Agree / Disagree

19 When I receive feedback in a group I need time to assimilate it. Agree / Disagree

20 I always look at my own behaviour before giving feedback to other group members. Agree / Disagree.

THE JOKER IN THE GROUP

In chapter three we looked at some of the roles that individual members often adopt. As part of this chapter we also discussed a Case study highlighting the role of the joker, in this instance, Paula, who belonged to a training group of fourteen students. It is worth extending the discussion about humour and joking in groups here, since this particular way of relating to others in groups has both positive and negative potential.

Almost as soon as a new group starts, it becomes obvious that at least one member favours a jocular or humorous style of communication with others. Humour is not uncommon at the beginning of a group, and it is certainly a useful way of easing tension and nervousness at this anxiety provoking stage. In addition, people often use humour in order to cope with what might otherwise be intolerable conditions in everyday living, so it is reasonable to expect that this same coping mechanism will be apparent in groups, especially when emotionally charged issues are being discussed.

Brandler & Roman (1999:232) describe the way in which humour is sometimes used in therapy groups to highlight the 'absurdity of suffering' and the coping strategies which people devise to deal with it. In this respect, humour can act as a very strong bond among group members, and it can also encourage more reticent members to self-disclose in an atmosphere which is less threatening than a sombre one. Moreover, the use of humour does not necessarily preclude expression of other strong feelings, including anger, loss, sadness and grief. In fact, in some instances, humour may be effective as an emotional catalyst in groups, especially when it serves to encourage deeper engagement with a wide range of feelings, both positive and negative. In this next Case study humour is evident, but it is just one of the many emotions expressed.

CASE STUDY: MURIEL

Muriel was a woman in her fifties who joined a support group for people recovering from cancer. As a result of drug treatment she had lost most of her hair, as had some of the other members of the group. Muriel had dreaded this effect of chemotherapy, so she was anxious to find out how other group members dealt with it.

Muriel: (Laughing) *The first time I looked in the mirror and saw myself bald as an egg it was a big shock I can tell you! Don't get me wrong, I knew what to expect because they told me ... I just didn't anticipate the actual shock of seeing it.*

Colette: *I know the feeling ... sheer panic. Then how to explain it to everyone ... as if you should have to explain it anyway.*

Joan: *Did you have that too? I couldn't believe how many people were fascinated by hair loss. It was like I had become a celebrity ... a bald celebrity!*

Beth: *It's because so many people are afraid ... hair loss is scary ... and dramatic hair loss is very scary.*

Muriel: (Starting to cry) *It most certainly is ... and the way it changes you ... the way you see yourself changes totally. It's the shock of it all ... and it only sinks in later.*

Joan: (Nodding) *And it's not just the hair loss is it? It's the realization of what could have happened ... that you're lucky to escape ... that I'm lucky to escape anything worse ... that I got treatment in time.*

Following these exchanges, members of the group were able to talk more openly about their fears and anxieties, in a way that they had not been able to do outside the group. By using humour to begin with, Muriel was testing the reactions of other group members to her feelings about hair loss and all the other traumatic changes she experienced. This led to a much deeper discussion among all the members who then felt safe enough to disclose their personal fears, their experiences of loss and their frustration when people outside the group proved insensitive or crass.

EXERCISE 32

THE HAPPINESS GROUP
Time: 1 hour.

This exercise should encourage you to identify the positive, and some negative, aspects of humour in everyday life, and to discuss the contribution which humour makes to happiness, health and general well being. Working in pairs, take turns to talk for about five minutes each on the following topics:

◆ The things that really make me laugh are:
◆ When I am really happy I:
◆ One of my apprehensions about happiness is:
◆ Something that made me laugh recently was:
◆ I remember when humour helped me to cope with:
◆ When I'm with really funny people I:
◆ Humour can be positive in groups when:
◆ Humour can be a problem in groups when:
◆ Laughter is good for general health because:
◆ Group leaders need a balanced sense of humour because:

When you have finished your discussion in pairs, join members of the whole group and share your ideas together. The group leader or facilitator should help members identify any recurring themes that emerge in the discussion, with special reference to identification of both positive and negative use of humour in the group.

When joking becomes a problem

We have considered the ways in which humour is helpful in groups, with special reference to its effectiveness in accessing other, deeply felt, and often painful emotions. Humour is not always a positive force in groups, however, and in some instances members who try to avoid confrontation with serious issues may use it. Occasionally one group member will adopt the role of joker in order to mask anxiety or to compensate for the lack of other, more appropriate, social skills. Strean (1994:190) suggests that group members may use humour as a way of maintaining self-esteem, or as a means of 'maintaining boundaries while sharing some threatening feeling.' If we list the more negative reasons for using humour in a group, therefore, we can see that the following are included:

◆ Anxiety
◆ Lack of other social skills
◆ To maintain distance
◆ To avoid confrontation with difficult issues
◆ To avoid painful feelings
◆ To boost personal confidence and self-esteem

If the behaviour is not addressed, a persistent joker is unlikely to make much therapeutic progress in a group. Eventually other group members will become tired of the relentless humour as well, though there may be some reluctance to challenge the joker, since to do so tends to invite a 'spoil sport' label which few are willing to risk. When therapeutic work is inhibited or lessened because of joking, the group leader (or counsellor) should address the issue in a way that is acceptable to the whole group and the member responsible. The following is one example of how this might be done:

CASE STUDY: MAX

Max, a student member of a counsellor training group, described how he liked to 'lighten the atmosphere a little' when discussion became too serious for him. There was a fairly relentless quality to his joking, and other members of the group began to show, by their non-verbal cues that they found his behaviour difficult. During a group discussion about self-awareness he resorted to humour again.

Max: *I have been told often enough what I'm like ... I think I know myself pretty well ... I'm, you know ... irresistible, good looking ...*

Group trainer: *You don't want to get into this discussion about feedback and self-awareness?*

Max: (surprised) *Don't get me wrong ... I'm all for it ...*

Group trainer: *But really asking for feedback from others can be threatening ... often uncomfortable?*

Max: *Hmm ... if you put it like that ... I'm not that used to it..*

Group trainer: *So one way of coping is to laugh it off ... make others laugh ... then you don't have to look.*

Max: *Yes, I suppose that's true.*

If the group trainer had not intervened to highlight his avoidance of serious issues, Max wouldn't have been encouraged to look closely at his behaviour, the reasons behind it, and the damaging effects on other group members and their discussion. However, interventions like this need to be properly timed, and should be sensitive to the needs of the group and the individual concerned.

BLAMING AND ATTACKING OTHERS

Conflict is not an unusual experience in groups. In fact, it is often an indication that members are interacting with each other openly and honestly. In addition, conflict is an integral part of certain stages in a group's life. In chapter four, for example, we noted that Tuckman's storming stage of development is characterized by conflict and sometimes rebellion against the leader, polarisation of opinion, resistance to the designated task and the formation of bickering sub groups. In some instances, however, conflict and aggression are not confined to particular stages of the group's life, but may be shown consistently in the behaviour of one member who habitually blames or attacks others. Those blamed may not necessarily be members of the group, and may even include places or things residing outside it. We know from chapter five that the group leader is often blamed too, especially when members are reluctant to identify their own coping resources and cling to dependence instead.

Blaming people, places and things outside the group is yet another way of refusing to acknowledge individual responsibility and commitment to change. The following short Case study shows this clearly.

CASE STUDY: SOMEONE ELSE SHOULD BE HERE

Janice was receiving help for her alcohol addiction, and was referred to a counselling group by her G.P. Though quite willing to join the group, Janice was by no means convinced that she was the person who really needed help. In group discussion she often referred to her husband's drinking and was emphatic that he needed help more than she did. Other group members were at pains to point out to Janice that she had come to the group on a voluntary basis, so she must, therefore, be aware that she did indeed have an alcohol problem. Finally the group counsellor intervened to ask Janice what she hoped to gain in the group. This question forced Janice to think carefully about her presence in the group. As a result, she was able to see that she was indeed there for a purpose.

Janice: (pausing) *I suppose I came because I have a problem.*

Counsellor: *The problem of drinking too much?*

Janice: *What do I want from the group? Support and help ... for my problem.*

Counsellor: *So you need to start with yourself ... not with your husband, with yourself?*

Janice: *Yes, that's true.*

By asking Janice what she wanted from the group, the counsellor encouraged her to focus attention on herself instead of her husband. Clients in counselling, and this includes individual as well as group counselling, often make the mistake of believing others should change before they themselves can make a decision to change. Part of the learning process for clients like this is the realization that we cannot change other people. What we can do is change ourselves. When this is achieved, others may then change in response, though this change in others is not always the kind we had hoped for.

Group blaming

Sometimes several group members band together to blame people or things outside the group. Edelwich & Brodsky (1992:117) refer to this tendency, and describe how effective process statements from the leader block it. Blaming outside factors or people can become a contagious habit in some groups, with almost every member present pointing to something external to censure for personal difficulties. These external factors can include jobs, bosses, partners, men, women, children, unreasonable bank managers, the police or the government. While this kind of blaming is happening, very little therapeutic work goes on in the group. By responding with process statements the group counsellor can call the group's attention back to its purpose and task. The following is an example:

I feel that the group has now gone into a blaming routine. There is a focus outside instead of inside the group, and I think this will stop us going forward. Could we get back to the group here and looking at personal responsibility?

Finding a scapegoat

Sometimes blame in a group is levelled against one particular member who, as we saw in chapter three, is often selected to carry unwanted unacceptable feelings experienced by other group members. We also saw that the scapegoat is frequently used to the role, and may, in fact, invite (through their behaviour) hostility from others. Brown (1998:126) suggests that the role of scapegoat may actually be 'functional and satisfying' for the victim, since a certain amount of negative attention may be preferable to no attention at all. Scapegoating is certainly an example of problem behaviour in a group, and as such, needs to be dealt with by the leader so that members are encouraged to confront and address personal issues avoided through its use. Focusing on group process is usually effective in helping members recognize what is happening. Examples of how this can be done were given in chapter three where comment and clarification were used to direct member attention to the scapegoating behaviour. If scapegoating behaviour is not confronted, the victim may, as Yalom (1995:301) indicates, be forced to leave the group.

BEING SEDUCTIVE

For some group members, sexuality and seduction form an integral part of the way they establish and maintain relationships. This particular interpersonal style is meant to attract as much attention as possible, and to induce an erotic response from others. The kinds of behaviour characteristic of this approach include flirtatiousness, blatant verbal exchanges and provocative dress. Once again it is essential to consider the underlying reasons for interacting with others in a specific and preferred way. Group members who relate to others in a one dimensional, overtly sexual way, often do so for the following reasons:

◆ Because they fear relationships will break down unless sex is a major component

◆ Because of early experience of sexual abuse

◆ Because of low self-esteem

◆ To acquire status in the group

◆ To avoid confrontation with painful personal issues

◆ To appear attractive and to manipulate others

CASE STUDY: LYNETTE

There were twelve members in a counsellor training group, none of whom had met before the first session. The group comprised eight women and four men, all slightly apprehensive about the training programme ahead of them. During the first meeting, the group trainer encouraged participants to say how they felt about this new situation. As part of the ice breaking agenda for the evening, participants were also asked to say what three inanimate things they would take with them to a desert island. When it came to her turn to speak, one group member, called Lynette, said she would take only one thing, her vibrator, since in the absence of a sexual partner it was all she would want or need. This revelation was greeted with laughter all round, as well as some surprised glances from the men. Lynette continued to surprise other group members with her frequent references to sexual matters, and she interacted with male members of the group in a provocative and sexual way. However, during a later training session, when group members were asked to participate in a group task, Lynette demonstrated another, more hostile, characteristic. During the group task, one of the men assumed a prominent position in relation to a decision being taken. In response to this, Lynette attacked him verbally, saying emphatically that she would not allow herself to be 'dictated to' by a man. So intense was her reaction that other group members (including the object of her anger) were reduced to surprised silence. Later on, during another group task, Lynette initiated a second angry confrontation with a male member of the group. This time she refused to participate in the task and simply withdrew from the group. During the process observation sessions that followed these episodes, Lynette was at a loss to explain her behaviour. At the end of the course, however, she was able to identify reasons for her angry reactions in the group. In an assignment she wrote:

I still feel awful after that last exercise, and wonder why I had been so violent in my verbal reactions to other members of the group. I do remember I didn't care about anyone else there at the time. I didn't care about my hurtful behaviour to both men and women present. I was full of self-pity and had no time for anyone else.

Later in her assignment, Lynette described how she gradually identified the underlying reason for her antagonism towards men in the group. She had been sexually abused as a child, and adult relationships with men had also been emotionally and physically damaging. In addition, she could see that her impulse to control men by seductive behaviour was linked to early experience. Back then she was expected to relate to others in an overtly sexual way, a habit she had retained without ever questioning it. Following these insights, Lynette sought individual psychotherapy, and abandoned further study until she felt she could cope with the demands which training often makes.

TAKING ON THE ROLE OF GROUP THERAPIST

Trained counsellors and therapists often slip into the role of helper when they themselves are members of a counselling group. This situation is easy enough to understand, since most of us have experienced difficulty occasionally, in separating ourselves from the professional roles we inhabit. Becoming the unofficial group therapist poses some problems, however, not just for the individual concerned, but for other members of the group as well. Edelwich & Brodsky (1992:119) make the point that an individual who assumes the role of therapist or voluntary assistant, does so in order to avoid confronting his or her own issues. One counsellor recounted her experience of being a group member in the following way:

> *Almost as soon as the group started I, along with another trained counsellor, slipped into our helping roles. When other members described their problems we were straight in there, wanting to help and support. During this time I never really thought about my own problems or my reasons for joining the group in the first place. Then the group counsellor intervened by focusing attention on what was happening in the group. She did not confront us directly, but instead asked the group as a whole to consider what was taking place. My colleague and I could then see clearly that we were assuming leadership / therapist roles, and avoiding our own issues in the process. I was disconcerted when I realized what I was doing, and I found it very difficult to change. Quite apart from my counsellor training, I was the eldest in a family of four and I was used to telling my siblings what to do. I was also used to looking after them at times too. When my 'helper' behaviour in the group was taken from me, I was at a loss to know how to behave. For a long time afterwards I became withdrawn in the group, and I had real difficulty in learning how to be me without the role.*

It was, in fact, some considerable time before this particular group member could modify her behaviour in a way that allowed her to acknowledge her own problems. In her personal account of what happened, she identifies several significant reasons for behaving as she did in the group. These include:

- A childhood history of helping siblings
- Professional training as a helper
- An inability to de-role
- Fear of self-disclosure
- Not knowing how else to behave

In addition to the reasons identified and listed here, there is another important reason for playing the role of the therapist in a counselling group. On a fairly obvious level, it represents a challenge to the designated leader / counsellor of the group. Group leadership challenge is certainly not uncommon, and can take many forms. When group members have training and qualifications similar to, or even more impressive than, those possessed by the leader, some challenge is almost inevitable.

THE ANGRY GROUP MEMBER

Earlier in this chapter we discussed the phenomenon of blaming and attacking others either inside or outside the group. We saw that anger can take different forms in a group, and may be directed against the leader, individual members, or the group as a whole. Sometimes one group member seems especially angry, and may express hostility by being overtly or covertly critical. Such members may also make a point of challenging the usefulness of the group, or they may refuse to participate as a way of showing disapproval or scorn. Repetitive questioning of the leader, or even interrogation of other group members, can indicate anger barely concealed. It is important to remember that anger need not necessarily be expressed verbally, but may be shown in body language or even in choice of seating position within the group. In a group of trainee counsellors, one student always placed her chair outside the group circle. On the surface she seemed pleasant and interested, but later, as group members became better acquainted, she expressed strong, angry feelings against the group as a whole. Because of the nature of the training programme, and its emphasis on self-awareness, she was able to work out the reasons for her antagonism and fear of intimacy with other members. These reasons stemmed from early relationships within her family, and once she became aware of them she was able to change her behaviour within the group.

We have also considered the reasons for dominant behaviour in one, or more, group members. We saw that anxiety, lack of confidence and a need to control were included as reasons for wanting to monopolize the group. Unacknowledged anger is another reason for behaving in this way. Unless checked, a member who talks a lot and interrupts others will have an inhibiting effect on the group. This is certainly one way of exercising control in the group, but it is also often a clear expression of anger too. Withdrawn members may also be expressing anger through their behaviour. If we consider the effects of early experience on later behaviour, it is easy to identify the 'logic' behind silence as a means of punishing others. A child who is never allowed to show anger openly will find other ways of expressing it. Silence and passive resistance are, therefore, often potent signals of animosity and displeasure.

Helping the angry person

Unless the angry person is helped to identify and change their habitual way of relating to others, their presence in the group will not yield therapeutic results for themselves, or indeed for anyone else involved. In one group, Cara, a particularly angry member, alternated between extended and frosty silences that were clearly discernible to other members, and an interrogatory approach when other people spoke. In order to highlight this behaviour, the counsellor decided to use process statements as a starting point. He did this by using 'I' statements as follows:

Counsellor: *I would like to look now at some of the recent interactions in the group. Cara, I'd like if I may, to say something about the questions you ask.*

Cara: (surprised) *Go ahead.*

Counsellor: *Well, when I'm not sure of myself, or angry about something in a group, I tend to ask a lot of blunt questions and put other people on the spot too.*

Cara: *Are you saying asking questions is a sign of anger?*

Counsellor: *I perceive it that way – that it is sometimes. It depends on the way questions are asked ... long silences can mean that too. But I wonder what you feel about it.*

Cara: *I never thought about it to be honest. But I know when I'm really fuming I tend to sit back ... afraid to come clean with it. I didn't notice myself doing it so much here though.*

Lelia: *I would like it if you would say more about yourself. I don't know what you're thinking, and when you fume like that I feel uncomfortable and can't get near you.*

Counsellor: *So not saying what you feel openly, not saying when you feel angry, hurt, sad or just plain mad at others, can make them uncomfortable. They would rather you spoke openly and expressed those feelings.*

Cara: *What, become angry you mean – how would that help anyone?*

Lelia: *No, not become angry, but talk about it. Say what you feel when others annoy you.*

Cara's angry behaviour was a problem for her, and other members of the group, so the counsellor was concerned to help her identify its cause and change to a less combative style. She had come into the group because she had experienced difficulty with relationships at work, and in her personal life. Anger, or rather her inability to express it appropriately, was a major problem for Cara, though she hadn't seen it clearly as such until it was highlighted in the group.

It is important to emphasize here that anger is often legitimate in a group, and as Barnes et al. (1999:12) suggest, may be expressed by one person 'on behalf' of other group members. It would be wrong, therefore, to give the impression that anger is out of place in groups. On the contrary, its total absence is nearly always an indication that something is being hidden or disguised. This may happen when members intuitively feel that the leader is uncomfortable or inhibited about expressions of anger. In such a situation the anger does not go away, but is expressed indirectly, either through poor time keeping, absenteeism or other demonstrations of subversive behaviour. This is why it is essential for group leaders, and especially group counsellors, to be aware of their own feelings in relation to anger and how it should be expressed. This kind of self-awareness can only be achieved through on-going training, supervision and, ideally, experience of membership in a therapeutic group.

Helping group members who are angry, therefore, begins with an acknowledgement that we all have angry feelings about some things, and in certain situations. This may seem obvious, but for some people it is not. In a training group for counselling students, one member called Hazel was adamant that she never got angry. To help her identify and acknowledge her true feelings the counsellor engaged her in the following dialogue:

Group trainer: *You say you never feel angry?*

Hazel: *No I don't ... I don't see any need for anger.*

Group trainer: *So you are never angry?*

Hazel: *No.*

Group trainer: *Never ever?*

Hazel: *I've said I'm never angry ...*

Group trainer: *You are saying you never feel anger ...*

Hazel: (becoming angry) *How many times do I have to say it, I am never ...*

Group trainer: Angry?

As a result of these exchanges Hazel did indeed feel angry, especially at the way she had been tricked into betraying her feelings. The group trainer explained why she had provoked her in this way, and considerable time was spent on processing and analysing the incident. This is not a technique recommended for use in a routine way. The trainer who used it knew her students well, and was aware that Hazel would be able to accept (though not necessarily like) the lesson learned from it.

> ### EXERCISE 33
>
> **SAYING HOW YOU FEEL**
> Time: 1 hour.
>
> Working individually, look at the following list of emotional responses and try to identify any group situations that might provoke these in you.
>
> ◆ Anger
> ◆ Resentment
> ◆ Anxiety
> ◆ Withdrawal
>
> Once you have identified the group conditions that might elicit these responses from you personally, you are more likely to understand how clients in group counselling respond in the ways they sometimes do. Discuss your answers with other group members, and consider the similarities that may be apparent.

> ### EXERCISE 34
>
> **BEHAVIOUR IN GROUPS**
> Time: 40 minutes.
>
> Sometimes people behave in groups in ways that we find difficult to understand or deal with. These include:
>
> ◆ Monopolizing

- ◆ Remaining silent
- ◆ Showing anger
- ◆ Blaming others
- ◆ Interrogating others
- ◆ Joking
- ◆ Intellectualising
- ◆ Challenging the leader
- ◆ Remaining dependent
- ◆ Arriving late / leaving early
- ◆ Missing sessions
- ◆ Breaking into sub-groups
- ◆ Scapegoating
- ◆ Showing intolerance
- ◆ Being seductive

Working in small groups, discuss these behaviours and identify those that cause you personal problems, either as a group member or as a facilitator. Look at the list of behaviours again, and discuss what you think they might mean.

INTELLECTUALISING

Some group members find it difficult to respond to others without recourse to theoretical speculation or intellectual discussion. In some instances this response is meant to emphasize a rational approach to problems, though it may also be accompanied by an explicit contempt for emotion or the expression of feelings, as the following Case study shows:

CASE STUDY: MATT

Matt, who was a student member of a counsellor training group, found it difficult to be concrete or specific, and instead tended to theorize as soon as a discussion began. He was also disdainful of emotional display, which was, in his view, 'self indulgence' and a means of gaining sympathy and attention. When another group member asked him why he was on the course, Matt replied that he had been funded by his agency to attend, and that he was interested, though not 'convinced.' During a discussion about the value of support groups, he interjected several times to express his views on the subject. The discussion arose because one group member (Halima) had a relative who was seriously ill and belonged to a support group.

Matt: *I think people can go round and round in circles when they get together. Things are never resolved in those groups. I read some interesting research suggesting that ...*

Kirsten: *Hey ... hold on a minute. Halima was talking just now about something very personal to her, something that was very difficult for her and her family.*

Matt: *Well I know, and I don't wish to seem disrespectful. But the fact remains that research suggests ...*

Halima: *Matt, it seems to me that each time someone refers to a painful subject, you fly off into the realm of theory and speculation.*

Matt: *I think someone needs to keep some perspective here ... otherwise, we're swamped with emotional stuff each time.*

Halima: *Perhaps what you mean is that you are afraid of being swamped.*

Group trainer: *When I'm apprehensive about feelings, not knowing if I can cope with them, I'm tempted to escape into theory sometimes.*

Matt: *So what are you saying, that I'm afraid of emotions?*

Group trainer: *It's worth thinking about. When we find ourselves trying to escape something, it's worth looking at why that should be.*

By commenting on her own propensity to intellectualise or resort to theory, the group trainer was able to confront Matt in a way that invited him to look more closely at his own behaviour in the group. Constant theorising often indicates a reluctance to dwell on our feelings, or to allow ourselves to be affected by the feelings of other people. Because the group referred to in this instance was for training purposes, it was possible for the leader/trainer to spend time in helping students understand the basis for certain types of behaviour, including intellectualisation, that is used as a defence. Achieving such results is possible in therapy and counselling groups too, even when the focus is not specifically a didactic or teaching one. Yalom (1995:235) suggests that clients who are overly intellectual may do better in groups as opposed to individual therapy. This is because some clients may be quite unaware of the problems they create in their relationships when they fail to recognize or acknowledge feelings. The group provides an ideal setting in which group members with an intellectual propensity can receive feedback from others present. This form of reality testing is, of course, essential for all members, regardless of their individual behavioural difficulties, and forms the basis of therapeutic progress in groups.

EXCESSIVE DEPENDENCE

In chapter one we referred to research carried out by Bion (1999) in which he described the strategies often used by group members to deal with anxiety. One of these strategies, dependence, is evident when the group appears to need (and expect) a strong leader with whom they can feel safe and protected. We know from our discussion in chapter four that group members often show this kind of dependence in the initial forming stage, when anxiety and tension are usually high. This stage tends to be transient, and group members gradually acquire confidence and some belief in their own abilities to cope and become independent. However, for some members this move to independence is more difficult.

It is important to remember here that staying dependent is not the same as being withdrawn or silent in a group. In fact, a dependent member may contribute verbally, and frequently, while remaining reluctant to assume personal responsibility. Occasionally such contributions take the form of references to personal, often seemingly insurmountable, difficulties and problems for which no remedy is ever seen as suitable. In some instances, certain members may become dependent on the group itself. This is more likely to happen when underlying factors, like loneliness and lack of other social contacts, exist. Again, as with all other forms of individual behaviour in groups, the group counsellor needs to understand why some members behave in dependent ways. Reasons include:

◆ Social isolation and loneliness

◆ A history of reliance on other 'stronger' people

◆ Fear of desertion

◆ Fear of rejection

◆ Lack of assertiveness skills

CASE STUDY: BEVERLY

Beverly, a member of an anxiety management group, showed excessive dependence on the group therapist from the outset. She suffered from anxiety in social situations, but her emotional difficulties were compounded by numerous physical symptoms, for which her doctor could find no cause. During group meetings, Beverly often referred to these symptoms, and to the fact that no one was able to help her. Though encouraged by the therapist and other group members to look more closely at ways of dealing with her own symptoms, she was adamant she had tried everything and that nothing had worked.

Beverly was a widow whose late husband, a much older man, had left her well off financially. During their time together he had taken care of all the practical details of their lives, paid the bills, and generally assumed responsibility for all aspects of daily living. Beverly couldn't drive (her husband said she didn't need to), nor could she deal with cheques, insurance companies and other financial matters. This all-encompassing dependence on her husband meant that she had no idea how to assert herself, or assume responsibility after his death. After a while she simply stopped trying, and it was around this time that her anxiety symptoms started to appear. Her doctor referred her to the anxiety management group at the local hospital, and Beverly quickly came to see it as a social support system that she could depend on to help her manage her life.

The group therapist was aware that Beverly's dependence extended far beyond the initial stage of the group's existence. Her task, therefore, was to help Beverly become more aware of her dependent behaviour, to understand its effects on herself and other people, and to change to more self-reliant ways of coping with her life. This proved to be easier said than done, since Beverly was very reluctant to change habits acquired over a lifetime of fifty years. Even as a child she had been protected by possessive parents who had never encouraged her to take risks or become psychologically independent. As a result of feedback from other group members, however, she did start to believe in herself a bit more, and even enrolled for a computer course. At the evening class she made some social contacts, and this encouraged her to become more adventurous and outgoing.

It could be argued that Beverly's involvement in computer studies at an evening class was more effective than the therapy group in helping her towards independence. This highlights the point that other factors, besides the group, are often instrumental in encouraging members to change. We noted in this Case study that Beverly tended to view the group as a social one, in which she could meet people and gain answers to her problems. Once she realized that she would have to work at changing herself, her enthusiasm for the group as a social support system diminished. She then looked for other, more appropriate, activities to fulfil her social needs. Once she made these contacts, she became less dependent in the therapy group.

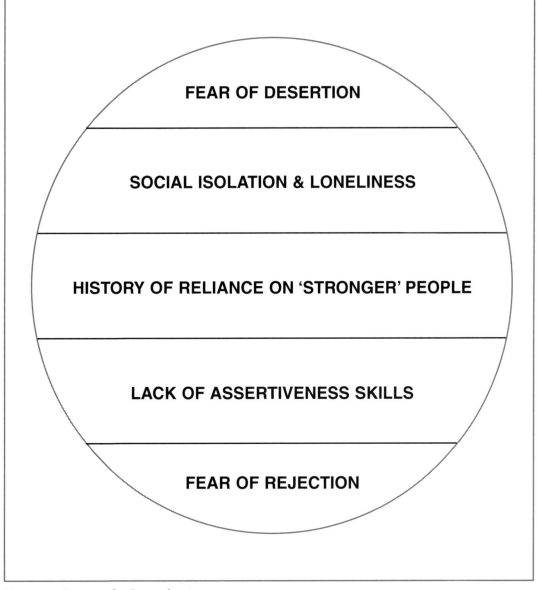

Figure 6.1 Reasons for Dependency

BREAKING INTO SUB-GROUPS

The formation of smaller group alliances is another form of behaviour that is potentially problematic for the group as a whole. In chapter four we noted that sub-group formation could be destructive in most groups, since it means that communication is no longer shared equally among all the members. However, it should be added that small group attachments are usual at certain stages of a group's existence, especially when group members learn they have common interests or concerns. When a group is just starting, for example, members may 'discover' others to whom they are attracted, and with whom they feel safe at this vulnerable stage. Difficulties arise when loyalty to small groups becomes more important than wholehearted participation in the life of the main group. When some group members establish sub-group alliances they clearly have reasons for doing so. These include:

◆ Fear of involvement in the whole group

◆ The need to voice concerns not voiced in the whole group

◆ The need to express hostility which cannot be expressed directly to the leader

◆ To gossip about other group members

In chapter four we saw that the issue of sub-grouping needs to be addressed by the group leader or counsellor. This is because a basic aim of group counselling is to explore interpersonal relationships, a task which is only achieved when all members present are committed to it. The allegiance of a small number of members to each other, and to the exchange of confidences, destroys group cohesion, inhibits therapeutic change and effectively excludes other group members. Interventions by the group leader/counsellor should focus on group process, and should invite sub-grouping members to discuss their experiences. In one counselling group, the leader became aware that two members frequently exchanged whispered confidences during meetings.

> **Group leader:** *Group, I want to focus again on our contract to discuss issues openly in the group. Maybe if there is something you feel nervous about sharing, we could look at the reasons for that.*

Following this intervention, there was a short silence. Then the conferring members, Diane and Susan, exchanged glances.

> **Diane:** *We just know some people in common, and we didn't think it would interest anyone else. Actually, it's this woman we know whose daughter became involved in drugs ...*

> **Group leader:** *So it's something you are interested in, something that concerns you ...*

> **Diane:** (looking at Susan) *It's just that we have had something similar in our families recently.*

> **Group leader:** *That similarity would emphasize your own experiences then?*

After this Diane and Susan were able to talk openly to the group about the traumatic events in their own family lives. By focusing on what was happening in the group, the leader succeeded in bringing the two sub-grouping members back into the here and now where they explored their difficulties and received the support of other members.

Yalom (1995:332) suggests that sub-grouping need not always be destructive, as long as the members involved are encouraged to talk about their experiences and needs. When the ethos of the group is conducive to openness, and when there is an absence of censure or blame, members who form small groups may feel able to discuss their chosen friendships, as well as their need to communicate in this way. Pre-group preparation is the most effective way of teaching group members about the goals of group counselling. Such preparation also highlights the need for commitment to group aims, which should be observed, even though certain distractions may present themselves and appear more attractive at times. Teaming up with one other person, or forming an exclusive clique, may seem more rewarding than total involvement in the group. What members should know from the outset is that communication within the whole group is infinitely more rewarding in the long term.

CONFLICT

Strictly speaking, conflict in groups should not be regarded as a problem, but as something that arises naturally when a number of people, all with different experiences and views, are interacting together. This point has been made in previous chapters, but since most group leaders (and members) feel apprehensive about dealing with conflict, it needs to be emphasized again.

Perhaps one of the reasons we tend to feel excessively fearful about conflict is that our previous experiences of it have been negative. Our memories of conflict in childhood may have been traumatic, and could have left us with the impression that it needs to be avoided at all costs. One member of a counselling group described how conflict was dealt with in her own family:

> *When there was any disagreement it tended to lead to shouting, people storming out, slamming doors and refusing to speak to others for days on end. Sometimes it led to physical violence, especially between my parents. I have been terrified of conflict ever since. I would avoid it at all costs, even if I lost out in the end because I couldn't hold my own.*

This group member's experience is certainly not unique. Students in training groups frequently describe their reasons for avoiding conflict in a similar way. When students have experience of unresolved conflict on a larger scale, within their own society, for example, their fear of dissention and disagreement may be even more pronounced. This is an effect that one trainer encountered while teaching students who had experienced unresolved conflict while growing up in their own society.

The students would do anything to avoid conflict in the group. All of them had witnessed violence as a result of conflict in society, so naturally they associated these two things (conflict and violence) at a very deep level. They took the view that conflict should always be avoided, and when it did occur in their own group, they were concerned to deny it and move on to something else.

As a result of later discussion, these students were able to see that conflict does not go away just because it is denied. On the contrary, it tends to surface in some other, sometimes violent, way. In addition they learned that what is important is the way we deal with conflict, and the group is an ideal medium in which to practise conflict resolution through the use of good interpersonal skills. The energy generated in conflict situations can be harnessed for creative, rather than destructive purposes. Indeed, without conflict it is difficult to see how individual differences can be heard and explored, and a conciliatory position finally reached.

If we look again at the developmental stages described by Erikson (1995), and referred to in chapter four, we can see that, according to his theory, different life stages are beset with conflict and crisis. It is interesting to note that the stages proposed by Erikson, are those during which major change is taking place, suggesting that in life, conflict is necessary for growth and change. The adolescent who rebels against his/her parents does so as a necessary prelude to adulthood. Members of a group also need to rebel, sometimes against the leader, sometimes against the views and opinions of others, in order to establish individuality and to grow psychologically.

The energy generated by conflict, can, if handled with sensitivity and skill, enhance the personal growth of all members and move the group forward to a more intimate and therapeutic level. To achieve these therapeutic results, however, the group leader needs to model attitudes of tolerance and respect when strong differences are expressed between members. It is particularly important to maintain and model these attitudes when argument is heated or angry. Group members should see that such feelings would not split the group apart, but can be contained and dealt with when basic communication skills are used to facilitate their appropriate expression. The following exchange took place when one member of a counselling group where members were discussing their experiences of addiction, interrupted others as they spoke:

Jordan: *Look, Sandy, I'm really pissed off with you cutting in. Who the hell do you think you are? This is the third time now I've tried to get a word in.*

Ariane: *Oh look, let's not fight. I can't stand this tension.*

Mimi: (Sounding angry) *Hold on a second, I agree with Jordan. Why shouldn't he say what he thinks?*

Group counsellor: *There are several viewpoints here. Let's take them one at a time. This time though, let's remember our agreement to listen when someone else speaks, even when we don't agree with them. I sense there are a lot of differences of opinion in the air now, and the group needs to hear them all.*

Dealing with conflict can be stressful for group leaders, so regular supervision is essential so that these and other challenging issues can be explored. Finally, it is worth reminding yourself frequently, that conflict is usual and necessary in groups; that it can be mobilized for the good of all the members; that it does not disappear if ignored and that its appearance is often an indication that members are interacting, often for the first time, with honesty and a real desire to clarify issues that concern them.

References

Barnes, B., Ernst, S. and Hyde, K. (1999) *An Introduction to Groupwork.* London. Routledge.

Baron, S., Kerr, N. L. and Miller, N. (1996) *Group Process, Group Decision, Group Action.* Buckingham, O.U. Press.

Bion, W. R. (1999) *Experiences in Groups and other Papers.* London. Routledge.

Brown, A. (1998) *Groupwork* (3rd ed.) Aldershot. Ashgate Arena.

Brandler, S. and Roman, C. P. (1999) *Group Work, Skills and Strategies for effective Interventions.* (2nd Ed.) U.S.A. The Haworth Press.

Douglas, T. (2000) *Basic Groupwork.* (2nd ed.) London. Routledge.

Edelwich, J. and Brodsky, A. (1992) *Group Counselling for the Resistant Client.* New York. Lexington Books.

Erikson, E. (1995) *Childhood and Society.* London. Vintage.

Strean, H. (1994) *The Use of Humor in Psychotherapy.* U.S.A. Jason Aronson INC.

Yalom, I. D. (1995) *The Theory and Practice of Group Psychotherapy.* (4th ed.) New York. Basic Books.

7

Groups with a specific focus – Unconscious processes in groups

INTRODUCTION

The next three chapters are concerned with different theoretical approaches in counselling and therapy groups. These approaches are especially relevant because of the way they focus on specific helping strategies, designed to assist group members with particular needs, preferences and therapeutic goals. In considering these models of group therapy, we shall focus on three broad categories as follows:

◆ Groups which highlight the importance of unconscious processes

◆ Groups which emphasize cognitive processes

◆ Groups which emphasize a humanistic or person-centred philosophy

In common with individual counsellsing and other forms of therapy, groups have been influenced by all the major theories of personality development. These theories include those proposed by Freud and his followers; those derived from research carried out by cognitive behavioural psychologists, and those with an underlying philosophy rooted in the Humanistic movement and its psychology.

In chapter one we traced the evolution of groups, starting with those appearing in the early part of the last century. After this we looked briefly at groups with a more specific focus, and those that emerged in the aftermath of the Second World War. When we consider the evolution of groups, we can see that their therapeutic potential was identified and developed gradually over a period of time. Once their therapeutic potential was established, however, psychotherapists of various persuasions started to use them to help patients and clients with a range of emotional, behavioural and relationship problems.

PSYCHOANALYTIC THEORY

Although Freud never conducted groups himself, he certainly recognized their therapeutic potential. In his work published in 1922 entitled *Group Psychology and the Analysis of the Ego*, he addresses different aspects of group phenomenon, including the significance of the leader's role and the relationships of members to the leader. However, it was left to others, most notably his one time colleague, Adler, to develop psychotherapy groups. Later on, in the 1930s and 1940s, group psychotherapy grew rapidly, as did the number of influential psychoanalysts and psychologists who contributed to our understanding of how groups work. In chapter one we looked at the pioneering work of Bion and Foulkes, both of whom applied psychoanalytic theory to groups. In the first section of this chapter we shall consider the theories formulated by Freud, and we shall also discuss how these theories apply to individuals and to their behaviour in groups.

GROUPS WHICH HIGHLIGHT THE IMPORTANCE OF UNCONSCIOUS PROCESSES

Groups influenced by Freudian, or Psychodynamic theory highlight the significance of unconscious processes, and the effect of these processes on individual members. In addition, unconscious processes are seen to operate at a collective level, thus affecting not just individuals, but also the group as a whole. The concept of the unconscious is central to psychodynamic theory, so it is worth looking at it more closely to determine its exact meaning.

THE UNCONSCIOUS

In his discussion about the unconscious, Easthope (1999:5) suggests that contemporary society tends to have an exaggerated respect for rationality and the 'rational individual.' This respect for rationality often blinds us to other forces operating at a much deeper, hidden level; forces that nevertheless have a profound effect on our behaviour and on our relationships with other people. These hidden forces derive from the unconscious, a concept first described by Freud in 1915. In speaking about this concept, Freud proposes that for all of us a vast amount of mental activity is unconscious and cannot be called into awareness without a great deal of effort. However, according to his theory, some information can be retrieved without too much difficulty. This information is located in what is known as the preconscious, an area of mental functioning that corresponds to memory. The preconscious is much closer to the conscious than to the unconscious, and it is largely within a person's control.

EXERCISE 35

TAPPING MEMORIES
Time: 1 hour.

This exercise is meant to tap into personal memories by focusing on sense impressions, especially the sense of smell. The exercise should be conducted by group facilitators or trainers who should make sure that members are given enough time to process any material arising from it. To start with, ask members to write down a list of smells they remember from the past, along with the memories they evoke. Members should be given the option of sharing these in group discussion, or keeping them private. Either way, the exercise itself can be discussed in the group, with special emphasis on its power to elicit feelings, ideas or actual events that were previously forgotten.

Latent and manifest content

The terms latent and manifest content (which we referred to briefly in chapter five) are often used in relation to groups, especially those with a psychodynamic focus. The latent content of a group is that which is happening at a hidden psychological (or unconscious) level, and is not immediately obvious, while the manifest content is what seems to be happening and is obvious to anyone observing. One example of latent content in a group is the anxiety that is often masked by joking. The use of humour is, of course, the manifest content that is there for everyone to see. However, what we see in groups is very often the opposite of what is really going on. This is easier to understand if we consider the numbers of people in a group, all with their own difficulties and hidden agendas. In addition, the group has a personality of its own which is formed by what Brandler & Roman (1999:182) refer to as the interacting personalities of all the members present. Latent content in a group can often be detected in members' body language, tone of voice or incongruent behaviour. Identification of latent or unconscious content is facilitated when the group counsellor monitors her own personal feelings, and uses these to help members look more closely at what is really happening in the group. An example of this process was shown in chapter five in the Case study entitled 'What's the joke?' Here the group leader used her personal responses to encourage members to consider the unconscious motivation at work in their jocular behaviour.

Brandler & Roman (1999) have developed a useful chart to help leaders identify latent or unconscious content in any given session. By paying attention to the charted variables, and by acknowledging personal feelings, the leader can assess what is, or might be, going on in the group during meetings. Included in their chart are the following areas:

◆ The group leader's own feelings
◆ The particular phase of the group and its issues
◆ The manifest content of the group

In other words, the group leader or counsellor needs to consider other variables in addition to her own feelings in relation to the group. The group phase is of particular importance because as we have seen, certain kinds of behaviour are common at different times in the life of a group. A long term group that is ending might, for example, be expected to feel regret or sadness, though such feelings may not be acknowledged by members unless the leader draws attention to them. Group composition is important too. If the group population is composed of members with a specific problem, survivors of sexual abuse, for example, the group leader is likely to take this variable into account when looking at unconscious dynamics among members.

The manifest content offers many clues to the underlying feelings in a group. Sometimes group members talk about a particular subject which on the surface might seem irrelevant or superficial. If we accept psychodynamic principles, however, we must conclude that unconscious or latent factors motivate all behaviour, however meaningless or aimless it may appear on the surface. In the following short Case study the leader is puzzled by the behaviour, and conversation of members as the group is ending

CASE STUDY: LATENT CONTENT

A counselling group of seven members was meeting for the penultimate session. In a previous session the counsellor had mentioned that the group would soon finish, but members were reluctant to discuss this. Almost as soon as the present session opened, members began to talk about a popular television soap opera which most of them followed and enjoyed. Two long-standing members of the cast were leaving, which meant that the programme would undergo considerable changes. In discussing these changes, group members expressed regret and disappointment that the cast were now split up. One group member said she felt angry that such steps had been taken without consultation with the public. In monitoring her personal responses to the group's behaviour the leader felt uncomfortable, ignored and rejected. They were speaking as if she were really not present. In addition, she could see by their body language and other nonverbal clues that members were indeed disappointed, even angry. In order to draw attention to latent themes the leader then spoke to them as follows:

Group counsellor: *Let's look at what is happening in the group at present. I sense some uncomfortable feelings in myself and in the group. Most people seem very concerned about big changes in the programme, changes that people feel will affect them personally.*

Sunita: *I suppose nobody really likes change much ... most of us like things to stay the way they are.*

Group counsellor: *We spoke about changes here last week ... about coming to the end of the group. I'm wondering if that might be in people's minds right now.*

Tim: *That's something I've put off thinking about.*

Group counsellor: *Maybe the group has come to it in a different way. Maybe some of the feelings people had about the programme could help us look at how we feel ending the group?*

> **Milo:** *Like Sunita says, change is hard work. Maybe we've just put it off as long as we can.*

Following these initial comments, the group was able to address the issue of leaving the group that had come to mean so much to them. By focusing on manifest content in the group, the leader encouraged members to identify their underlying (or latent) anxieties about the termination of the group. Her own feelings of discomfort and rejection were accurate indicators of the group's mood, and she was able to use these to draw attention to unconscious material that was not being addressed. Members did indeed feel some anger towards her, since she was, after all, the person responsible for setting time limits to the group. They dealt with these angry and hurt feelings by ignoring the leader before she had a chance to 'ignore' or leave them. All these issues arose as a result of the initial discussion about a television programme, a discussion that, at the time, seemed random, trivial and unconnected to the major concern that it actually highlighted.

Free association

In psychoanalytic terms, the notion of the unconscious underpins every other aspect of both theory and practice. Psychodynamic psychotherapy – which is the treatment derived from psychoanalytic theory – depends for its effectiveness on helping clients to bring crucial unconscious material into conscious awareness. It is not enough to simply tell a client in therapy about the possible causes of his or her symptoms. Information delivered in this way is almost certain to be rejected, because the rational thinking part of that person's mind will censor it as irrelevant or incorrect. If intellectual and emotional understanding (or insight) is to be achieved, some other, more effective, way of gaining access to, and presenting the information, needs to be used. The therapeutic procedure used by Freud and his followers for this purpose is known as free association. The technique is one whereby the client is encouraged to speak freely, verbalizing whatever comes to mind at any given time so that all associations are freed from conscious control. Much of this spoken material may seem, on the surface, to be meaningless, inconsequential, or even downright silly. However, over time, clients who use the technique, find themselves making associations between verbalized material, preconscious memories and ultimately the unconscious conflicts responsible for their difficulties. With help from the therapist, and through the process of interpretation, the client's associations should be clarified, so that meaning and insight result. In the next Case study we can see how the technique of free association helps the client (Morag) recall important details from her past.

CASE STUDY: THE MATCHING JUGS

During psychotherapy a fifty year old woman called Morag was talking freely about her enthusiasm for home decoration and interior design. While she was talking Morag referred to two matching jugs she had inherited from her mother. This is how she described them:

They are quite ugly in a way, not expensive, showing desert scenes of a camel, an oasis and so on. I remember my mother said that her mother got them from a hawker, a travelling salesman. My mother was a child then, so it was a long time ago, oh almost eighty years now. They were in our house for as long as I can remember. Yes, I can just see them now. They were on the mantle-place in the living room. Well isn't that strange, I've just remembered something. My mother used to keep loose coins in one of them, and keys, things like that. If I was helpful, what I mean is if I were helpful and 'good' in her eyes, she would give me some money from the jug. I just thought of something else. One Monday morning I needed money for something at school, yes it was for a trip to the church hall to see Hamlet. But she wouldn't give me the money. She was in a bad mood, so I just knew not to argue. The humiliation was terrible when I had to tell the teacher at school. Miss Kerr was her name – the teacher – she couldn't understand it. She knew I loved Shakespeare, so she must have been surprised. She wanted to pay for me herself, but I couldn't do it. I loved that teacher. She was my first real love. Then she died two years later; I mean Miss Kerr died. My mother died five years ago. I was never able to talk to her about things that mattered. After the Hamlet shambles I shut off from her. Yes, that was the start of our estrangement. I never really thought of it before. I just pieced it together now, when I thought of those two damned jugs.

EXERCISE 36

FREE ASSOCIATION
Time: 1 hour.

Group facilitators or trainers should organize this exercise. It is meant to highlight the process of free association among members. Choose a subject and introduce it to the group. Ask members to say, in turn, whatever comes into their heads in relation to it. The subject may be one of your own choice, or one of the following:

◆ Home

◆ Family

◆ Love

◆ Responsibility

◆ Work

◆ Endeavour

◆ Achievement

◆ Ambition

◆ Friends

◆ Memories

Spend about thirty minutes on the first part of the exercise, making sure that each person gets a chance to speak. Afterwards, discuss the process, paying particular attention to any significant material that has surfaced for individual members. Because of the nature of the exercise, with its tendency to elicit unconscious material, you need to schedule adequate time to process it afterwards. Another way of conducting it is to ask group members to draw individual clusters, see fig. 7.1, and afterwards talk to the rest of the group about their associations.

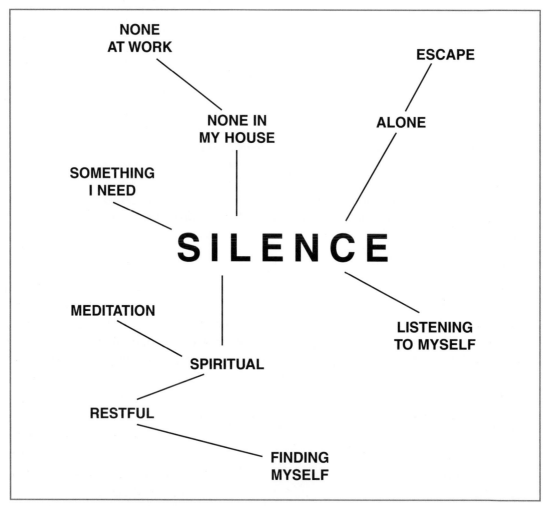

Figure 7.1 The concept of free association at work.

FREE ASSOCIATION IN GROUPS

The previous Case study clearly shows the association of ideas occurring in a particular client's mind as she speaks freely in individual therapy. In group therapy, members can use the same technique of free association when they speak to each other. This kind of interaction occurs when members are spontaneous in giving feedback to each other, and when they are uncensored in their expressions of feeling. This might sound like a recipe for chaos, but clearly such processes need to be monitored by the leader if they are to prove safe and therapeutic for everyone present. In referring to this form of group communication, Foulkes

(1964) describes it as 'free-floating discussion', a description that neatly sums up the verbal exchanges between participants in psychodynamic groups. When group members have come to know and trust each other, they tend to become less wary of expressing themselves in more open and honest ways, so that cohesion is strengthened and active participation encouraged. It is also possible for the leader to lend direction to the process of free association among members. Formalizing the procedure can do this, so that each member is asked to speak in turn on a specific subject. Another method is to ask participants to express their feelings about each other in turn. These two, more formalized, approaches to free association were first suggested by Wolf (1949). He also proposed that use of these techniques would lead to self-awareness for group members, as well as awareness of other people's perceptions of them. While members are interacting in this way, the group leader co-ordinates contributions, making links and connections where appropriate, and occasionally explaining or 'interpreting' behaviour and group processes.

Interpretation

Interpretations could be described as the use of informed guesses or inferences, arrived at by the group therapist through knowledge of the group and its members. In order to interpret what is happening in the group, the leader or therapist must be aware of each individual member's behaviour and feelings, but she must also be aware of her own (counter-transference) feelings towards individual members and her responses to what is happening in the group as a whole. In a reference to interpretation, Freud (1995:25) states that though it requires 'tact and practice', it *is* nevertheless not 'hard to acquire.' This is good news for students of group counselling, many of whom are reluctant to engage in a process that is often seen as highly specialized and difficult to learn. Storr (1997:32) is also optimistic about the student's ability to master the art of interpretation, which, he says, can be done after a short period of training. People in group counselling may have problems which are incomprehensible to them, and one of the reasons they seek help in the first place is to try to make sense of their difficulties. To do this, they need the help of someone who is willing to observe, listen, and attempt to identify unconscious feelings, attitudes and motives so that group members learn and gain personal insight. This is precisely what the group counsellor working in a psychodynamic group, and with proper training, is required to do. It should be added here that everything that happens in a group is potentially open to interpretation, including the following:

◆ Behaviour in the group, including lateness, leaving early, absenteeism
◆ Responses to the leader and to other group members
◆ Dreams
◆ Fantasies
◆ Jokes and slips of the tongue
◆ Avoidance of certain issues
◆ Links between early life, problems or conflicts in everyday life, and behaviour in the group

In chapter three we looked briefly at the use of interpretation skills by the leader of the group. We saw that all group facilitators, regardless of their theoretical approach or orientation, use interpretation. In the context of working with psychodynamic counselling or therapy groups, however, the use of interpretation has special meaning precisely because it is concerned to uncover unconscious attitudes, feelings and motives. In the following Case study the group counsellor uses the skill in this way.

CASE STUDY: INTERPRETATION

A number of group facilitators working for a voluntary agency asked for a one day training workshop to update their skills. The group counsellor prepared a detailed programme for the day. This included reference to all the subject areas he had been asked to address. The group counsellor (Aaron) noticed that the subjects of conflict, and dealing with difficult group members, were given a prominent position in the request he received prior to the start of the training day. As the workshop began, Aaron was aware that group members were unusually quiet, even though they had known each other for some considerable time. Gradually it became clear to him that there was some tension in the group. Members seemed to lack enthusiasm for the programme, and contributions to discussion were slow and grudging. Aaron decided to address the issue by commenting on group process, which he did in the following way:

Aaron: *I have a sense that the group is not enthusiastic about the way we are going at present. Is that a perception anyone else shares?*

Ciaran: (after a pause) *I'm looking at this programme and thinking to myself that it's all very theoretical.*

Aaron: *Does anyone else want to comment?*

Bob: *It seems to me there are a lot of things we could learn from the programme....but*

Aaron: *But you could just as easily learn it from a book?*

Ciaran: *Well, yes ...*

Aaron: *The subjects of conflict and difficult behaviour stand out in the request you sent me. I feel some conflict in the group now ... about how we should proceed.*

Bob: *To be honest I think we would be better off looking at ourselves here.*

Aaron: *So the subjects proposed perhaps refer in some way to this group. Perhaps difficulties within this group could be addressed instead of just looking at theories about conflict and so on?*

Bob: *I think that's the issue. We devised that programme between ourselves. There was a general pretence that we wanted to acquire more knowledge about facilitating groups ... when in fact we must have known deep down that we have mega conflicts among ourselves in this group, and with our agency. Why else would we have chosen those particular subjects?*

This Case study shows how the group counsellor interpreted the mood of the group in which members had asked for specific subjects to be taught. The members who had all requested the inclusion of conflict and difficult behaviour had devised the programme. Group members were genuinely unaware that when they made their request it represented another (unconscious) agenda. The real agenda was the conflict among themselves and with their agency, which, for various reasons, no one wanted to openly acknowledge. By bringing the unconscious wish of the group into the open, the counsellor was able to help members acknowledge, express and begin to work through the many difficulties they currently experienced.

Resistance

Free association and interpretation are not, of course, always as simple or easy as they sound. This is because all of us are resistant to hearing certain things, especially when they make us uncomfortable or worried. Even though, at a conscious level, people may want to gain knowledge and insight, strong unconscious drives may repress material which is deemed to be threatening in some way. Demonstrations of resistance may include long silences in the group; avoidance of certain topics; speaking about issues in a superficial or intellectualised way; forgetting important topics; poor time keeping; absenteeism; or even displays of feigned emotion. The group counsellor's task is to help members become aware that resistance is actually taking place, to show them how the resistance is demonstrated, and finally to help them discontinue the resistant behaviour so that free association can continue in the group. When members are habitually late, for example, the group leader should address this issue in the group, but only when the latecomers are there to hear it. It is inappropriate for group members to talk about an absent member, since this can easily descend into gossip, and draw attention away from the group itself. One way of drawing attention to resistant behaviour through lateness is as follows:

> **Group counsellor:** *I need to know what's going on in the group now, with people coming in late or staying away. I know if I did that it would send some kind of message to the group ... perhaps that I wanted to avoid something.*

If the group counsellor does not address signs of resistance as they appear, they are likely to continue to such an extent that group cohesion is damaged as a result.

Other defence mechanisms in the group

Resistance is just one of the ego defence mechanisms that people use in groups and in everyday life. In Freudian terms, the word ego refers to the conscious thinking part of a person's psychic make-up and is responsible for managing reality. The ego can call upon a variety of mechanisms that serve to mask the unwelcome impulses or desires emanating from the unconscious. Included here are some of the common defence mechanisms:

Repression
When something is repressed it is relegated to the person's unconscious and forgotten.

Events or experiences from childhood may be dealt with in this way. Some of these events or experiences might prove painful, or even intolerable, if they were allowed into conscious awareness. In group counselling members may uncover repressed material, especially when free association is used. This repressed material may relate to early childhood experience or events.

Regression

The term regression describes the way in which someone may revert to an earlier stage of development. Regression is often a reaction to stress, anxiety or some form of threat. Regression may be evident among group members at the beginning or forming stage of the group when levels of anxiety and insecurity may be high.

Projection

Projection is a mechanism whereby a person disowns threatening impulses or emotions and then locates them in someone else. These threatening impulses may relate to racist, sexist or homophobic feelings to name just a few. Thus an individual who accuses others of a negative attitude, including any of those mentioned, may be unable to face these feelings personally. Projection, which is an unconscious process, is often seen in groups, and is especially evident when members blame each other instead of owning their own feelings. This is shown in the next Case study.

CASE STUDY: PROJECTION

A group of counselling students in training were asked to complete a group exercise. The exercise required that they should reach a group decision relating to a specific task. One male member of the group was particularly dominant, and frequently dismissive of opinions offered by others. Tension in the group was quite high, and afterwards during discussion about the exercise, several members referred to this. Several members spoke of sensing anger in the group, yet no one was prepared to own up to feeling angry personally. Instead, accusations of anger were thrown back and forth like a football. This continued until the group trainer asked members to stop, observe, and process what was happening in the group. When this was done, members were able to identify their own anger, and to say why they felt this way. A useful discussion then followed on the subject of anger, and why group members were reluctant to acknowledge it in themselves.

Displacement

A person may experience an unacceptable impulse or feeling (like rage or resentment) towards another person and yet be unable to express it. This can happen when the recipient of these feelings is especially powerful or threatening in some way. A man might feel angry with his father and displace it onto other male authority figures like policemen or politicians. In a similar way, group members may feel angry with the leader and displace this onto a scapegoat. Anger against the leader may also, as Yalom (1995:301) suggests, be displaced to people outside the group. These people who are sometimes the targets of displaced anger, include other authority figures like doctors and teachers.

Denial

Denial is a defence that is frequently used in everyday life. When we deny a particularly frightening aspect of reality, we simply block it out and pretend it is not happening. Members of a counselling group may deny painful or disturbing issues by refusing to discuss them, or by simply saying that they don't exist. One woman in a support group for people with asthma described how she denied she had the condition until she became very ill and had to be hospitalised.

Rationalization

When we rationalize something we usually do so by offering 'good' reasons for thinking or behaving in certain ways. One man in a counselling group rationalized his excessive alcohol intake by pointing to research suggesting that wine was good for the circulatory system. Group members often rationalize aspects of their behaviour by highlighting the difficulties they experience in relation to others. A teenager in a substance abuse group rationalized his drug taking by castigating his parents who were neglectful and often absent. One important aspect of the group counsellor's role is to help members see how they perpetuate their own difficulties when they rationalize them and blame others for their problems.

◁ EXERCISE 44 ▷

EXERCISE 37: DEFENCES
Time: 40 mins.

This exercise should encourage you to look more closely at the defences which you and other group members sometimes use. Working in groups of three to four, read the following short Case studies, and identify any defences that might be evident in them.

1 Ingrid is talking to group members about her difficulty in sustaining relationships. She describes herself as fun loving, humorous and supportive, but she is unable to meet anyone who will take her seriously.

2 Jason tells the group that he recently applied for a job but was unsuccessful. Though it was a job he thought he really wanted at the time, he has now decided that it was too far to travel anyway.

3 Lydia, who has found herself in conflict with several group members, mentions her boss at work and describes her in less than flattering terms. According to Lydia, her boss is difficult and demanding.

4 Chris describes the break-up of an intimate relationship. His partner, who was unfaithful, exploited him financially and then left. Chris did not have a chance to confront him, or to say how angry and hurt he felt. Now, in the group, he frequently shows flashes of anger towards the group leader.

5 Group members are anxious about an upcoming residential weekend that is part of their training course. As the trainer tries to sort out administrative details, the members fool around and make jokes. They talk about the fun they might have on the residential course, if only the trainer wasn't going to be there.

Although defence mechanisms often overlap or merge so that two or more may be present at the same time, it is nonetheless, possible to suggest the presence of a particular one in each of these Case studies. Ingrid is obviously keen to show herself in a particular light, but since her relationships break down so often, it may be that she is denying aspects of her true personality. Jason may be using the defence of rationalization to mask his disappointment at not getting the job. Lydia, who has a tendency to initiate conflict, blames her boss for many of the problems she encounters. It may be, therefore, that she is denying her own hostility and anger, and attributing these to her boss instead through the mechanism of projection. Chris is unable to confront the partner who betrayed him, so he displaces this towards the group leader. The group members, who are anxious about their residential weekend, engage in behaviour that seems to suggest some measure of regression.

TRANSFERENCE AND COUNTER-TRANSFERENCE

In chapter five we looked at the concepts of transference and counter-transference and considered how these affect or distort relationships in the group. In groups with a psychodynamic focus, the issue of transference and counter-transference has special meaning. This is because psychodynamic groups highlight links between the past and present, between childhood experience and relationships in the present. Ettin (1999:100) emphasizes the potential for 'many and varied' transferences within a group. Members are likely to find parental substitutes in the person of the therapist(s). In addition, other members of the group may come to represent siblings, friends, partners, children, people who are admired or despised, or even figures from the past that were significant or important in some way. Collectively, the group itself can also represent different things to different members. A group may symbolize either safety or danger. It may represent a place where some members feel they can take risks, experiment and try out new behaviours. For others, and at certain times, it may seem threatening and strange, especially at the beginning when people have just come together.

Because of these many and varied transference responses, the group is an ideal medium for members to compare their present experiences with those stemming from the past. Rutan (1999:152) suggests that the group offers opportunities for members to talk about their relationships, and then to see them demonstrated in the group. He extends this by saying that though psychodynamic therapy is often seen as rooted in the past, transference and counter-transference phenomena are very much located in the present.

Transference interpretation

In relation to transference interpretation, the group counsellor's role is obviously different, and in some ways more complex than the counsellor's role in individual therapy. This is because the group therapist or counsellor is concerned to help individuals in the group, while at the same time clarifying the dynamics of the group as a whole. In addition to helping individual members analyse their responses to others in the group, the counsellor monitors group process as it unfolds, and then shares his/her observations in a way that helps members understand their collective, and mostly unconscious, motives for behaving in certain ways. In the Case study entitled 'Interpretation' at the beginning of this chapter we saw how the group counsellor clarified group process in order to help members understand their own unconscious motivation. The counsellor could have extended this by focusing on a possible transference issue in their reluctance to ask openly for help. Were they afraid of punishment by the leader if they admitted openly to conflict among themselves? A much safer, and indirect way of conveying their need for help was to distance themselves from their problems by requesting a programme instead.

Projective Identification in Object Relations Theory

In chapter five we looked briefly at the subject of projective identification. This is the term sometimes used to describe the group leader's counter-transference responses to members of the group. Melanie Klein (1946) first highlighted the mechanism of projective identification. She was the originator of Object Relations Theory, a development of psychoanalytic theory. Earlier in this chapter we discussed the defence mechanism of projection, and saw that it meant a refusal to recognize our own personal impulses or deficits which we then "project" onto other people. Freud used the term projection, but Klein extended his concept to suggest that what is projected is much more than impulses or personal deficits. In Kleinian terms, one individual can actually project or induce in someone else, various feelings, thoughts and fantasies. When this happens, the recipient feels unconsciously compelled to comply with the induced roles. This is easier to understand if we consider the often repeated expression 'she makes me feel stupid, clumsy, inept etc.' An example of this in the group context is the member who unconsciously makes the leader feel a particular way, which could be anything from bossy and controlling to ineffectual and tired. This unconscious (and primitive) form of communication is derived from early childhood when verbal communication was not possible, and is meant to convey 'this is how I feel.' A group leader who becomes influenced by a member's projective identification is liable to change into the object or person that the particular member wishes him or her to be. Grinberg (1979) makes this point in relation to therapists working individually with clients, but the principle applies in groups too. We can see from this how important it is for the group counsellor to monitor and examine his/her own responses in an ongoing way. In this next short Case study, the group counsellor monitors her responses in relation to a member who seems confident and vocal in the group.

CASE STUDY: SHANE

In a counselling group of eight members, Shane appeared confident, vocal and very much in command of the situation, even during the first meeting. This surprised the counsellor, Stephanie, since most group members are somewhat anxious to begin with. In her interactions with Shane, however, Stephanie felt anxious herself. She also felt ineffectual at times, and began to wonder if she might be losing her skills in groupwork. During a supervision session she talked about her feelings and came to realize that her experiences in relation to

Shane are the exact opposite of how he presents himself in the group. In a later meeting Stephanie spoke to the group about the anxiety that people usually experience when a group begins. Later, Shane says that he is good at hiding his feelings, and then goes on to add that sometimes he doesn't really know what his feelings are. The group continues to work on this theme of feelings and how to identify them. In this way, verbal communication is established in the group, and takes the place of communication through projective identification. In her initial responses to Shane, the group counsellor acted as a container for the anxieties he was unable to talk about. The word container was originally used by Bion (1970) to describe the therapist's mental capacity to 'hold' a client's emotions safely, in much the same way that a mother takes in negative or frightening feelings from her baby. The group counsellor's task is to become aware of members' projections of distress or anxiety into him / her, then to define these projections through careful interpretation, and finally to help members integrate this new experience of communication through verbalization.

Feeling and thinking

The identification and expression of feelings has a particularly important place in groups with a psychodynamic focus. However, as Rutan (1999) points out, thinking (or cognition) is obviously important too. When individual members have expressed strong emotions in the safety of the group, the experience needs to be processed and placed in perspective. Corey (1995:156) states clearly that insight means gaining 'awareness of the causes of one's present difficulties.' In making connections between the causes of their current difficulties, group members can then decide to change, not just in the group, but in everyday life as well. However, this process of change is much more difficult than it sounds, since as we have already seen, most of us are strongly resistant to change, especially when it entails hard work, as it invariably does. A particular strength of group membership is that it does give members the opportunity to re-experience strong emotions connected to problems of the past. With support and empathy from other group members, and in a protective and holding environment, the individual is able to integrate emotion and understanding. This is often referred to as the 'corrective emotional experience.' Alexander (1948). However, it does not 'replace' the old experience, but instead offers a new beginning by recreating and integrating the old experience in the present.

◁ EXERCISE 44 ▷

EXERCISE 38: IDENTIFICATION OF FEELINGS
Time: 1–1½ hours.

In chapter six we noted that many people are reluctant to dwell on feelings, or to allow themselves to be affected by the feelings of others. Failure to recognize or acknowledge feelings is a major cause of problems in relationships, work and social life. Goleman (1996:96) emphasizes the importance of paying attention to emotions and feelings, not just in close relationships, but in business and management too. Students who start group training are often surprised that so much attention is given to the identification, acknowledgement and expression of feelings. Some students may also experience difficulty in relation to their own feelings, and may find the experience of talking about them strange and unsettling to begin with. This exercise is meant to help you locate your own feelings and identify how you experience these in your body. To complete it you will need a large sheet of drawing paper and some coloured pens or crayons. Working individually, copy the diagram (Figure 7.2.) and spend some time thinking about the following:

◆ In which part of your body do you experience feelings of love and affection?

◆ Which areas of your body do you associate with anger or resentment?

◆ Where are you most likely to feel anxiety or fear?

◆ Which part of your body do you associate with laughter and humour?

◆ Where in your body do you feel sadness and loss?

◆ Where in your body do you feel peace and contentment?

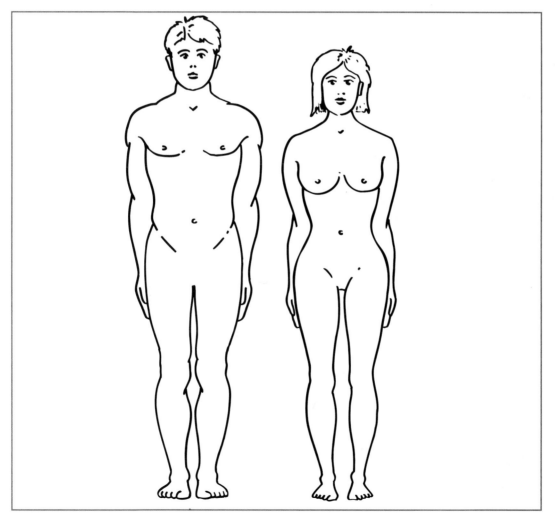

Figure 7.2 The identification of feelings.

Using coloured crayons or pencils, shade in the areas you have chosen in your answer to each question. Select the colours that you identify most with particular feelings. When you have finished, share your ideas with other group members. Group leaders should ensure that enough time is allocated for processing this exercise and for group discussion about feelings generally.

USING DREAMS IN THE GROUP

Dreams, as most people are aware, rarely have a literal meaning. In psychodynamic theory, dreams are regarded as important because of their potential to convey unconscious material and repressed experiences. During sleep, the ego or thinking part of the brain is relaxed so that repressed impulses and other forbidden material is allowed to emerge. Dreams are, of course, expressed in symbols, a language that is also seen in stories, myths, legends and art. Though it is possible to study symbols and to attribute certain meanings to them, it is not possible to apply these in a formulaic way to individuals and the dreams they experience. This is because dream symbols are used in a very idiosyncratic way that is applicable to the dreamer alone.

Freud (1995:28) refers to two different aspects of dreaming and describes these as manifest and latent content. The manifest content of a dream is that which we remember on waking, while the latent content refers to the unconscious, or censored, aspect of the dream. Occasionally this unconscious aspect does break through, causing intense anxiety (or an anxiety dream) for the dreamer. A question arises as to why the latent or unconscious aspect of a dream should be censored in the way Freud describes. According to him, dreams represent the disguised fulfilment of repressed wishes. These repressed wishes are usually unacceptable in conscious waking life, either because they are violent, sexual or indicative of other basic impulses. Freud (1991:352) offers an example of such unacceptable wishes when he describes a dream recounted by one of his patients. This patient referred to a recurrent childhood dream in which a crowd of children are playing in a field. Suddenly all the children grow wings and fly away, leaving her alone. Freud interpreted this as a dream of sibling rivalry in which his patient displayed hostile impulses towards her brothers and sisters. If they all flew away (or died), then she is left alone to enjoy her parents' undivided attention and love. Without some form of censorship, the true, or latent, meaning of this woman's dream might have proved too frightening to her as a young child, yet the basic impulse to be rid of her brothers and sisters was nonetheless there.

In order to understand the relevance of dream interpretation in psychodynamic groups, or indeed in any other context, it is important to understand how symbols disguise the true meaning of the dream itself. Within the group context, dreams can be viewed from an individual perspective, or they can be viewed as an expression of something that is happening in the group as a whole. In other words, one member of the group may recall a dream, along with his individual associations and reactions to it. Other members can then respond to it too, offering suggestions and further associations in the process. In the next Case study one member of a training group recounts a dream he had the night before, and the other members contribute to a discussion about it.

CASE STUDY: DREAMS

One member of a training group (Robert) recalled a vivid dream he had the night before. His description was as follows:

I am on my way to work and I look down to see that my legs have completely gone. They are just not there anymore. Then I get to work and I feel fine. I don't remember anything about my shock earlier on. After a while it's lunchtime and I go out to the deli to get a sandwich. I feel really hungry, but I sense that there's something wrong with my legs again. I look down and they're just not there. That's it.

After this description of his dream Robert was stuck and unable to interpret it. Invited by the leader to apply free association to it, he did so as follows:

Going to work, no legs, legless. Wishing to forget, hungry for food. Looking for support and nourishment. Then legless again.

As soon as he used the word 'legless' Robert understood the symbolism of his dream. During a meeting the previous week, the group had a discussion about alcohol abuse. Though he wanted to talk about his drinking problem then, he did not feel sufficient trust in the group to do so. Robert was also able to make connections between the food symbolism of the dream and his desire for support and 'nourishment' from the group. As group members talked about the dream other associations emerged for them too. The themes of risk and trust were explored, and the difficulties inherent in making oneself vulnerable were discussed. This proved to be a very useful exercise for the group as a whole, and it arose because one member used a personal dream to stimulate group associations relevant to everyone.

EXERCISE 39

USING DREAMS
Time: As required.

For this exercise you need to think of a recent dream that you can bring to your group. The exercise should be planned along with your trainer or group facilitator, who should also allocate time for those members who wish to use their dreams in the group. It is best if you focus on a dream that you have had within the life span of the group. This is because such a dream is more likely to have relevance (as Robert's dream had) to the group as a whole. To make the dream more vivid and immediate, recount it in the first person, present tense. When you have finished, apply free association to the dream, saying whatever comes into your head in relation to it. Invite other group members to offer their own associations to the dream. Afterwards, analyse and discuss the process, paying special attention to any insights, wishes, or anxieties that emerge for individual members as a result.

Recalling and recording dreams

Not everyone is skilled in recalling and recording dreams, but the process can be learned over time, and without too much difficulty. The first and most important step is to make a decision to become interested in what is happening in your unconscious while you sleep. The next step is to leave a pen and pencil by your bed so that you can record your dreams fully in writing as soon as you wakeup in the mornings. Record the dream quickly so that you catch the main elements of it. Always use the present tense when recording dreams, and begin with the dream setting, for example, 'I am walking on a beautiful beach,' etc. Give the dream a title, and describe the emotions you associate with it. Say what themes emerge in the dream. Another way to capture a dream is to draw it. At this stage, do not try to interpret the dream, just record the essential elements of it. Is the dream asking you a question? If so, record this too. Next, choose a symbol in your dream. This could be a feeling, a person, a thing, a time of day, a colour, an event or indeed any other element that figures in it. Next, use the technique of free association to clarify it, listing its characteristics, what it is used for and so on. In the following example a group member chooses one element of her dream (a bathroom) and free associates to it.

> A bathroom is a place of elimination and cleansing. It is a place where I can be naked. It is a place that is private, where I can be alone. A bathroom has an abundance of water. There are many pipes in a bathroom, most of them underground and out of sight .It is possible to dispose of waste in a bathroom, to feel renewed, to relax. Bathrooms can be utilitarian and cold, or they can be warm and luxurious.

Having talked like this about the bathroom in her dream, the woman was able to interpret what it meant for her. She frequently dreamt about bathrooms, and about her inability to get privacy in them. This group member led a particularly busy life. She worked in a caring profession where she felt unsupported. In addition, she lacked regular supervision, and it was this inability to 'eliminate' and be 'cleansed' which caused her most concern. When some other members of her group took up the theme of underground pipes, they likened them to the unconscious. Like the unconscious, the pipes were out of sight, but were nonetheless active and important. If they were forgotten, or neglected, they were liable to cause problems and to make their presence felt in some spectacular or unpleasant way. These associations led to other important insights for the group as a whole. Conflict, which had not been addressed, was now acknowledged and discussed. This acknowledgement of conflict caused significant change in the group, and communication improved as a result.

JUNG AND THE UNCONSCIOUS

Carl Gustav Jung (1875–1961) added another dimension to our understanding of the unconscious. For some time he was an associate and admirer of Freud, accompanying him to the United States and defending his theories. In addition, Jung became a psychoanalyst, teaching the subject at the university of Zurich and serving as the first president of the

International Psychoanalytic Association. However, Jung was an individualist, and over a period of time, came to view the human personality quite differently from Freud.

On one significant point, however, Jung did agree with Freud. This concerns the importance of bringing unconscious material into conscious awareness, and about the necessity of acknowledging the shadow or dark side of human personality. Unlike Freud, though, Jung's view of the unconscious is that it is creative as well as shadowy and potentially base. Moreover, according to Jung, our unconscious can guide and enlighten us. His concept of the collective unconscious is a radical departure from Freud's theory, since it adds an historical dimension, suggesting that we have predispositions, memories and guidelines inherited from the beginning of time. In the context of dreams and dream interpretation, analytical psychology (the title of Jung's approach) also highlights several important points of difference from the purely Freudian perspective.

Jung and dreams

In common with Freud, Jung believed that dreams provide significant clues about the hidden realms of the mind. However, he added to this by suggesting that we are all capable of collective as well as personal dreams. A personal dream might, for example, concern family relatives or friends, whereas a collective dream will deal with larger issues, perhaps affecting a whole community or group. In addition, collective dreams will contain archetypal images or symbols that convey powerful ideas, usually with universal appeal. Mother Nature is one such archetype, so too is the archetype of evil, often symbolized as the devil or Satan.

It is not difficult to see how relevant such concepts as the collective unconscious and dreams could prove in a group context. Boyd & Dirkx (1991:41) suggest that although analytical psychologists have tended to avoid 'theoretical or clinical applications' of Jungian theory to families and small groups, there is a strong case for saying that Jung's psychology is ideally suited to groups. This is because of the social implications of his approach. Intrinsic to Jung's theory is the notion of individuation, a term which describes each person's lifelong journey of self-discovery or self-realization. It is difficult to imagine such a process unfolding in isolation from other human beings. As Boyd & Dirkx also point out, individuation always takes place within a social context, in the course of our everyday living. If we consider the group context once again, we can see that it presents many of the conditions necessary to facilitate the individuation process. Strong social relationships are possible in groups, for example, so too are group cohesion and commitment to goals. These unique conditions foster intimacy, trust and a willingness on the part of members to take the kind of risks necessary for self-exploration. If we accept that self-exploration encourages self-discovery and the unfolding of one's inherent and unique personality, then the group seems an ideal place to start the process or continue it.

IMAGES AND ACTIVE IMAGINATION
Time: 40 mins + discussion time.

It is impossible within the scope of this chapter to do justice to a subject as detailed as Jung's psychology. However, it is worth looking more closely at the subject of images, imagination and the way these influence views about ourselves. Looking at images can also help us in the process of self-exploration and individuation. While discussing these in the group context we can receive feedback from other members about ourselves, and their perceptions of us.

The exercise should be organized by the group trainer or facilitator, and members should be given sufficient time to discuss their images, self-concepts and perceptions of others. Group members should also be familiar with Jung's work on the subject of 'active imagination.' This is a process of concentrating on mental images so that they develop, expand and present us with a more detailed picture of others and ourselves (Jung (1976)).

To start with, ask group members to relax and to imagine themselves as one of the following:

◆ An inanimate object

◆ A plant

◆ An animal

◆ A hero/heroine of a story

◆ A famous person

In the process of visualizing these images, group members are likely to reveal much more about themselves than they would through sharing factual information. Ettin (1999) suggests that use of structured imagery encourages 'a more introspective accounting' from participants. If we look at the following short Case study we can see how this happens.

CASE STUDY: STRUCTURED IMAGERY

One member of a group described herself as a store cupboard full of provisions that other people needed. There was no lock on the cupboard, so others could come and go as they wished. When stocks were low, she was obliged to replenish them, though there were times when she worried about her ability or resources to do this. The provisions in the cupboard were mostly edible, foods to suit everyone's taste. As a cupboard she found it difficult to get privacy and space for herself.

In thinking about this description of herself, the group member became much more aware of how she related to other people. She was a single parent with a busy job and two very small children. Her widowed, and particularly demanding father lived with her. At work she took on extra tasks and helped people out when they asked her. In fact, so many demands were made on her time (and on her 'provisions') that there was very little left for herself. In sharing her image with other group members she could see herself in a clearer light. This in turn increased openness in the group, which was further enhanced as other members described and discussed their personal images too.

References

Alexander, F. (1948) *Fundamentals of Psychoanalysis.* New York. W. W. Norton & Co.

Bion, W. R. (1970) *Attention and Interpretation: A scientific approach to insight in Psychoanalysis and groups.* New York. Basic Books.

Boyd, R. D. & Dirkx, J. M. (1991) 'Methodology for the study of the development of consciousness in the small group' in Boyd, R. D. *Personal Transformations in Small Groups.* London. Routledge.

Brandler, S. & Roman, C. P. (1999) *Group Work: Skills and Strategies for Effective Interventions.* U.S.A. The Haworth Press.

Corey, G. (1995) *Group Counselling.* (4th Ed) California. Brooks Cole.

Easthope, A. (1999) *The Unconscious.* London. Routledge.

Ettin, M. F. (1999) *Foundations and Applications of Group Psychotherapy.* London. Jessica Kingsley Publishers.

Foulkes, S. H. (1964) *Therapeutic Group Analysis.* New York. International Universities Press.

Freud, S. (1967d) *Group Psychology and the Analysis of the Ego.* New York. Liveright.

Freud, S. (1974) *Introductory lectures on Psychoanalysis.* Harmondsworth. Penguin.

Freud, S. (1991) *The Interpretation of Dreams.* London. Penguin.

Freud, S. (1995) 'An Autobiographical Study' in Gay, P. (ed) *The Freud Reader.* U.S.A. W. W. Norton & Co.

Goleman, D. (1996) *Emotional Intelligence.* London. Bloomsbury.

Grinberg, L. (1979) *Countertransference and Projective counteridentification in Contemporary Psychoanalysis.* 15: 226-247.

Jung, C. G. (1976) *The Symbolic life. Collected works. Vol 18.* U.S.A. Princeton University Press.

Klein, M. (1946) *Notes on Schizoid mechanisms.* International Journal of Psychoanalysis. 27, 99–110.

Rutan, J. S. (1999) 'Psychoanalytic Group Psychotherapy' in Price, J. R., Hescheles, D. R. &

Price, A. R. (eds.) *A Guide to starting Psychotherapy Groups.* San Diego. Academic Press.

Storr, A. (1997) *The Art of Psychotherapy.* (2nd Ed.) Oxford. Butterworth/Heinemann.

Wolf, A. (1949) *The Psychoanalysis of Groups. 1.* American Journal of Psychotherapy, 3: 525–558.

8

Behavioural and Cognitive-Behavioural Groups

INTRODUCTION

This chapter deals with a theoretical focus that is quite different from the one described in the last chapter. Here we are concerned to look at models of group counselling which are more orientated towards cognitive processes, observable behaviour, problem solving, and pragmatic approaches to coping with a range of difficulties encountered in everyday life. Within the chapter we shall concentrate on two main contributions to this area of group-work. These include Aaron Beck's Cognitive Behaviour Therapy, and Rational Emotive Behaviour Therapy (R.E.B.T.) formulated by Albert Ellis, another model widely used in individual counselling and in groups. We shall also consider the work of Eric Berne and the importance of Transactional Analysis as a theory of personality, and as an approach ideally suited to helping people in groups.

BEHAVIOUR THERAPY

Behaviour therapy has its origins in the work carried out by several psychologists during the early part of the twentieth century. Ian Pavlov is perhaps the best known of this group, since it was he who developed the Classical Conditioning model of learning theory. Pavlov was able to show that dogs will respond (by salivating) to the sound of a bell, once they associate this with the presentation of food. The experiments carried out by Pavlov were extensive, and obviously more complex than the synopsis given in this section. However, as Richards and Mc Donald (1990:5) indicate, the basic paradigm formulated by Pavlov is straightforward, and can be applied quite easily to human as well as animal behaviour. In the following short Case study a man describes the birth of his child at home forty years previously, and events shortly afterwards.

CASE STUDY: FOOTSTEPS

Our little girl, Polly, was born at home. She arrived at three o'clock in the morning, after a fairly long but uncomplicated labour. Rita, my wife, was exhausted, and I was tired, but we were both over the moon and so excited. Polly was in her cot beside the bed, and just as we thought we were about to get some sleep, she started to cry. I got out of bed and held her for a while until she became quiet again. Then I put her back in her cot and tried to get some sleep again. After a while though, she cried again, and I lifted her up and comforted her. This pattern continued for quite a while, and then something interesting happened. Just as I was getting out of bed once again to pick her up, Polly stopped crying. She heard my feet on the floor and clearly knew I was coming to get her. It struck me at the time how quickly she had learned to associate the sound of my footsteps with comfort and reassurance.

We can see from this Case study that the kind of learning described by Pavlov is evident in humans from a very early stage. Problems arise, however, when the pairing of two stimuli result in maladaptive learning which continues into adult life. It is not difficult, for example, to imagine a situation in which a small child comes to associate adult footsteps with fear and abuse, rather than comfort and reassurance.

OPERANT CONDITIONING

If we consider the example in the Case study once again we can see that (the baby) Polly, came to associate the sound of footsteps with comfort and reassurance. What she had also learned, however, was that a certain kind of behaviour (in this case crying) led to certain consequences. In other words, crying served to activate someone in the room who would then come forward and lift her. B. F. Skinner is another behavioural psychologist who has added to our knowledge of the way people learn. His work introduced the concepts of Operant Conditioning and reinforcement. The latter is a term that describes the rewards following a certain course of action. When behaviour is reinforced, there is every possibility that it will be strengthened and repeated. Polly's behaviour received reinforcement when her father acted as he did, so she continued to cry as a means of gaining attention. As a result of the research carried out by Pavlov, Skinner, and many other behaviour psychologists, we have a much clearer picture of how people learn to behave in particular ways. We can also see how aspects of behaviour can become problematic, not just in childhood, but in adult life too.

APPLICATION OF LEARNING THEORIES TO COUNSELLING AND THERAPY GROUPS

Behavioural psychotherapy (or counselling) is based on the premise that learned behaviour can, in fact, be unlearned. Thus, it is possible to help people who have acquired maladaptive behaviour in early or later life by a process of behaviour modification. Put simply this means teaching clients, both in individual and group therapy, to change to more healthy ways of functioning. A variety of techniques are used to achieve this outcome, including social skills training; stress management training; assertiveness training; relaxation therapy; systematic desensitisation; role play; positive reinforcement and modelling of appropriate behaviour. The techniques mentioned here are probably familiar to most students of counselling and groupwork, but it is worth saying more about them, since practitioners of this approach use them so effectively.

Systematic desensitisation

Systematic desensitisation is a technique based on Pavlov's classical conditioning (described at the beginning of this chapter) and is widely used to help people with irrational fears and phobias. Anxiety responses which are learned or conditioned can be treated through gradual exposure to the stimulus that caused the anxiety in the first place. In order to do this the client is guided through a process of relaxation that forms an integral part of the overall approach. If we look at the example of someone suffering from a social phobia, for example, we can see how systematic desensitisation helps to break the vicious cycle caused by avoidance of the triggering factor(s) or stimulus. A person with a social phobia is likely to avoid going out as much as possible. This social avoidance serves to produce more anxiety and fear, and the development of elaborate strategies to maintain isolation. One way of breaking the deadlock is to support the client while s/he is exposed to the anxiety-producing situation, though this is achieved in a gradual way. Thus, the intensity of the exposure is increased step by step until anxiety decreases over a period of time. Going outside to look at the street might be the first step for a person with a social phobia, while taking a bus into town might represent a real and lasting breakthrough.

Systematic desensitisation is frequently used in individual therapy, though it is often used in group therapy too. An example of its use in a group context is the provision offered by certain airlines to help people with flying phobias. Such programmes bring people together in groups so that they can become acquainted with the inside of an aircraft to begin with. Talks and teaching seminars form a part of these courses, so that gradually group members are sufficiently confident to travel on a short flight. In addition to the taught element of such programmes, and the gradual exposure to aircraft and flying, members support each other, talk about their difficulties, and generally gain a great deal from the experiences of others.

Relaxation training

Relaxation training plays a central role in behaviour therapy. The ability to relax is a fundamental requirement of any programme undertaken to overcome anxiety, panic attacks or phobias. However, the kind of relaxation referred to here is much more than just resting or unwinding. Bourne (1995:67) stresses this point, and suggests that the kind of deep relaxation essential for dealing with anxiety and other problems should be practised daily. Group members need to be taught how to relax in this way, since it is not something that anxious people are used to doing. Though there are various approaches to deep relaxation, all of them focus on the practice of abdominal breathing, progressive muscle relaxation, and often the visualization of a peaceful scene and, or, meditation. It is important that group members are encouraged to practise at home on a daily basis, so that relaxation forms part of their general routine. The next exercise is an example of progressive deep relaxation.

EXERCISE 41

PROGRESSIVE RELAXATION
Time: 30–40 mins.

This exercise can be conducted with a whole group. The group leader or trainer should guide members through the stages. It is important to ensure that there is sufficient room for members to lie back comfortably. Relaxation should take place in a quiet area that is warm and free from interruptions. The following are the stages through which members should be guided:

1   When you are comfortable place one hand on your abdomen

2   Breathe in deeply through your nose, into the bottom of your lungs, counting slowly to five. Your hand should rise as your abdomen expands

3   Hold your breath, counting to five again

4   Breathe out slowly through your mouth, counting to five

5   Continue to breathe as you would normally

6   Now repeat the three steps again, breathing in counting to five, holding your breath to a count of five, and breathing out counting to five

7   Clench your fists, hold them steady like this, then release

8   Tighten the muscles of your arms, hold them like this, then release

9   Tense the muscles in your face by raising your eyebrows, hold like this, then relax

10 Tighten the muscles of your jaw by opening your mouth widely. Hold like this, and then relax

11 Concentrate on the muscles of your neck by pulling your neck backwards. Hold like this, and then relax

12 Take another deep breath, hold it and count to five, then release and count to five

13 Raise your shoulders as far as you can, tighten them, and then relax

14 Tense the muscles of your back. Push your shoulder blades back, hold the tension, and then relax

15 Concentrate on your chest muscles. Take a deep breath, hold and count to five. Release slowly, counting to five. Imagine the tension in your body flowing away as you breathe out

16 Tense the muscles of your abdomen, hold and then relax

17 Arch your lower back, tensing the muscles, hold, and then relax

18 Tighten the muscles in your hips and thighs, hold, and then relax

19 Tighten the muscles of your lower legs, hold, and then relax

20 Concentrate on your feet. Curl your toes downwards so that your muscles are tightened, hold, and then relax

21 Take a deep breath, counting slowly to five, hold to a count of five, and breathe out counting to five

22 Imagine all the tension in your body easing away. A great wave of relaxation is spreading all over you

23 Just stay quiet for a while and breathe normally

Stress management

Behaviour therapy in groups will often include some elements of stress management. A central focus of stress management is to show group members how to cope more effectively with the ordinary stressors that are a part of everyday living. Stress is usually caused when we are required to adapt physically, mentally and emotionally to a change in our lives. However, this is not always an entirely negative process, for as Peiffer (1996:3) points out, stress may follow something positive like a promotion which we have worked hard to achieve. It is true that certain personality types are more prone to stress than others, and members of a behaviour therapy group may not cope well with either positive or negative stress. It is for this reason that management forms such an important part of many group programmes.

Corey (1995:363) suggests that stress management programmes operate from an assumption that what we do and think will 'actively contribute' to our experience of stress. We can see from this how important it is to teach group members coping skills *and* to discuss with them how they contribute to and create their own stressful problems. Later in this chapter, when we look at cognitive approaches in groups, we shall see some examples of the ways in which members contribute (through faulty thinking) to their own difficulties in relation to stress. Members are also taught to identify the situations that cause them most stress. These might include factors in the working environment, domestic disagreement or tension, difficulties with children, or indeed any changes that disrupt daily life or routine. In addition, members are encouraged to monitor their own responses to stressful situations; they are also shown how to identify the warning signs of stress, including those that affect

⟨ EXERCISE 42 ⟩

PERSONALITY AND STRESS
Time: 1 hour.

In this exercise you are encouraged to look at your own beliefs, values and attitudes in relation to stress. Read the following list of questions, and give yourself points as follows: for each yes answer give yourself 2 points, and for each no answer, 0 points. Spend about ten minutes on the exercise and afterwards discuss it with other members of the group.

1   I am often anxious and afraid. Yes / No

2   I am easily hurt when criticized. Yes / No

3   I am always conscientious and like things to be perfect. Yes / No

4   People often take advantage of me. Yes / No

5   I tend to worry about what others think of me. Yes / No

6   I often feel down or depressed. Yes / No

7   I feel guilty when I'm not working. Yes / No

8   I sometimes feel at the mercy of forces outside my control. Yes / No

9   I tend to put other people's needs before my own. Yes / No

10 I often feel angry but unable to express it. Yes / No

Results of your score – 12–20 points indicates high levels of stress. 6–8 points indicates medium levels of stress. 2–4 points indicates low levels of stress.

If your score represents medium to high levels of stress you should look again at your lifestyle and seek help for any obvious problems that you have. Even if you have answered yes to one or two of the questions, it is worth thinking about any changes you could make, or possibilities for dealing with the issues highlighted in the questionnaire.

behaviour, physical well-being, emotions, and mental health.

Assertiveness training

Assertiveness training groups have grown in popularity from the 1960s and 70s onwards. Indeed, many organizations now provide assertiveness courses as part of their training programmes. Perhaps the most important reason for the ongoing development of these programmes is that people want to feel good about themselves, and about their behaviour. If we consider the word behaviour in this context, we can see clearly how assertiveness training is linked to behavioural group therapy. Fritchie & Melling (1991) emphasize this behavioural aspect of assertiveness, and point to the various ways people act in difficult situations. They suggest that many individuals react by becoming loudly aggressive and demanding, behaviour that they often regret later on. Alternatively, they may remain silent and passive, doing nothing and later regretting their inaction, a situation that leads to diminished self-respect. Assertiveness training helps group members to identify their usual responses in a variety of situations, and to change these responses if necessary. It is quite possible for someone to be assertive in one situation, while failing to respect their own, and other people's, rights in many other situations. The following are some of the goals of assertiveness training in groups:

◆ To encourage members to become more self-assured and better able to deal with conflict

◆ To encourage members to balance their own needs with the needs of others

◆ To teach members to recognize their right to be listened to and consulted

◆ To teach members that other people have the right to be listened to and consulted

◆ To show members that their individual views and thoughts are important and should be contributed

◆ To encourage members to assume responsibility for upholding their own rights

◆ To help members express their feelings in appropriate ways

◆ To teach members the difference between passive, aggressive and assertive behaviour

◆ To encourage members to transfer and apply what they have learned in the group, to everyday situations outside the group

As part of assertiveness training in groups, members are often asked to complete homework assignments. This may take the form of a journal, or record of stressful situations and how these were dealt with. Skills practice and role rehearsal are also often included during group sessions, and members are encouraged to try out new ways of behaving in different situations. Stress management may be integrated with assertiveness training, along with relaxation training and anxiety management when necessary. The leadership style in assertiveness groups is a teaching one, and the emphasis is on changing maladaptive behaviour and the acquisition of new skills.

While teaching assertiveness skills in groups it is important to remember that people from various cultures differ in their attitudes to self-expression and how they perceive themselves in relation to family, friends and their own social group. However, it is also true to say that everyone, regardless of cultural background, is likely to respond positively to any programme that places emphasis on the needs of others as well as the needs of group members. In other words, assertiveness training makes good social sense, since it is designed to help participants become confident and competent, and more respectful of others in the family, socially and in the workplace.

◁ EXERCISE 43 ▷

PERSONAL ASSERTIVENESS

Time: 1 hour.

Read the responses to each of the situations described in this exercise. You can complete the exercise individually to begin with, but it is a good idea to compare your answers to those given by other group members. Identify which response you consider to be the most assertive in each case.

1 A friend asks you to drive her to town when it is not convenient for you to do so. You respond by saying: (A) I'm terribly sorry I haven't got the time. I really am sorry. (B) Look, I'm not a taxi driver, you know. (C) I have made other plans for the day, so no, I can't do it.

2   You buy a new vacuum cleaner that breaks down the first time you use it. When you bring it back to the store the manager says it is a minor fault and refuses to give you a refund. In response you: (A) Take his word that the machine is now mended and leave the store. (B) Say: 'It may have been a minor fault but I would still like a refund.' (C) Become angry and threaten to report it to Trading Standards.

3   You are at the cinema and the people behind you are making a lot of noise by talking and eating crisps and popcorn. Feeling frustrated you: (A) Show your irritation and move at once to another seat. (B) Turn round and say: 'I'm finding it difficult to hear, could we have a bit of hush please?' (C) Turn round and say: 'Shut up.'

4   You are a member of a training group in which there are several dominant members. Each time you offer a viewpoint it is dismissed as irrelevant or silly. You put up with this for a while and then: (A) Feeling fed up leave the group session. (B) Say: 'Obviously nothing I suggest is taken seriously, so I'm going to keep quiet from now on.' (C) Address the group leader and say: 'It seems to me that we need to look at the ground rules again. We did say we would respect each person's opinion and avoid being disrespectful or dismissive.'

5   A relative asks to borrow money several times. Finally you: (A) Refuse to answer the phone next time she calls. (B) Say: 'I have a lot of expense at the moment, what with paying the car tax, a big electricity bill and saving for a holiday that I really need. I'm terribly sorry.' (C) Remind her that she borrowed money two months ago and add: 'I can't lend you any more money. I simply cannot afford it.'

6   In a restaurant you order a steak well done. When it arrives the steak is medium cooked. You point this out to the waiter who adopts a superior tone and replies that most people like it that way. In response you say: (A) 'That may be so, but I do like it well done, so please take it back to the kitchen.' (B) Give up and accept the steak as it is. (C) Become angry and ask to speak to the manager at once.

7   You phone the health centre for an appointment and the receptionist asks for details of your condition. You reply: (A) 'I don't want to talk to you about that, I don't think it's anything to do with you.' (B) 'I understand why you need certain information, but this is something I'm not comfortable talking about on the phone.' (C) 'Please just give me an appointment.'

8   The painter and decorator fails to complete all the work he was contracted to do. When he asks for payment you say: (A) 'You won't get a penny until all the work is done.' (B) 'I don't think you've done everything you said you would do. Let's check that first before I pay you.' (C) 'If you're really sure everything is done, ok.'

9   Your partner wants to have relatives to stay for a week. The timing is inconvenient for you, but you are reluctant to disappoint your partner. Your response is to: (A) Argue that the proposed visit is unreasonable because you will end up doing most of the work. (B) Ask your partner to set aside some time that evening to discuss the request. (C) Feel resentful but agree to the visit anyway.

10 A friend phones to ask for a favour. She says she needs to know fairly quickly if you can help. You reply: (A) 'I'm sorry, I would like to help, but I'm up to my eyes right

now.' (B) 'It does sound urgent for you, but I need time to think about it. Let me call you back tomorrow when I have checked my commitments.' (C) 'Isn't there anyone else who can help you?'

Answers to assertiveness questionnaire:

No. 1 – C, No. 2 – B, No. 3 – B, No. 4 – C, No. 5 – C, No. 6 – A, No. 7 – B, No. 8 – B, No. 9 – B, No. 10 – B.

Social skills training

We have already looked at some aspects of social skills training when we considered the example of someone suffering from a social phobia. In that example, systematic desensitisation was used to help a client overcome a fear of going out. However, there are now many groups set up specifically to address difficulties that people experience in a variety of social situations. Such groups could be composed of members who lack interpersonal skills, for example, or who have been out of work for some time and need practice before going back into employment. As with other aspects of behaviour therapy, social skills training is designed to help members alter problem behaviour and to acquire new ways of responding in situations which have formerly been challenging or difficult.

Before starting therapy in the group, members are given precise information about the purpose of the group. They are also encouraged to identify the specific situations that are problematic for them. Group members are further encouraged to define the exact nature of their individual problems. People with a social skills deficit tend to reinforce their own maladaptive behaviour, either through avoidance or anxiety. It is for this reason that they require training and practice in an environment that is non-threatening and supportive. In helping members address their problems, the group leader is likely to include a variety of therapeutic interventions within the group. These include problem-solving skills, coping skills, coaching and teaching, role-playing, modelling appropriate behaviour, relaxation training and work in small groups. In common with assertiveness training, social skills groups often include some homework practice and a requirement to keep a written record of progress from week to week.

Reinforcement

At the beginning of this chapter we looked at the role of reinforcement in shaping animal and human behaviour. It is for this reason that reinforcement is emphasized and demonstrated in the group context too. Group counsellors working from a behavioural perspective often use various forms of reinforcement, including approval and praise. What makes the group especially effective, however, is the fact that reinforcement is provided for individuals by other members, as well as by the leader. Corey (1995) stresses the importance of self-reinforcement also, and suggests that members should be taught to support their own achievements in an ongoing way. By doing this, group members make greater progress, and become more self-reliant and confident.

Role play and modelling

The terms role play and modelling have been mentioned several times in this section. This is because they are frequently used in both individual and group therapy. The term modelling refers to an intervention the group leader could employ to demonstrate different ways of responding to challenging situations. A group leader might model a social skill like walking into a restaurant to order a meal, for example. People with social phobias may find situations like this very difficult, and may actually benefit from watching someone else negotiate it with confidence. Modelling can also be enhanced through the use of video technology, which can be used as an alternative to modelling by the leader. This is especially effective for groups whose members need to see and practise employment related skills like job interviews, for example. In addition, members can actually use video recording to practise new behaviours and then view them afterwards. This is one form of role play in groups, though it should be stressed that technology is not essential for this kind of intervention. In fact, for some very apprehensive group members, the introduction of cameras or other forms of technology might prove just too threatening, especially at the beginning when participants are nervous anyway. Certain group members may benefit more if they use role play at their own pace, with the individual support and encouragement of the leader.

THE COGNITIVE-BEHAVIOURAL DIMENSION

Cognitive-behavioural therapy (also sometimes referred to as cognitive therapy) has evolved from the purely behavioural approach, and stresses, as its name suggests, a thinking dimension to problem solving and behaviour change. Rose (1999:99) describes the approach as one that makes use of behavioural *and* cognitive techniques, including modelling, reinforcement, relaxation training, problem solving and cognitive restructuring to enhance the coping skills of group members. Group processes are also used as a means of helping members address any relational and interpersonal difficulties that may contribute to their everyday problems. The inclusion of group process observation in cognitive-behavioural groups has not always been highlighted in studies, and as Rose (1999:100) points out, cognitive-behavioural group therapy has traditionally relied on the use of interventions for addressing behaviour problems. However, there is now increasing recognition of the benefits of process observation in cognitive-behavioural and other groups.

AARON BECK

Aaron Beck is one of the most influential names in the field of cognitive-behavioural therapy. Beck started his career as a psychoanalyst in Philadelphia, but developed doubts about the effectiveness of this approach in dealing with many psychological problems. In particular, he believed that psychoanalysis did not address the cognitive factors associated with depressive illness. Much of Beck's seminal work was carried out during the 1960's when his

behaviour, but he was concerned that these were not formerly reflected in the terminology.

Like Beck, Ellis became disenchanted with psychoanalysis as a treatment for psychological problems, so he began to devise his own approach, which has, in fact, much in common with the work of Beck. In describing the theory of R.E.B.T. Ellis (1995:2) outlines what he calls an ABC model of human disturbance. In the first place, he suggests, people generally have goals in life which include those relating to general survival and the wish to be reasonably happy. As part of everyday living, however, we encounter difficulties or 'adversities' that tend to hinder our desire for happiness and success. These adversities are known as activating events, which lead to cognitive, emotional and behavioural consequences. It is not, however, what happens at point A (the activating event) that causes our disturbance. What matters is our interpretation or self-talk about the event, and this occurs at point B, where our beliefs and inferences have a great deal of influence on our interpretation of events generally. Finally, beliefs and inferences about the activating events lead directly to certain emotional and behavioural consequences. This is illustrated in Figure 8.1:

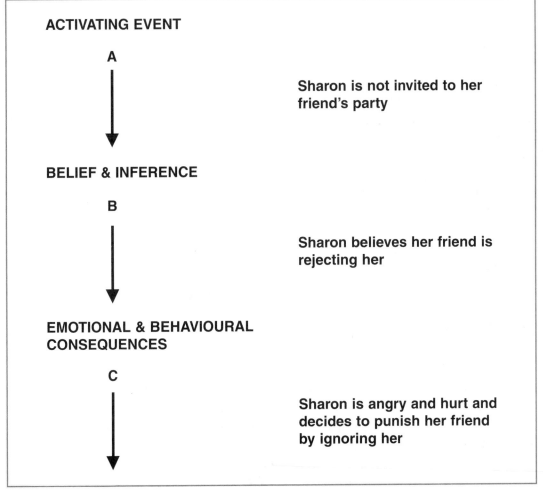

ACTIVATING EVENT

A

Sharon is not invited to her friend's party

BELIEF & INFERENCE

B

Sharon believes her friend is rejecting her

EMOTIONAL & BEHAVIOURAL CONSEQUENCES

C

Sharon is angry and hurt and decides to punish her friend by ignoring her

Figure 8.1 Adapted from the ABC Sequence described by Ellis (1995)

We can see from the example shown in the diagram on page 183 that Sharon believes her friend has rejected her because she isn't invited to the party. This in turn causes her to feel hurt and angry, and she makes a decision to punish her friend by ignoring her. But Sharon, because of her interpretation of events, is causing her own unhappiness according to the ABC model. She could quite easily interpret the activating event in an entirely different way, as the next example (Figure 8.2.) shows.

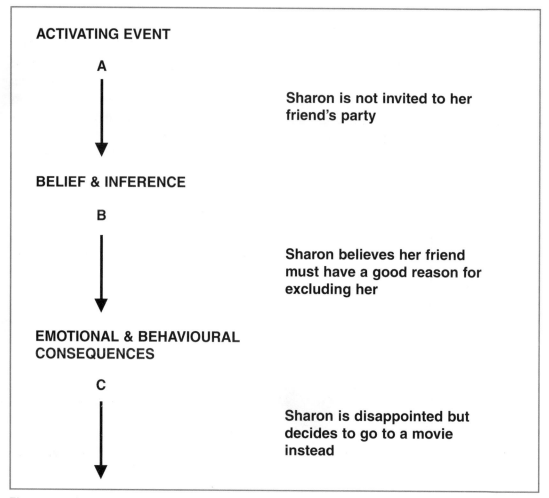

ACTIVATING EVENT

A

Sharon is not invited to her friend's party

BELIEF & INFERENCE

B

Sharon believes her friend must have a good reason for excluding her

EMOTIONAL & BEHAVIOURAL CONSEQUENCES

C

Sharon is disappointed but decides to go to a movie instead

Figure 8.2 Sharon's alternative ABC model.

In this second example Sharon's belief and inference about not being invited to dinner are more measured, thoughtful and realistic. She is clearly disappointed, but instead of mentally castigating her friend, she remains optimistic and upbeat, and decides to treat herself to a night out. The activating event (exclusion from the dinner party) does not depress her, nor does it make her angry as it did in the first example. According to Ellis, people can indeed choose how they will respond to events. In order to do this, though, they must first identify their own patterns of self-defeating beliefs, and understand how these lead to emotional disturbance and unhappiness.

R.E.B.T. and group counselling

R.E.B.T. is similar to Beck's cognitive therapy in its teaching and educative focus. In addition, it is an approach that can be used in either individual or group counselling. Beck (1995:21) describes how he began to apply R.E.B.T to groups in the 1950s. At that time he realized just how much support group members derived from each other, especially when they learned and used R.E.B.T. together and became adept at discussing and disputing irrational beliefs. Ellis also points out that R.E.B.T. is suitable for use in many different types of groups, including those designed specially for women, workshops and shorter intensive courses. During group counselling a range of techniques can be used, but by far the most important is teaching members how to dispute their own irrational beliefs. These irrational beliefs include the many 'shoulds', 'oughts' and 'musts' that hinder or disturb people and lead to numerous psychological problems. People often believe, for example, that they ought to do or achieve something, without ever really testing or disputing the validity of such an absolute. The group therapist's task is to teach members to use what Ellis (1995:16) calls Empirical or Realistic cognitive disputing to counter these absolutes. The following Case study is an example:

CASE STUDY: DISPUTING IRRATIONAL BELIEFS ──────────────

A group member called Clive was depressed because he believed he should follow in his father's footsteps and become a lawyer. The group therapist disputed with him as follows:

Group therapist: *Why should you follow in his footsteps?*

Clive: *I think that's what he expects.*

Group therapist: *But where is the evidence that he expects it?*

Clive: *He hasn't actually said so, but I feel it.*

Group therapist: *So you have a feeling. How does this mean you should be a lawyer?*

Clive: *It's because of my father. I feel sure he would want me to do it.*

Group therapist: *Though he has never actually said so, and you feel depressed at the thought of becoming a lawyer?*

Clive: *I don't feel I can ever be really happy unless I fulfil his ambitions for me.*

Group therapist: *Is it possible to be depressed and happy at the same time?*

Clive: *Well, probably not.*

Group therapist: *Probably not?*

Clive: *Well, it's highly unlikely, I suppose.*

Group therapist: *Which brings us back to what you would like to do.*

Clive: *As I said when I came into the group, I would like to be a journalist.*

Group therapist: *Which you've had some success at already?*

Clive: *Yes.*

Group therapist: *Where is the evidence for believing that you* should *do something you have no aptitude for, while forfeiting something else you are good at and like?*

Clive: *None. Except this feeling I have about my father.*

Group therapist: *Is that logical?*

Clive: *No, it isn't.*

(Adapted from Ellis, 1995)

This Case study shows how the group therapist actively challenges or disputes Clive's irrational beliefs about how he should conduct his career. The technique used is a vigorous and confronting one, and is designed to illustrate how Clive perpetuates his own difficulties when he clings to the belief that he must do what he *imagines* his father would like him to do. Other R.E.B.T. techniques include giving group members homework, so that they can practise disputing their own irrational beliefs. There are also many self-help forms designed specifically for use in R.E.B.T. groups, and members are encouraged to complete them as part of homework assignments. Humour also forms an integral part of the approach, especially in relation to irrational beliefs, and group members are encouraged to spot the absurd and incongruous in their belief systems and cognitive errors. A technique called reframing is used as part of R.E.B.T group therapy, and involves asking members to change or reframe some of the 'awful' things they believe will happen, or have happened, to them so that the positive aspect is revealed. Thus, someone whose relationship has ended is encouraged to look at the opportunities to form new ones, and to look at the time now available to do other things.

As a therapeutic approach, R.E.B.T. places a great deal of emphasis on the correct use of language, particularly in the context of how group members describe their feelings. Ellis believes that people often use language incorrectly, especially when they over-generalize and blame themselves needlessly. Semantic Correction is the term used by Ellis to highlight the way clients and group members are shown their inaccuracies in language. Someone who says, 'She made me feel inadequate', for example, would be asked to change this around to say instead: 'I choose to be inadequate when we argue'. Coping Statements are also encouraged, and group members are shown how to formulate and retain these for use when necessary. The most important way in which members can deal with negative or irrational beliefs is by countering these with positive coping statements. This technique includes writing down and rehearsing coping statements that directly invalidate or refute negative or irrational beliefs. In writing about this technique, Bourne (1995:179) emphasizes the time element, and suggests that because most people have had years of practice in negative self-talk, time, practice and consistent effort are needed in order to overcome them. This time and effort might act as a deterrent for some, but in a group context, there is support from other members, along with encouragement and feedback from the leader.

EXERCISE 45

SELF DIALOGUE

Time: 30 mins.

In this exercise you are asked to work individually to begin with, and to make a list of any strong beliefs you hold, especially those containing a 'must', 'should' or 'ought'. When you have completed your list, take each belief in turn and ask each of the following questions in relation to it.

◆ Is this always true for me?

◆ Does this belief help or hinder me?

◆ Did I choose this belief, or did I inherit it?

An example of how this is done is shown in the following sequence:

Belief:

'I should always help others when they ask me, otherwise I'm not much good as a person.'

Question:

Is this always true for me?

Answer:

It is certainly good to be helpful when another person is really in a tight spot. Occasionally I need someone to be there for me too. I can't be there for every person in trouble, especially when I'm feeling low or tired myself. At times like these, it is better if I care for myself, or even to learn to ask for help myself.

Question:

Does this belief help or hinder me?

Answer:

If I always say yes when I'm approached for help, I might feel good for a short while. If I agree to help in a situation where a friend or relative is clearly distressed, then I do feel satisfied that I've done the right thing. On the other hand, I feel resentful in the long term if I agree to every request for help. That has a knock on effect on my relationships with people I'm close to, because I'm tired, sometimes angry and feel I've been exploited. The answer is that it's not good for me to be available all the time to help others, though it is good when it's really necessary.

Question:

Did I choose this belief or did I inherit it?

Answer:

When I think about it, my parents were neglectful and always expected me to do a lot of the practical work around the house. They owned a business and spent all their time there. I learned early on that the only way to get their attention, approval and support, was to do as much for them as possible so they didn't have too much trouble when they got in from work. The answer is that I didn't choose this belief for myself; it was something I simply absorbed from childhood onwards. I firmly believed I could only be loved if I kept on doing things for other people.

Exercise conclusion

When you have completed the individual part of the exercise, discuss it with other members of the group, and compare your responses to the various beliefs listed.

Procedures not used in R.E.B.T.

Ellis (1995) is explicit about those procedures he considers unhelpful in his approach. Included in this category are free association, intense focus on early life experience, exploration of dreams, overemphasis on feelings, too much stress on positive thinking in place of disputing irrational beliefs, and finally, anything that would prompt or encourage dependency on the therapist or group leader.

Although R.E.B.T. does stress interpersonal and family relationships, Ellis is more concerned to help clients and group members recognize how they actually disturb themselves about their relationships. There is a focus on relationships, therefore, but it takes the form of encouraging people to see how their irrational beliefs lead to disturbance and poor cooperation with family members and others.

Transference

Ellis (1995:186) takes the view that transference responses do occasionally occur during therapy, but when they do they are usually linked to irrational beliefs on the part of the client or group member. When transference becomes apparent during therapy, therefore, the therapist must look for the irrational beliefs underpinning it, and then show the group member how irrational it is. If we consider the example of a young man who develops deep loving feelings for a middle-aged group therapist, *as if she were his mother*, then R.E.B.T. would view this as an irrational belief that needs to be highlighted, clarified and changed. We can see from this that R.E.B.T group therapy differs significantly from groups that emphasize unconscious processes and transference responses among members, and to the leader.

Brief therapy

Both R.E.B.T. and Beck's Cognitive therapy are often used in time limited therapy groups.

Curwen et al. (2000:2) define brief therapy as an approach in which 'maximum benefits' can be achieved with the advantage of low cost to group members or clients. They also outline other defining characteristics of short-term therapy, including its pragmatic and optimistic focus stressing each individual's resources and strengths. In addition to being less expensive, short-term group therapy has other obvious advantages for clients, especially those who cannot afford the time and investment required for longer therapy. When people are troubled emotionally or psychologically they usually want fairly speedy results. In fact, both R.E.B.T. and other cognitive therapies have always tended to be brief, and this is something that Ellis (1997) highlights. Within the past decade the demands for time limited helping approaches has certainly increased, and the cognitive-behavioural therapies have responded to this. Time limited or brief therapy can, of course, mean different things to different people. Curwen et al. (2000) do not suggest a time span for brief therapy, though they concede that different cognitive therapists place limits on the number of therapy sessions that they can offer. They also point to research indicating the average number of brief therapy sessions to be from six to ten.

Strengths and limitations of the R.E.B.T. and Cognitive-behavioural approach in groups

One of the most obvious advantages of the cognitive and cognitive-behavioural approaches in both group and individual settings is the fact that it is often available as part of N.H.S. provision for addressing psychological problems. It is also readily available privately, is easy to understand and is emphatically problem focused and practical. Group therapy may be unsuitable for people who are deeply or clinically depressed, however. This is because individual support (and / or medication) is often needed to help people in these circumstances overcome the critical phase of their illness. In common with all the other theoretical approaches in groups, R.E.B.T. and other cognitive therapies stress the importance of the relationship between group members and the leader or therapist. Though the cognitive approaches are clearly didactic and directive, they also emphasize respect for client autonomy, and, in the case of groups, the ability of members to support and help each other. Avery (1996) points to a possible weakness in cognitive therapy when he suggests that its benefits may not always be lasting. Cognitive therapy does indeed tackle the presenting problems that group members have, but there is the possibility that deeper, unconscious dynamics are ignored or discounted in favour of rational and logical explanations for all psychological difficulties.

Perhaps one of the most impressive aspects of R.E.B.T and cognitive therapy in groups is the attention paid to the design and structure of programmes and the content of individual sessions. Additionally, Free (1999:6) points out that it is much easier to evaluate cognitive therapy in groups, since its procedures are so clearly and specifically set out. Another benefit of this design and structure is that programmes can be 'manual based', which means they can be used by therapists in different settings. Free makes the further point that when procedures are clearly set out like this, and practitioners or group therapists are following prescribed guidelines, it is less likely that subsequent evaluations of them will be affected by bias.

ERIC BERNE AND TRANSACTIONAL ANALYSIS

Transactional Analysis is another form of group and individual therapy stressing an educative approach to helping people overcome their problems. Its originator, Eric Berne, was born in 1910 in Montreal, Canada. He studied medicine, and later psychiatry at Yale University. Later still he became a psychoanalyst, and it was this experience of working with patients in therapy that prompted his ambition to decode and simplify the arcane language used in psychoanalysis. To do this he devised his own formula for describing the various elements that make up the inner emotional world of each individual. Berne published two important books in the early 1960s: *Transactional Analysis in Psychotherapy* (1961) and *Games People Play* (1964). Both these books give detailed accounts of Berne's theory of personality, and are immensely readable and easy to understand.

Parent, Adult and Child

Berne decided to use very familiar words to describe the three elements or ego states which, in transactional analysis, make up an individual's personality. These ego states or states of 'self' are common to all of us, and are responsible for our thoughts, feelings and behaviours. If we look at this closely, we can see that Berne is referring to three separate ways of thinking about, and responding to, other people and the external world in general. These ego states form the very core of the self, so they are not the same as roles or different moods that people can try out as they wish. The Parent ego state which is divided into two components – Controlling Parent and Nurturing Parent – is that part of us which is derived from parental influences and other authority figures from the past. In many ways it resembles a recording of everything we have heard from, or observed in, the adults who have been important to us in the past. The Controlling Parent and Nurturing Parent describe, as their names suggest, different aspects of parental behaviour and influence. These aspects are shown in various situations and transactions with other people. When we help someone in distress, for example, we are quite likely to look, feel and behave like a caring parent who is concerned and supportive. This is the Nurturing Parent part of our personality. The Controlling Parent is usually shown when we want to lay down the law, lecture someone, uphold the rules, or generally 'control' others or the situation we are in.

The Child ego state describes that part of us containing all the emotional responses felt and used in childhood. These emotional responses are carried into adult life, and can be triggered at any time in a variety of situations. Like the Parent ego state, the Child ego is also divided into two aspects or components. These two aspects are known as the Free Child and the Adapted Child. When a person is in the Free Child ego state s/he is likely to feel fun loving, uninhibited, unbound by rules or restrictions, and sometimes even thoughtless. The Free Child state is often shown when we feel energetic, creative, or in the mood to party. The Adapted child is, on the other hand, more constrained and 'adapted' to the socialization process that is part of early childhood experience. Early on young children do learn to adapt to the moods and expectations of their parents or parental figures. In later life, people often respond to certain situations in the same way that they responded as children. If someone criticizes our work, for example, we may respond by becoming as angry or depressed as we did when criticized unfairly in childhood. In addition, we may become unduly anxious when faced with important deadlines or tasks. The following Case study illustrates this last point.

CASE STUDY: GILL

In a transactional analysis therapy group a member called Gill recalled her behaviour at a recent work seminar.

I was asked to give a talk about the new assessment procedures we were about to implement at the university. Since I was involved in the design of these procedures I knew all about them, so I shouldn't have been nervous about speaking to colleagues. Just before I was due to speak, however, my boss said he didn't like the emphasis I had put on certain key areas. He added that he would prefer a different approach, focusing on issues that he believed were more important. I just felt wiped out by the criticism, and I found myself becoming anxious and depressed as he spoke. The feelings were exactly the same as those I experienced as a child when my father criticized my hand-writing. It seemed so unfair to me then, since it was my handwriting, not his. In the same way, I felt the seminar presentation was mine; therefore my boss should not have interfered. Anyway, his timing was certainly meant to unsettle me. In retrospect, I real-ize that I could have chosen to respond in my Adult ego state, instead of responding as I did in the Adapted Child.

In the Case study above, Gill refers to her Adult ego state. This is the ego state that is in touch with reality, and is evident in our feelings, attitudes and behaviour. When in this state, our behaviour is calm, thoughtful and reasonable. The Adult ego state represents that part of our personality that is able to think clearly in difficult situations, so that an effective working solution becomes possible. Adult behaviour is assertive, though never bullying. It means respecting others, as well as respecting ourselves. When in the Adult ego state, we are unlikely to be overwhelmed by strong feelings. This does not mean that feelings are absent, however, but it does mean that we recognize and control them. In the Case study, Gill became anxious and depressed because her boss criticized her work just before the presentation. If she had chosen to respond to her boss Adult to Adult, she might have said something like this:

I can see that you don't agree with me on all the points, but I'm quite sure this is how I'd like to present it. In any case, it's too late at this stage to discuss it in detail. Perhaps this is something we could talk about after the seminar?

Transactions

In addition to describing the three ego states, Berne also analysed and described the transactions that take place between people. He used the term 'Strokes' to denote the exchanges that we all engage in socially. These strokes include non-verbal communication and physical contact, as well as verbal exchanges. According to Berne's theory we all need strokes since they represent recognition, and children especially will go out of their way to receive them, even when they are negative. Problems are perpetuated in adult life when we continue to search for strokes in a dysfunctional or unhealthy way.

Scripts

Scripts are beliefs about ourselves, others and life in general which we have acquired in childhood. In transactional analysis the word 'script' refers to early conditioning and its effects on an individual's thinking, feeling and behaviour in the present. Early in childhood people adapt to the adult world around them, and in doing so form certain beliefs about themselves and their future. A child might be told that he is clumsy or stupid, for example. Later on, as an adult, his 'script' might dictate that he feels, acts and thinks clumsy and stupid. In transactional analysis such scripts are discussed and group members are encouraged to understand why they feel and believe certain things about themselves. Once understanding is achieved it is then possible to initiate change. Re-decision is the term used to describe the process of changing out-dated beliefs relating to earlier life decisions. This re-decision is achieved over a period of time, and is supported by other group members and the therapist.

Transactional Analysis and the group

Transactional Analysis teaches group members about positive and negative communication. It also shows how the ulterior transactions or psychological games which are sometimes conducted by people, point to the distorted emotions and attitudes of those concerned. Language is central to Transactional Analysis, and this is the first facet of it that is taught to new group members. This gives everyone the tools to explore and describe their feelings, behaviour and attitudes. The language of Transactional Analysis may seem strange when members first join a group, but after a while its use becomes almost second nature, especially when everyone is using the same terminology.

Transactional analysis can be used in individual therapy, but it is commonly conducted in groups where its effectiveness is enhanced by the range of communication taking place in such a context. It is an educative and experiential approach which is also very accessible, easy to grasp and usually available in most areas. It is sometimes available in community centres and colleges where it is likely to be offered on an education course in communication skills. Business and management organizations also often train their personnel in transactional analysis through the provision of short courses or seminars. However, it is important to remember that the transactional analysis used in these settings is quite different from the kind of therapeutic groupwork that we are concerned with here.

Practitioners in group therapy undergo a lengthy training, and are accredited by the Institute of Transactional Analysis. In addition, they receive regular supervision, and very often receive therapy themselves.

EXERCISE 46

EGO STATES

Time: 1 hour.

In this exercise you are asked to think about your own ego states and the situations in which you experience them. Work individually to begin with, concentrating on the following questions:

◆ Are there situations where I find it difficult to control strong feelings?

◆ Do I ever find myself acting, feeling and sounding as I did when I was a child?

◆ Do I ever find myself speaking to others as my mother or father might have done?

◆ How do I respond when others criticize me?

◆ Do I ever find myself taking care of others as a parent might do?

◆ Are there situations in which I am defensive or uptight?

◆ Is my tone of voice calm, clear and confident when I speak at meetings?

◆ Am I ever excessively apologetic or dependent on the good opinion of others?

◆ Do I analyse and look at the facts before responding to others?

◆ Do I often have bright or creative ideas that energize myself and others?

When you have considered your own responses, discuss these with other members of the group. A useful addition to this exercise is to ask other group members for feedback about your responses in the group. In this way, you should gain some understanding as to why you get certain reactions from others. It may also help you to change any behaviour that causes problems in your relationships, both inside and outside the group.

References

Avery, B. (1996) *Principles of Psychotherapy.* London. Thorsons.

Beck, A. T. (1991) *Cognitive Therapy and Emotional Disorders.* Harmondsworth. Penguin.

Berne, E. (1968) *Games People Play.* London. Penguin Books.

Berne, E. (1996) *Transactional Analysis in Psychotherapy.* London. Souvenir Press.

Berne, E. (1992) *What do you say after you say hello?* London. Corgi Books.

Bourne, E. J. (1996) *The Anxiety and Phobia Workbook.* California. New Harbinger Publications Inc.

Corey, G. (1995) 4th ed. *Theory and Practice of Group Counselling.* California. Brooks/Cole Publishing Co.

Curwen, B. Palmer, S. and Ruddell, P. (2000) *Brief Cognitive Therapy.* London. Sage.

Ellis, A. (1995) 'Fundamentals of Rational Emotive Behaviour Therapy for the 1990s' in Dryden, W. (ed.) *Rational Emotive Behaviour Therapy: A Reader.* London. Sage.

Ellis, A. (1995) 'Rational-Emotive Therapy Approaches to Overcoming Resistance' in Dryden, W. (ed.) *Rational Emotive Behaviour Therapy: A Reader.* London. Sage.

Ellis, A., Gordon, J., Neenan, M. and Palmer, S. (1998) *Stress Counselling: A Rational Emotive Behaviour Approach.* New York. Springer Publishing.

Free, M. L. (1999) *Cognitive Therapy in Groups.* Chichester. John Wiley & Sons Ltd.

Fritchie, R and Melling, M. (1991) *The Business of Assertiveness.* London. B.B.C. Books.

Peiffer, V. (1996) *Principles of Stress Management.* London. Thorsons.

Richards, D. and McDonald, B. (1990) *Behavioural Psychotherapy: A Handbook for Nurses.* Oxford. Heinemann.

Rose, S. D. (1999) 'Group Therapy: A Cognitive Behavioural Approach' in Price, JR., Hescheles, DR. and Price, A. R. (eds.) *A Guide to Starting Psychotherapy Groups.* California. Academic Press.

9

The Humanistic Influence in Groups

INTRODUCTION

The Humanistic influence in groups is directly related to the work carried out by Abraham Maslow and Carl Rogers, both of whom subscribed to an optimistic and essentially positive view of human nature and its potential. In this chapter we shall discuss their contributions to therapy generally, with special emphasis on the application of their theories to groups. In addition we shall consider the work of Fritz Perls who pioneered Gestalt therapy, since he too is often grouped under the heading of Humanistic therapeutic approaches. The Existential approach to personal growth in groups will also be discussed, along with some reference to the fundamental questions that it poses in relation to human nature, existence, and the philosophical dilemmas that people face throughout their life. Because so many theories are included in this chapter, it is not possible to describe each of them in detail. For this reason, we shall concentrate on the distinguishing characteristics of individual approaches, with special focus on their defining principles and use of techniques.

THE WORK OF ABRAHAM MASLOW

Abraham Maslow is probably best remembered for his hierarchy of needs, which he believed, is common to all of us and lends meaning to our existence and to our relationships with others. Maslow, who was born in 1908 in New York, suffered an unhappy childhood. At his parents insistence he studied law, but abandoned this after a very short time. Later, he studied psychology, and gained his doctorate in 1934. Though he was initially attracted to Behaviourism, he gradually came to believe that it could never adequately explain the uniqueness and diversity of human experience and potential.

Maslow wrote several influential books, including *Towards a Psychology of Being* (1968) and *Motivation and Personality* (1970). In both these texts he outlines his psychological theories and concepts, and emphasizes the need to consider the whole person along with the effects of the environment and culture when looking at human behaviour and experience.

THE HIERARCHY OF NEEDS

As stated earlier, Maslow's most important contribution to our understanding of human personality is his description of the needs hierarchy that drives people onwards towards self-actualization. Maslow believed that our innate tendencies are constructive and move us towards growth and loving relationships with others. However, events, early experience and negative influences in the environment, often conspire to inhibit these positive tendencies, so that negative, self-defeating and often destructive behaviour is produced instead. The hierarchy offers a clear picture of the needs that motivate people, and the difficulties that arise when these are inadequately met.

Physiological needs

The needs that are taken as a starting point in Maslow's hierarchy are those relating to basic physiological drives. Included here are hunger, thirst, the need to rest and sleep, the need to eliminate, and the need for sexual satisfaction. These needs are similar to those that motivate lower animals too, but as far as human beings are concerned they must be satisfied before the next level of needs can be contemplated. It is, of course, possible to be deprived temporarily in any of these physiological needs areas, but persistent deprivation will obviously inhibit any ambitions to proceed to a higher level in the hierarchy.

Safety needs

If these physiological needs are gratified, a new set of needs emerges which relate to safety, stability, structure, and the avoidance of pain and anxiety. In referring to these safety needs, Maslow states that fortunate, healthy people in society are secure and satisfied. There are, of course, those who are not so fortunate, and in their case the lack of security will have a damaging effect on their outlook, since practically everything seems less important than security and protection.

Because our need for safety and stability is so strong, it affects our general attitude to many things. This is especially true in relation to our feelings about change, for example. Maslow (1970:19) points out that certain people with psychological or emotional problems often fear change so much that they react against it by developing obsessions or compulsions in a desperate attempt to impose lasting order and stability on an otherwise unmanageable world. This is an important point to remember in the context of group therapy, since there are invariably members whose life experience has been unstable at some point, often in early childhood. Such people frequently find it difficult to deal with the unknown, the unfamiliar or strange, and in an effort to impose order they may seek to live in a highly disciplined and restricted fashion which may cut them off from normal social interaction with others. The experience of group participation can help to ameliorate some of these negative impulses by showing that human intimacy is not always threatening or abusive.

Relationship needs

Giving and receiving affection are important to most normal people; so important in fact, that we tend to feel deeply unsatisfied when we do not have meaningful relationships, or when we do not belong to a family or other group. However, certain aspects of contemporary life, including the transient nature of many relationships, may lead to significant failure in meeting this particular need. Ironically, this is one reason for the increasing attraction of counselling and psychotherapy groups, mainly because these often serve to redress this relationship deficit and to provide the intimacy and connectedness lacking in personal life. Maslow (1970:20) points to this phenomenon, and suggests that its appearance is motivated by a general hunger for 'contact, intimacy, and belongingness.'

Being in a group is one way of overcoming feelings of loneliness, which, as Maslow says, are highlighted by the breakdown of traditional groups, and by increasing mobility. A problem arises, however, when a counselling or psychotherapy group is seen as a permanent substitute for what is missing in a person's personal and social life. As we noted in earlier chapters, group members need to be aware from the outset that the group will one day come to an end. This is why preparation for group membership is so important, and also why it is important to stress the transient nature of the group experience from the beginning.

Esteem needs

All of us need to feel valued by family, friends and work colleagues. Our need for a sense of personal worth and esteem starts in early childhood and continues throughout our life span. Sometimes this is referred to as a desire for respect, a good evaluation of self, and a need to be appreciated and recognized by others. In order to have real self-esteem (as opposed to an inflated and false sense of superiority) people have to develop competence and some sense of achievement, especially in relation to their innate abilities and skills. When people have true self-esteem, it leads to feelings of usefulness and a sense of being a vital part of society and the wider world. Maslow (1970:22) stresses that true self-esteem is based on 'deserved respect' from others, rather than on false adulation associated with fame or celebrity. When we do not accept ourselves, and are not accepted by others, feelings of discouragement and inferiority are likely to follow.

In addition to esteem needs, Maslow emphasises the importance of cognitive and aesthetic experience. This involves an awareness and appreciation of beauty, a desire for knowledge, and a quest for understanding and explanation. Maslow (1970:24) states that psychologically healthy people are attracted to knowledge, mystery, and the unknown, whereas those people with emotional difficulties tend to cling to the familiar and dread the unknown. Another group of people, those with minimal ability and intelligence whose cognitive and aesthetic needs are consequently frustrated, often suffer from low self-esteem, boredom and very often, depression. One way in which group counselling and therapy can help members whose cognitive and aesthetic needs have not been met, is to develop their self-awareness and interpersonal skills so that they can become more confident. When this happens, there is the possibility that they will then address and fulfil their cognitive and aesthetic needs.

Self-actualization needs

Maslow emphasizes that people need to do what they are individually motivated and fitted to do. In other words, an individual with a special talent like art or music must be allowed to pursue and develop their particular skill in order to self-actualise. Self-actualisation is the highest form of need and consists of the identification and fulfilment of our innate abilities. Such identification and fulfilment is obviously different for each person. Some people strive towards self-actualisation by climbing mountains, others by writing poetry, and still others by research into science or the study of life itself. It is important to stress here that not everyone achieves self-actualisation. This is because it is only possible in an environment that has satisfied one's basic lower needs. Freedom of speech and action are necessary concomitants of self-actualisation, and these, unfortunately, are not conditions that can be obtained for everyone. Not everyone is at liberty to pursue a specific course, either of study or action, which would lead to self-actualisation. Once again, it is possible to look at one of Maslow's needs in the context of group counselling or psychotherapy. It is often the case that group members have been unable to fulfil their need for self-actualisation for a variety of reasons. These reasons may include discouragement in childhood, illness, disability or other forms of social or material deprivation.

CASE STUDY: RAFFINA

In one counselling group a member (Raffina) described her struggle for self-actualisation, though she did not use Maslow's term when talking about her experience. Instead, she referred to her efforts to 'do what she felt good at' which meant developing her artistic talent, an ambition that had been discouraged by her parents when she was younger.

My parents had clear ambitions for me, but these didn't happen to be what I wanted for myself. They were very keen that I should do well academically, and they really pushed this from the moment I started school. When I said I wanted to study art and become a dress designer, they were scathing. This didn't fit into their scheme of things for me. My father was a doctor, my mother had been a nurse, and I think they both thought I would follow into medicine too. I was very depressed at secondary school, and when I was fifteen I took an overdose of tablets and had to be rushed to hospital. When I recovered I could see that my parents were extremely disappointed in me, even more disappointed than they had been previously when I expressed my artistic ambitions. It took a long time for us to get back on real speaking terms, and the upshot of all this was that I made a decision to shelve what I wanted to do for myself, and go along with what they wanted. Then when I was at university my father died suddenly. Afterwards, my mother became depressed too. I dropped out of my course and got a job as an assistant window dresser. This satisfied my artistic feelings to some extent, but I still wanted to study art and do a proper course in design. It was only when my mother went into a residential home that I felt courageous enough to apply for a place on a course. I did qualify eventually, but getting there took its toll on me. I felt a lot of guilt about my mother, and I am still saddened that my father was so disappointed in me. On the plus side, though, I lost many of the physical symptoms I suffered from, including the skin rashes that had plagued me since childhood. Also, I just felt more like my real self.

The above Case study highlights the problems that people often face in order to achieve self-actualisation. Even when she did manage to secure a place on a course, Raffina felt guilty about disappointing her parents and thwarting their ambitions for her. However, through her participation in the group, she was able to express and deal with her feelings of guilt. She was also able to forgive her parents (and herself) for all their differences of opinion in the past.

THE APPLICATION OF MASLOW'S THEORIES TO GROUP THERAPY

Maslow did not develop a specific school of therapy, though he did write about psychotherapy and the importance of the therapist / client relationship in helping people to understand and overcome their psychological problems. However, his work has had enormous influence on practitioners of both individual and group therapy, and has increased our understanding of what it is that people need in order to achieve and maintain emotional health. Maslow does refer to the use of groups (1970:104) and stresses his respect for the medium, which, he says, helps participants to deal with feelings of isolation, guilt and the sense of uniqueness that often troubles those with psychological problems. In addition, he makes the point that although groups may differ in terms of theoretical orientation and procedures used they all have the same 'far reaching goals' which include the realization of individual potential. However, Maslow warns us that groups should be conducted by competent people, otherwise they can be useless or even harmful. This is a point that we shall take up again in the next chapter when we look at some of the possible damaging effects of groups.

The hierarchy of needs is an invaluable paradigm for looking at basic and more advanced human needs. It also sheds light on the reasons that people often become 'stuck' and unable to make progress above certain levels. It is difficult to imagine how anyone could develop true potential while, for example, feeling insecure, unsafe, or even hungry. Conditions of insecurity and hunger are increasingly seen in our society among deprived groups, and some group leaders have experience of working with them. One group facilitator called Ronnie spoke of his work with a group of asylum seekers. Most of them were extremely traumatised, insecure and unsure of what the future might hold for them. He described their predicament in the following way:

I am often reminded of Maslow's hierarchy when working with the Tuesday group. These people have experienced conditions that we can only imagine. One group member talked last week about losing almost all his family, his home, and in fact every single thing they owned. Now he is here he wants to work, but cannot at the moment. He doesn't want to be a burden on society – he has his pride after all, but his self-esteem has taken a battering. If he, and the others, could only get that back, their self-esteem I mean, then I'm sure they could then move forward. But if so many people are against you, don't understand your circumstances and background, and really just resent your presence, where do you start? What I do know is that the group has been a lifeline for them. For the moment it is the one place where they can say what they feel because others will have had similar experiences and will understand.

Towards self-actualisation

Maslow places a great deal of emphasis on the need to help clients and group members fulfil their own particular potentials. When needs are frustrated, therefore, the focus in therapy must be on helping individuals to achieve gratification of these very needs. One of the most interesting aspects of Maslow's work is the attention he gives to diverse forms of helping, including the kind of helping that is available from untrained helpers and 'good human relationships.' In describing these different forms of support, Maslow (1970:98) stresses that it is the human relationship itself that is psychologically healing. Needs cannot, in his view, be satisfied by things other than good relationships with friends, lovers, parents, or children.

On the subject of psychotherapy he offers some poignant observations when he says that it offers what some people may never have had, namely a good human relationship. This interpersonal definition of therapy means that practitioners (or at least those who are influenced by Maslow) must view the people they are helping as absolute equals. The concept of equality is something that most therapists and groupworkers tend to take for granted, but both Maslow and Rogers (whose theories we shall discuss later) make it very explicit. The group as a medium for counselling and therapy certainly promotes the ideal of equality and sharing, and because the potential for good interpersonal relationships is multiplied, by virtue of the fact that so many people are present, group members are more likely to get the kind of support needed to address their needs deficits. In individual therapy clients have the opportunity to establish one good relationship, and hopefully transfer this to what Maslow calls 'their social life in general.' (1970:104) The group offers more than this, however, because it gives members the chance to practise their interpersonal skills with different people, with the support and help of the facilitator or therapist.

EXERCISE 47

SELF-ACTUALISING PEOPLE
Time: 1 hour.

In 1950 Maslow published his study of self-actualising (or fully human) people. The research was designed to identify the characteristics of psychological health, and included the following fifteen definitions.

1 **Accurate perception of reality.** In Maslow's study, self-actualising people were realistic in their evaluations of events, ideas, the world and other people. They were

able to make accurate judgements about most areas of life, and were less prone to deception and illusion.

2   **Acceptance of others and self.** Self-actualising people are more likely to accept themselves and their own human nature. They also accept others, and are not shocked by the frailties and weaknesses of humanity. This kind of acceptance leads to more enjoyment of life in general, and an absence of excessive shame and anxiety.

3   **Spontaneity of thought and behaviour.** Self-actualising people are less inclined to be rigid and inflexible in their thinking and behaviour. According to Maslow (1970:132) they are more simple and natural than people with psychological problems. In addition, self-actualisers are autonomous and unconventional, though they do not go out of their way to be deliberately so.

4   **Problem centring.** Maslow's subjects were more likely to focus on problems outside themselves than on their own personal problems or worries. They tended to become involved in projects or tasks that were of benefit to the wider community or to humanity in general. Self-actualising people are interested in philosophical and ethical issues, and they are unlikely to become worried about minor details or concerns.

5   **Solitude.** Maslow's subjects were happy to be alone and to enjoy a healthy detachment from others. Self-actualising people have the capacity to remain calm and serene, though their detachment is often mistaken for aloofness, which can cause problems in social relations with other people. A corollary of this detachment is personal autonomy in others areas, including decision making, responsibility, and making choices.

6   **Independence and Autonomy.** Maslow's self-actualising people also appeared to be more independent than most, and more capable of individual autonomy. This independence and autonomy means that self-actualisers are more resilient when things go wrong and they are less likely to become frustrated. They are, as Maslow says, 'self contained.' (1970:136)

7   **Appreciation of life.** Self-actualising people appreciate life with all its complexity. Experience of beauty, especially beauty in nature, never becomes stale for them. This implies that they also live richer and more fulfilling lives, and are grateful for all the benefits and good fortune they already have.

8   **Peak experiences.** This characteristic is directly linked to the last one because it describes a capacity to experience heightened satisfaction and delight in nature, pleasure, love, art and the wonders of the natural world. Self-actualising people may even experience deeply mystical, sometimes ecstatic episodes in their lives.

9   **Kinship.** Self-actualisers feel close to other people, and have greater feelings of kinship, sympathy, connection and genuine affection. They also tend to be non-possessive in their relationships, and because of this they are often misunderstood and viewed with suspicion by others who feel less secure in their relationships.

10 **Respect and humility.** Self-actualisers have greater respect for people of all classes. They find it relatively easy to be friendly with anyone, regardless of race, education,

social class, religion or ethnic origin. In addition, they are willing to learn from any-one who has something to teach them, regardless of any other characteristics that the 'teacher' might have. In this respect, self-actualisers are truly democratic in their character structure and outlook.

11 **Relationships.** According to Maslow, self-actualising people have deeper, more intimate and meaningful interpersonal relationships. They are capable of greater love, identification and connectedness than other people would find possible. Because of this, they have more secure ties with a relatively small number of peo-ple, but are at pains to spend time with, and support those they number among their close friends.

12 **A sense of right and wrong.** Self-actualising people are also strongly ethical – they know the difference between right and wrong, and they have a true sense of morality. In their day-to-day lives they make choices based on these standards. Maslow refers to such people as 'religious' though not in the conventional sense. In fact, many of the people he describes are agnostic or atheists, but they do pos-sess a deeply spiritual side.

13 **Sense of humour.** Although Maslow's self-actualising subjects were seen to have a keen sense of humour, it was not of the common type that pokes fun at others, or is hostile to outsiders or those who are different. The sense of humour he describes is more sophisticated than this, and is more likely to be self-deprecating, or of the thoughtful philosophical type.

14 **Enhanced creativity.** Maslow's subjects were more creative and original than other people. In referring to creativity, Maslow uses the term in its broadest sense, and indi-cates an ability to approach everyday tasks with a freshness of thought and attitude. Creative people, of the kind that Maslow describes, are less inhibited than usual, more spontaneous, natural, and inclined to experiment with new ideas and concepts.

15 **Resist enculturation.** The word 'enculturation' is used by Maslow to describe the way in which people become identified with the prevailing culture. His subjects were less likely to become slaves to cultural expectations and prevailing standards, and more likely to maintain a certain 'inner detachment', especially when aspects of the culture are perceived as unhealthy by them.

Having read Maslow's list of characteristics, can you say how many of them you per-sonally share? Discuss your views about the characteristics with other group members, and say how you think group participation might help people acquire or develop such attributes.

It is difficult to imagine how anyone could possibly display all these characteristics, and Maslow indicates that self-actualisation is, in fact, a matter of degree, and that few people possess the characteristics to perfection. In addition, less healthy people may, on occasion, exhibit some or many of them, though they are unlikely to sustain them long term. Self-actualising people are, on the other hand, more consistent in their demonstration of the characteristics described, though they are still liable to display faults as well, including occasional bad temper, irritation, boredom or even discourtesy towards others.

> ◁ **EXERCISE 48** ▷
>
> ## MASLOW'S HIERARCHY
> Time: 40 mins.
>
> This is an exercise that you can do individually to begin with. When you have completed the first part of it, work in small groups and discuss your experiences.
>
> Look at the diagram of Maslow's hierarchy (see Figure 9.1) and identify any need (or needs) that may have been blocked for you at any point in your life. What were the circumstances at the time, and how did you respond when you were unable to satisfy a particular need? Was there anything, or anyone, that helped you at that stage of your life?

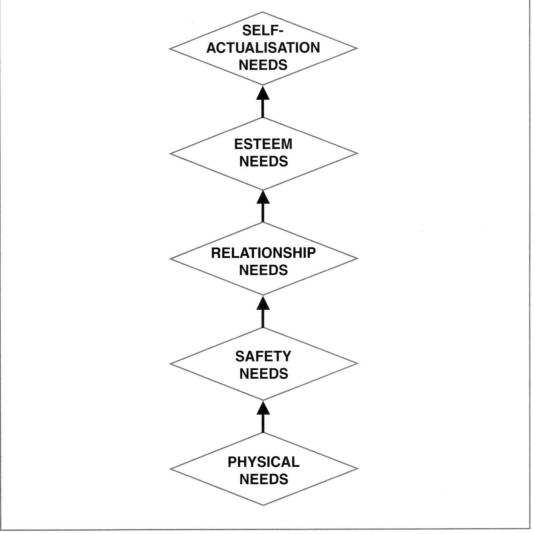

Figure 9.1 The Hierarchy of Needs (Maslow)

CARL ROGERS AND PERSON CENTRED THERAPY

Like Maslow, Carl Rogers believed that human nature is essentially healthy, and inclined towards growth, wholeness and self-actualisation. Rogers, who was born in Illinois in 1902, moved with his family to Chicago when he was twelve years old. He lived a fairly solitary existence on a farm where he read extensively about scientific farming methods and rearing animals. Later he studied agriculture at the University of Wisconsin, but later still became interested in pursuing a career in one of the caring professions. For some time he was attracted to the idea of becoming a minister of religion, but eventually studied psychology and psychotherapy and received a PhD from Columbia University in 1928.

Rogers had a broad education in psychology, and was familiar with its various branches, including Freudian theory. However, his main field of interest was clinical psychology, and though he was not a qualified psychiatrist, he worked for some time at a child guidance clinic in New York. Here he had many confrontations with orthodox psychiatrists, many of whom believed he should not be working in the area of mental health. However, Rogers was able to weather these disputes, and started to formulate his own approach to counselling and psychotherapy. In 1945 he moved to the University of Chicago where he established a counselling centre. After this he proceeded to the University of Wisconsin to conduct further research into counselling theory and practice. In 1963 he resigned from the university and joined the Behavioural Sciences Institute in La Jolla, California. Here he founded the Centre for Studies of the Person, and continued his research into interpersonal relationships. He died in 1987.

The Actualising Tendency

As stated earlier, Rogers' view of human nature is positive and optimistic, and he emphasizes our innate tendency to develop and actualise. Rogers believed that each person has the capacity and ability to reach maximum potential, a tendency that he referred to as the actualising tendency (1991:487). This concept is extremely important in the context of the person centred approach to therapeutic groupwork and counselling. We can see how similar this is to Maslow's theory which also stresses the most positive aspects of human nature and the external forces that conspire to inhibit them. Like Maslow, Rogers too is very aware of the human capacity for destructive, callous and cruel behaviour. However, he attributes these characteristics to circumstances and influences outside the person, rather than to intrinsic or innate forces.

The Self-concept

The self-concept is a term that Rogers uses to describe each person's view or image of who they are. It is based on life experience, and on the reflected appraisals of other people. The development of self-concept begins in infancy and continues throughout our life span. If early experience is favourable and nurturing a person's self-concept is likely to be positive. On the other hand, negative or damaging early experience will produce a poor or deprecating self-concept that will persist into adulthood. Rogers believed that consistent love, support and approval from significant people in a child's life were absolutely necessary in the development of a positive self-concept. If, however, love and care are inconsistent, or dependent on the child behaving or conforming in certain ways, conflict will arise. This conflict stems from the fact that the child needs and wants approval, but also wants and needs to fulfil his or her innate potential. Long term and persistent conflict produces a false or inaccurate self-concept, and the 'true' or real self becomes buried or even forgotten.

The Organismic or True self

The organismic or true self is the real inner part of an individual's personality that is never lost, although often neglected or forgotten. It is a basic life force, present from birth, and capable of regulating each person's psychological and emotional growth. Because it is innate and instinctive, the true self can always be re-activated, especially when someone reaches a crisis point in life that prompts a need for change or reassessment. It is this inner, true self that grows towards self-actualisation and deeper awareness. Group members, and clients in individual therapy, are often motivated to look beneath the outward self-concept, in an effort to identify what it is they really need to do in order to improve their lives and relationships. It is, of course, possible for people to conduct their whole lives without ever expressing any interest in this kind of self-exploration. As we noted earlier though, it is often a crisis or trauma that prompts some people to start on a journey towards self-discovery.

The Therapeutic Relationship

Rogers (1991:20) places a great deal of emphasis on the nature of the relationship between clients and their helpers. In describing a therapeutic relationship he stresses the significance of the helper's attitude in relationship to the person receiving help, and suggests that this attitude should be one of respect, not just for clients, but for oneself as well. A corollary of respect, moreover, is an acknowledgement that clients (or group members) have what Rogers refers to as the 'capacity for integrating' themselves. If we acknowledge this capacity, then it follows that therapy, whether individual or in groups, should be 'non-directive' and geared towards helping people identify and maximise their own potential. (1991:24) Rogers uses the term unconditional positive regard to describe the kind of respect and valuing he wishes to stress. Unconditional positive regard is a non-judgemental, non-possessive respect that denotes caring for another person that does not include any desire or wish to direct or tell that person what to do. Unqualified acceptance of this kind will, according to Rogers, enable clients to explore their deepest feelings, fears and anxieties without any threat of criticism or judgement.

Empathy is another 'core' condition or attribute that Rogers considers necessary in counsellors and group facilitators. To be empathic, a helper must endeavour to understand a client in the deepest sense. This means striving to see things from the client's point of view, or to perceive things as the client perceives them. This is not, of course, easy to do, and requires close attention to the client's verbal and non-verbal messages, including body language, tone of voice, hesitations and all the other subtle signals that people use to convey what is difficult to express in any other way. Empathy is an invaluable aid to helping clients feel understood in a safe, accepting and supportive environment. When clients experience an empathic relationship they are, in Rogers' view, more likely to feel at liberty to explore all those hitherto hidden or frightening issues that cause problems for them (1991:31).

The person centred approach to helping stresses another attribute or 'core condition' that a counsellor or group leader should have. This quality, attribute or condition is sometimes referred to as congruence, though it is also described as genuineness, or the ability, on the helper's part, to be transparent in the therapeutic relationship. Being transparent or genuine in relation to others means being in touch with one's own inner experiences, and sharing these when it is appropriate and helpful to do so. This willingness to share in an open way does not, however, mean that group leaders or counsellors should burden those they are helping with their personal problems or difficulties. To burden others in this way would be unethical and unprofessional, and would have the added effect of reversing roles and causing unnecessary stress for those people who have asked for support for themselves. A willingness to share in a transparent way does mean, though, that group therapists and counsellors should avoid hiding behind professional jargon, defensive facades and any other form of pretence or deception. Ewen (1993:388) suggests that when group therapists and counsellors are open and transparent it offers a model of genuineness to clients or members, so that honest communication is likely to follow.

APPLICATION OF PERSON CENTRED THEORY TO GROUPS

In chapter one we looked at the evolution of groups, and discussed the contribution made to them by Carl Rogers. Rogers was aware from the outset that groups had enormous potential to help people increase personal growth and overcome the difficulties that impeded their progress towards self-development. We noted that Rogers, who was part of the humanistic movement in therapy, could see that group participation was the ideal setting in which to encourage and demonstrate the qualities of empathy, genuineness and respect for others. He was also aware of the factors that drew people towards group therapy, the most important being a need for true communication with others, closeness, and the opportunity to express oneself emotionally and spontaneously. People, in Rogers' view, seek relationships that are genuine and not based on outward success or appearances. Groups do provide a setting in which participants can achieve these ideals, as the next Case study shows.

CASE STUDY: ERIC

Eric, who was thirty, decided to give up his highly paid job in finance and set up his own garden centre, something he had always wanted to do. When he was ten, Eric's father had committed suicide, and the memory of this made him determined that his own life would be a lot less stressful than his father's had been. Because of the pressure of his previous job, Eric had never developed a committed relationship. All his energy, interest and free time, had been devoted to his career or to making money. Having money made him feel secure in the past, but recently it failed to give him the same satisfaction. He had started to think about his father, and about the reasons for his suicide. When he was much younger Eric refused to think about his father's death, but now, when he thought about it, he became depressed as well.

Setting up the garden centre lifted him out of the depression for a while, because in typical fashion, he threw himself into it with great energy and a determination to forget, once again, the disturbing thoughts about his father. After a while, though, he could feel the depression returning, and this was when he sought help from his doctor. He received antidepressant medication, which did help, but because he didn't want to continue with this long term, he decided to join a men's therapy group. Once in the group Eric found that he could talk openly, and for the first time, about his father's death and how it had affected him. He described his experience like this:

> Talking about my father was what helped most. I had never been able to do that before, because my mother clamed up and my brother would never talk either. But another thing that really helped was the way other people in the group accepted me, even though I was no longer a big shot making a lot of money. They were able to see the real me, the part that I had hidden for years. They, and Liam the group counsellor, accepted me and never judged me in any way. Of course, it was not all about me. Naturally, others in the group talked about their concerns too, and I really felt good I was able to help them as well. We all helped each other. Before that I never knew how group therapy worked, but now I know it's all to do with open communication, being able to say what you feel without fear of rejection or not being accepted. It was strange to begin with, but we learned from Liam how to listen and see things from another person's point of view. I learned about the importance of being genuine and true to yourself, about supporting others, and establishing good relationships. All the men in the group were concerned about relationships, their changing roles, how to handle work in a balanced way, and, above all, how to deal with negative feelings and communicate more effectively.

The counselling group that Eric joined was person centred in its approach. The facilitator, Liam, had been trained in person centred counselling, and had then gone on to complete group therapy training. It is clear from the account that Eric gives of his experiences, that Rogers' core conditions of respect, transparency and empathy influenced the group ethos a great deal.

ADVANTAGES OF THE PERSON CENTRED APPROACH IN GROUPS

Hobbs (1991:278) refers to several advantages of the person centred approach in groups. Group members, he notes, learn what it is like to give emotional support as well as receive it, and members who are isolated in their everyday lives, will gain a great deal from the interaction and communication that is part of the group experience. These benefits are highlighted in the previous Case study (Eric), and another advantage stressed by Hobbs, that of helping more than one person at a time, is also evident. Although this is a characteristic of groups generally, it is more evident in those with a person centred ethos, since here the helping capabilities of all members are respected and encouraged, thus raising the overall therapeutic potential.

Perhaps the most significant advantage of the person centred approach is the degree to which it respects each member's personal experience. Moreover, as Corey (1995:286) points out, it also encourages group members to assume responsibility for their own level of commitment to the group. The emphasis on listening, reflecting back what others say, clarifying, summarising, showing affirmation and respect for others and the development of empathic understanding are key features of the person centred model of groupwork.

If these guidelines are adhered to, group leaders and members are unlikely to cause problems of the kind that sometimes develop in other types of groups. These problems are often caused by inappropriate use of confrontation, advice giving, directive strategies, or rigidly following programmes that switch attention from individual group members to external matters. This is not to say that it is impossible to integrate procedures borrowed from other models of group counselling, and, in fact, there are probably a sizeable number of practitioners who do use a variety of techniques, if and when they seem right and effective for a particular situation or group. When the core concepts of respect, empathy and genuineness are truly enshrined in a group's philosophy, however, members are likely to feel valued and appreciated. They are also more likely to develop self-esteem, deeper awareness of their own potential, and the actualising tendency that Rogers refers to. Corey (1995:284) adds the very important point that groups can be most effective and productive when there is structure and some direction. The provision of these elements need not exclude a person centred ethos in the group. In fact, they may be an indication that the group leader is sincerely person centred, especially when structure and direction are used at key stages to facilitate members of the group, and to help them deal with anxiety or insecurity. When a group is starting, for example, the leader may use techniques or exercises designed to help members identify and to talk about their initial anxiety about being there. The group leader can, moreover, demonstrate the core conditions while doing this. The following is an example:

> **Group counsellor:** *Everyone is here now, so I think we'll make a start. It can be a little strange at the beginning, especially when we don't know each other. Let me introduce myself first, and then perhaps we could go around the group so that other people can introduce themselves. You probably all remember my name anyway ... I'm Meryl.*

After this the group members introduced themselves, hesitantly at first. They were all quite anxious, so the group counsellor acknowledged this, thereby showing empathy and demonstrating genuineness too.

> **Group counsellor:** *I can appreciate how difficult it is to speak out and introduce yourself in a group of people you are meeting for the first time. That is something that can make me anxious too. Would anyone like to tell us what feelings they are having about this new situation?*

Following these comments from the group counsellor, individual members began to say how they felt. Gradually everyone was able to see that these feelings of nervousness and anxiety were not unique. It is obviously usual for members of a group to feel nervous at the beginning, so it is a good idea to bring this out into the open and acknowledge it. By referring to her own anxiety, the group counsellor gave the signal that it was appropriate to be genuine and honest in this way. However, it would not have been useful or appropriate for her to dwell on this. Leader self-disclosure, when it is related to group process, as it was here, is beneficial for members, since it models openness and transparency. If it were taken further than this, it might increase group members' anxieties, especially about the group counsellor's ability to fulfil her function as a leader.

The group leader

In the person centred group the leader's role is to model and demonstrate the core concepts of empathy, respect and genuineness. To do this, it is obviously important that the leader is a person who is self-aware, sensitive to the needs of all group members, and holds a strong belief in the innate capabilities of each individual. Hobbs (1991:305) suggests that the best preparation for group therapy is experience in client centred individual therapy. However, he also adds that the group makes additional and new demands on the therapist, owing to the number of people present, and the emotional 'cross currents' that are commonplace in this context. In a group, the leader is required to respond to many individuals, keep track of his or her own personal feelings, and at the same time clarify and monitor group process. Hobbs is also emphatic that group therapy, and not individual therapy within the group, is the goal in the person centred approach. What this means is that attention is directed to what is happening in the group, as it happens. In other words, the group generates its own therapeutic potential, and members learn about themselves and their interactions through attention to group process. The group leader does not dominate developments, but accepts that members will often act as therapists themselves. However, if a member's feelings are ignored, denied or simply difficult to express, the leader must intervene to address and clarify the issue.

Empirical research

Rogers was very interested in research and wanted to clarify the elements that are effective in the therapeutic relationship. Much of the research in person centred therapy deals with the core conditions of respect, empathy and genuineness. One over-riding question in relation to these concepts, and to person centred therapy as a whole, is whether or not the process actually helps clients and group members to change. In referring to various studies on the matter, Rogers (1991:186) draws together some of the findings to show that the person centred model does indeed prompt change. This change includes more self-directed or autonomous behaviour in those people who have experienced person centred therapy; more responsible and less defensive in terms of behaviour; a more objective view of self and reality; less psychological tension and a greater ability to remain calm and deal with frustration and stress.

EXERCISE 49: EMOTIONAL INTELLIGENCE

Time: 1 hour.

Carl Rogers (1991:384) was critical of the prevailing ethos in teaching which, he believed, placed too much emphasis on cognitive intelligence, while virtually ignoring the emotional aspects of experience. The concept of emotional intelligence has been highlighted in recent times, most notably by Goleman (1996), who also defines what he considers to be its five elements: self-awareness, self-control, motivation, empathy and social skills. It seems clear from the contributions made by both Rogers and Goleman that empathy is a fundamental requirement for emotional literacy or intelligence. This exercise is meant to encourage you to look at your own capacity for empathy. It needs to be organized by the group leader who should ask members to think about someone they dislike, or someone they have difficulty in communicating with. It is not necessary to say who the person is, but it is best to avoid choosing public figures, since it is impossible to 'know' them as we would a family member, colleague at work, or neighbour. Ask group members to consider the following questions in relation to the person they have chosen.

◆ When I am talking to her/him I always take time to listen. Yes / No

◆ I am aware of my own body language when talking to her/him. Yes / No

◆ I am aware of the other person's body language too. Yes / No

◆ I am aware of the factors that prompt our differences. Yes / No

◆ I know what the situations are that cause us problems. Yes / No

◆ I know what his/her strengths are. Yes / No

◆ I think s/he knows what my strengths are. Yes / No

◆ I have a good idea of how s/he perceives me. Yes / No

◆ I tend to give feedback to this person, not criticism. Yes / No

◆ I would like more feedback about myself from him/her. Yes / No

◆ I see aspects of myself in him/her. Yes / No

◆ I can think of three positive things about him/her. Yes / No

◆ I can think of ways I would like her/him to change. Yes / No

◆ I can think of several ways s/he would like me to change. Yes / No

◆ I can often see things from her/his point of view. Yes / No

◆ I am aware of the personal difficulties this person has. Yes / No

◆ I am quite willing to admit my faults and mistakes when we disagree. Yes / No

◆ I focus on his/her negative side because I don't like to look at my own. Yes / No

- ◆ I would really like our relationship to be better. Yes / No

- ◆ When I am with this person I think of my own needs more than his/hers. Yes / No

This exercise should help you consider just how much you know or understand people you dislike. It should also encourage you to look carefully at how they might perceive you, and how you behave in relation to them. Empathy is essential for good communication, and, as we have seen, it forms the basis of emotional intelligence and literacy. When you have completed the exercise individually, discuss it in the whole group. How much do you really try to stand in the shoes of another person? Would your relationships be better if you really tried to do this?

GESTALT THERAPY

The German word gestalt, meaning a pattern, shape or configuration, was first used by a group of psychologists who were working at the beginning of the twentieth century. These psychologists were interested in human perception and the way it determines each person's view of reality. One of their most important theories concerns the principle of perceptual organisation, which means that when we perceive something, music, for example, we perceive it in its entirety. We do not usually analyse the individual notes making up a symphony (unless we are conductors or musicians). Instead we tend to appreciate the overall tune, the harmonious whole, and the total effect of the music as we hear it. Gestalt psychology maintains, therefore, that the whole is greater than the sum of its parts, and it is this emphasis on 'wholeness' that appealed to Fritz Perls, who, along with his wife Laura, developed Gestalt Therapy in the 1940s.

FRITZ PERLS

Fritz Perls was born in 1892 in Berlin, where he later trained in Freudian psychoanalysis. During the 1920s he met a psychiatrist called Kurt Goldstein who influenced him a great deal. It was through this association with Goldstein, and later through the influence of his wife Laura, a Gestalt therapist, that Perls came to develop his own individual model of psychotherapy. Like many of the other innovative therapists we have discussed in this book, Perls was disenchanted with classical psychoanalysis. He wanted to promote a more positive theory of personality, one that would invest the mind and body with equal importance, and place greater emphasis on the innate potential for growth and development that Perls believed we all have.

Perls and his wife moved to the U.S.A. after World War Two, and in the 1960s held a prominent position at the Easlen Institute in California. Thereafter, Gestalt therapy developed rapidly, coinciding as it did with other social phenomena, including meditation, Zen Buddhism, drugs and the cult of the guru figure. Perls was a larger than life person who certainly did not conform to the stereotype of doctor or psychotherapist. He was dynamic, often shocking in terms of his behaviour, style of dress and language, and in common with many of his contemporaries, also dabbled in drugs. However, his contribution to theory and practice is substantial, and since Gestalt is a humanistic psychotherapy usually conducted in groups, it is appropriate that we discuss it in this chapter.

GESTALT GROUP THERAPY

As we have indicated, Gestalt therapy is usually conducted in groups, though it is widely used on an individual basis too. Perls originally developed the approach with groups of people, and in this context he often worked with one volunteer individual at a time. This practice is still used by many practitioners, though as Philippson & Harris (1992) indicate, group leaders are often 'process orientated' too, and may focus on group rather than individual issues, especially when this is helpful for the group's overall development.

Perls took the view that people have an innate drive towards growth, and all the resources needed in order to live full and satisfying lives. However, any reduction in awareness and contact will inhibit this human propensity to grow and will inevitably lead to unhappiness and frustration. The word 'awareness' refers to a state of being in the 'here and now', fully in touch with our experiences and surroundings. According to Perls (1992:64) 'awareness is the only basis of knowledge, (and) communication.'

When we are totally aware of ourselves, and the environment, we are more likely to deal effectively with difficulties and problems, as they occur. The word 'contact' denotes an extension of awareness and refers to our ability to be aware, at a deep level, of our own inner experience, in terms of the psychological, spiritual, physical and relational. However, this deeper contact with ourselves is pointless unless we can connect it with outer experience too. Awareness and contact, therefore, go together, and when they are disrupted problems arise for the individual who may lose the capacity to respond appropriately to situations as they arise. Harris (1989:22) gives the example of driving a car to illustrate this point. While we are driving we often have spells when we drive without thinking too much about the process. However, when danger looms, we become aware again, and make the necessary responses to avoid an accident. It is not difficult to imagine what would happen if our level of awareness is seriously reduced, however. Stress, psychological problems, relationship difficulties and illness may blunt our awareness while driving, or indeed in any other situation. Heightened awareness ensures that we are more in command of ourselves, and our immediate environment. In Gestalt group therapy, the emphasis is on increasing our awareness and our ability to stay in the 'here and now.'

What happens in Gestalt groups

Spontaneity and staying in the 'here and now' are highly valued in Gestalt group therapy. Members are encouraged to be open and direct in their discussions, with a focus on present rather than past experience. This means that group members are also encouraged to take responsibility for their own lives, as opposed to blaming events or people from the past for their problems. Perls was very aware of the destructive influences stemming from the past that often inhibit a person's awareness, and he believed that these destructive influences could produce a variety of negative effects in adult life. These negative effects include relationship problems, repressed feelings, and being out of touch with one's body and physical experience. The following exchange illustrates this last point:

> **David:** *People are constantly on my back. I can't seem to get it right for anyone at the moment.*

> **Group counsellor:** *As you said that I could see you arching your back, and holding it as if you are in pain.*

> **David:** (surprised) *Yes, it is giving me problems; it's giving me hell in fact.*

> **Group counsellor:** *Could you repeat that, using the word I instead of it.*

> **David:** *I am having problems. I am having hellish problems and I am in pain.*

The group counsellor was concerned here to help David become more aware of his physical and emotional experiences, and to see the connection between them. People often speak of their bodies as if they were somehow separate from their feelings and emotions. In Gestalt therapy there is an emphasis on language, and especially on the kind of verbal leakage that may signal the root of a problem. A person might say, for example, 'It's a real headache' and yet remain unaware of the link between the relationship problem they describe, and the migraine headaches they experience.

Techniques

A central goal in Gestalt therapy is to increase awareness of all areas of personal experience, of others and the environment. Integration of thoughts, feelings and behaviour is another focus, and to this end a variety of techniques is used. One of these is known as the empty chair technique. Here a chair is used to represent part of the self, or another person, who may be either living or dead. A group member who regrets the row she had with her deceased mother, may be encouraged to pretend her mother is sitting in the opposite chair, for example. With the encouragement of the group therapist, the member may then address her mother and express her regret and her other feelings to her. We have already referred to the focus on language in Gestalt therapy, and to the way people often distance themselves from their own experiences, both physically and emotionally. This lack of awareness may well be demonstrated in the group context. If someone says 'It was devastating,' for example, the group therapist would probably ask him to rephrase it in a way that acknowledged ownership. 'I am devastated' is obviously much more immediate and intense than the first statement, and certainly more likely to help that particular group member get closer to his own feelings and experiences.

Dreams

Dreams are a central focus of Gestalt therapy too, though they are not analysed or interpreted as they might be in the psychodynamic or other approaches to therapy. Instead, group members are asked to bring their dreams to life and to re-live them in the present. To assist this process the dream is re-told in the present tense, so that it becomes a part of the person who is telling it. Perls (1992) took the view that each part of a dream is a projection of the dreamer, often indicating opposing parts, 'inconsistent sides, contradictory sides' and other conflicts hitherto unacknowledged. As the dream is told or acted out in the present, the dreamer recognises and assimilates its existential message, and as Perls puts it, is given an opportunity to 'find the holes' in his or her personality (1992:90). In the following Case study a group member recount a recurring dream.

CASE STUDY: NICOLE

I am standing beside a car that is parked by the roadside. It is dusk, and I'm unable to see very much. Suddenly the car starts to move away, as if the handbrake was off. I am terrified that it will cause an accident, so I run alongside the car and just manage to get inside and gain control of it. I am so relieved and I start to cry.

Group therapist: *Become the car in your dream and say what you are doing.*

Nicole: *I have no brakes on and I'm heading for an accident ...*

The exchange (which is part of a much longer dialogue between Nicole and the group therapist) highlights the immediacy and clarity that this approach can achieve. It enabled Nicole to acknowledge and tackle a drugs problem she had previously denied. Gestalt therapy is especially powerful, even confrontational in this respect, which is why practitioners need to be properly trained to use it. When, in the next chapter, we look at ethical issues in groupwork, we shall discuss the importance of training and supervision for practitioners. Gestalt therapy incorporates many other creative and innovative techniques that could not possibly be adequately described in a short section like this.

EXERCISE 50

LISTENING TO THE OTHER PERSON
Time: As required.

In this exercise group members are asked to conduct a dialogue with someone they know, using the empty chair technique. The exercise is best organised by the group leader or trainer who should ask for volunteers from members of the group. Group members should know a week in advance that the exercise will be used, and they should also understand just how challenging it tends to be. Ask members to think of someone they either disagree with, or fail to understand. The idea is for one person at a time to work with the empty chair. The exercise is as follows:

That other person, the one you disagree with or don't understand, is sitting in the chair opposite you. Address the person, stating your disagreement, or your lack of understanding as the case may be. Next, take the opposite seat and become the other person and reply to what has been said. Continue to conduct the dialogue in this way. If you really take the place of the other person, you will gradually start to see things from their point of view, and hopefully, become more understanding in the process. Gestalt techniques tend to be very powerful so take some time afterwards to process your experience and discuss it with other group members.

Perls (1992:49) believed that the central task in therapy is to help people become alive to their immediate or present experience. For this reason he did not place too much value on interpretation or intellectual insight. This has, unfortunately, led some group facilitators to use Gestalt techniques which elicit strong emotions in group members, emotions they do not fully understand. In my experience, group members who make themselves vulnerable to strong feelings must be given sufficient time and support to make sense of them. In addition, participation in such techniques or exercises should always be voluntary, and people should never be put under pressure to do what they clearly do not want to do.

EXISTENTIAL THERAPY

Existential therapy is a philosophical approach that is applicable to both individual work with clients or to groups. It stems from a long tradition of philosophical thinking whose main contributors in Western Europe include Kierkegaard, Nietzsche Heidegger and Sartre.

Perhaps the most outstanding existential psychotherapist of modern times is Rollo May who was born in Ohio in 1909. May studied theology to begin with, though later turned to psychology and psychoanalysis. During his late thirties May suffered from tuberculosis, an experience that influenced his choice of existential psychotherapy as an approach to helping clients who came to him. May published several important books on the subject, including *Man's Search for Himself* (1953), *The Meaning of Anxiety* (1977), *The Discovery of Being* (1983), and *The Cry for Myth* (1991).

What it is to be human

Existential psychotherapy is concerned with the question of what it means to be human and alive in the world. May (1983:15) emphasises, however, that it does not rule out the technical discoveries of Freud or the other theorists who have contributed to our understanding of human personality. What May's approach does seek to do is to form a new understanding of 'the nature and image of the human being'. This new understanding is intended as a counterbalance to what May regards as the 'dehumanising' tendency in science.

In his analysis of the major inner problems affecting people in modern society, May suggests that many people do not know what they want, and because of this lack of self-knowledge, suffer from powerlessness and emptiness (1953:14). In other words, a fundamental human problem for us is a deep sense of 'angst' or existential anxiety. A goal of therapy, therefore, is to help clients who are troubled in this way to become more authentic, responsive to life, and more accepting of all its limitations and possibilities. This process obviously takes time, since it entails self-exploration through deep and honest reflection of all the beliefs, attitudes, feelings and views of the person seeking help.

THE EXISTENTIAL APPROACH IN GROUPS

To some extent all groups have an existential focus, since a central concern for members is to become more self-aware and more authentic in relation to self and others. However, there are some groups that do tend to address and highlight existential issues and concerns. Included here are groups specifically set up to help members consider the meaning of their lives, their relationships with other people, the work they do, and the inevitability of suffering, loss and ultimately, death. These are weighty issues, and it is fair to say that people seldom get the opportunity to address them openly and honestly in the normal course of events. However, groups do provide a context for such discussion, as the following Case study shows.

CASE STUDY: DECLAN

Declan, who had joined a men's group, suffered from depression and had taken cocaine on several occasions. His marriage had broken down and he was unhappy at work, though he was reluctant to do anything about his job since the pay was good. Declan's main concern was his deteriorating relationship with his two children. Because of ongoing difficulties with his ex-wife, he did not see them as often as he should. In the counselling group, Declan was able to talk openly about these immediate worries, but he was also encouraged to address wider issues, especially those relating to masculine identity in a society with rapidly shifting roles and responsibilities. Other group members shared these concerns, since all had experienced difficulties in relationships and at work. Many of the group members felt that work dominated their lives, so that family, friends and relationships were often neglected. In addition, many of them had previously defined themselves by their work, but were now starting to question this philosophy. Declan described the feeling of 'emptiness' that he often experienced, and several other members said they often felt this way too. In order to deal with the emptiness, Declan sometimes took drugs, though he was filled with self-loathing when he did so.

As stated earlier, Rollo May (1953:14) regarded emptiness as the main psychological problem facing people in the middle of the twentieth century when he was writing. However, it is clear that the feeling of emptiness is very familiar in contemporary times too. It is also a fact that this issue will surface at some stage in most psychotherapy groups. When it does emerge it may be described in various ways, including feelings of isolation, meaninglessness, lack of autonomy, the inability to experience emotion or make decisions, or a general dissatisfaction with all relationships and a fear of intimacy. These are certainly existential concerns, and when group members articulate them they find that they are not alone, that others share these experiences. This is what Yalom (1995:5) refers to as 'universality', which means the recognition that we all do indeed have difficulties and anxieties in our lives.

Group members and responsibility

As Corey (1995:242) points out, members of an existential group are faced with the inescapable fact that they have responsibility for their own lives. The subject of personal responsibility is a recurring motif in any therapy group, but it does have special meaning in a group set up specifically to address participant's existential concerns. It is obviously difficult for many people to accept that they are capable of becoming more autonomous and self-directing. A central task for the leader, therefore, is to challenge members to identify and accept their innate capabilities and strengths, and to use them. In the previous Case study it was clear that many group members knew what they needed to do to improve the quality of their lives. Knowing what to do is quite different from actually doing it, of course, but recognition, discussion, and above all, support from others, are often sufficient to prompt action and responsibility. It should be emphasised that existential group therapy does not aim to change people. Rather, it is intended to help group members come to terms with themselves and with life, including all the difficulties, challenges and contradictions that are part of the human condition.

EXERCISE 51

EXISTENTIAL GROUPS
Time: 1 hour.

Existential group therapy is effective for some people, but not for others. There are certain contexts in which it is highly effective, and others in which it is less so. Working in small groups of three to four, look at the following situations and discuss how effective (or otherwise) you think the existential approach might be in each. Afterwards discuss your views with members of the whole group.

◆ Depression

◆ Addiction

◆ Crisis

◆ A desire for personal growth

◆ A need for greater self-awareness

◆ Severe anxiety

◆ Childhood abuse

◆ Feelings of frustration and emptiness

◆ Unrealised personal potential

◆ Conflict within a group

Existential therapy is probably most effective for problems that are rooted in a dissatisfaction with relationships and life in general. It is also good for those people who want to increase self-awareness, or their personal growth and development. It is probably least effective for people in immediate crisis who are more likely to benefit from participation in groups set up specifically to help them manage the crisis. The existential approach is an intellectual one, and is therefore attractive to members who are prepared to discuss issues in depth and at some length. This is not to say that it would never be suitable for people with acute depression or addiction. Such clients are just as likely as anyone else to benefit from existential discourse, but they may not be able to participate fully until the acute phase of the illness has passed. In relation to the last situation given in the previous exercise (conflict within a group) we have noted throughout earlier chapters that it is inevitable at some point, and if acknowledged and understood will often lead to greater cohesion and creativity.

References

Corey, G. (1995) 4th ed. *Theory and Practice of Group Counselling.* California. Brooks/Cole.

Ewen, R. B. (1993) 4th Ed. *An Introduction to Theories of Personality.* New Jersey. Lawrence Erlbaum Associates, Publishers.

Goleman, D. (1996) *Emotional Intelligence.* London. Bloomsbury.

Harris, J. B. (1989) 2nd ed. *Gestalt: An Idiosyncratic Introduction.* Manchester. Gestalt Centre.

Hobbs, N. (1991) 'Group-Centered Psychotherapy' in Rogers (Ed.) *Client Centered Therapy.* London. Constable.

Maslow, A.H. (1968) 2nd ed. *Towards a Psychology of Being.* New York. Van Nostrand Reinhold.

Maslow, A.H. (1970) 3rd ed. *Motivation and Personality.* New York. Harper Collins.

May, R. (1953) *Man's Search for Himself.* New York. Dell Publishing.

May, R. (1977) *The Meaning of Anxiety.* New York. W. W. Norton & Co.

May, R. (1983) *The Discovery of Being.* New York. W. W. Norton & co.

May, R. (1991) *The Cry for Myth.* New York. W. W. Norton & Co.

Perls, F. S. (1992) *Gestalt Therapy Verbatim.* New York. The Gestalt Journal.

Philippson, P. & Harris, J. B. (1992) 2nd Ed. *Gestalt: Working with Groups.* Manchester. Gestalt Centre.

Rogers, C. (1991) *Client Centered Therapy.* London. Constable.

Yalom, I. D. (1995) 4th Ed. *The Theory and Practice of Group Psychotherapy.* New York. Basic Books.

Principles of good practice in groups

In the preceding chapters we discussed, in context, a number of ethical and other considerations relating to groups and the people responsible for planning and leading them. We saw, for example, in chapter five that sexism, racism and other forms of oppressive behaviour can and do occur in groups. For this reason, leaders need to set ground rules that incorporate anti-oppressive guidelines about general behaviour in groups. In chapter six we highlighted a range of problem behaviours, and suggested skills that group leaders could use to encourage members to identify them and to change. This chapter will address other, often problematic, phenomena in groups, and will indicate key factors in helping leaders understand their dynamics and the impact they have on members and the group as a whole.

EXPERIENCE AND THEORY

Perhaps one of the most important things to state at the outset is that experiences in groups are often uncomfortable for participants. Experiential learning is, by definition, only accomplished through personal experience. Often these experiences are quite intense and challenging, and group members need a good level of self-awareness (and support) in order to integrate and make sense of them. Understanding at both cognitive and emotional levels is essential if experiential learning is to prove beneficial for members, and the group as a whole. If prospective members are adequately prepared before the group starts, they are obviously much better equipped to deal with, and learn from, any experiences they may have, even when these experiences are challenging and uncomfortable.

It is not just preparation of group members that matters, however. Equally important are considerations relating to the leader's level of training and experience, issues that we shall discuss in more detail later in this chapter. In this first section, though, it is important to stress the relevance of these professional concerns, since so many people are now showing an interest in working with groups in a variety of contexts. In chapters one and three, we identified the importance of your own personal experiences in groups, and added that a combination of experience and theory are essential foundations for people hoping to work as group counsellors or facilitators. A major problem arises when one of these two important components is missing, as the following Case study shows.

CASE STUDY: JUDE

A student on a university degree course described his first experience of studying on a groupwork module. The student (Jude) described the first meeting of members and group facilitator, a meeting that ended with most of the students walking out.

There were twelve of us in the group, and not one of us knew anything about the subject, except that we wanted to learn. We arrived for the first session, and waited fifteen minutes before the lecturer/facilitator arrived. When he did arrive, he told us to get into a circle, which we all understood and were happy to do. After that, however, he removed himself from the group and sat outside the circle, silent and impassive. Since none of us knew what was happening, we became very frustrated, some more than others, and a few people walked out. We asked him questions, but he refused to give us any real information. His only response was to ask us what we would like to happen, which, of course, made a lot of people even more angry and resentful. By the end of the evening most of us had decided not to return. In the event, just two of us turned up for the next session, which meant that the module couldn't continue. After that I resolved to keep far away from all groupwork studies, and no one has ever explained to me what happened, or what we were expected to do, on that first module.

It is clear from the description given by Jude that the twelve students on the module were treated in an unfair, even disrespectful manner. The behaviour of the group facilitator was reprehensible, and betrays a lack of experience in working with members who had no previous knowledge about groups. On one level, it is easy to see what the facilitator was hoping to achieve. He probably envisaged a situation in which students would have direct experience of the kind of anxiety common at the start of a group. The students did indeed experience anxiety, but this was so intense that it meant they refused to complete the module. Students on a groupwork module have added anxieties about being assessed, and it is quite likely that members of this particular module felt they were being graded already.

Apart from his job as a teacher, the facilitator responsible for this debacle had no real experience of working closely with people in groups. He did, however, have extensive knowledge of theory, so he knew that people become frustrated when they find themselves without guidance or a leader in a new group. He therefore acted on theory, in the hope that he could discuss the students' feelings and reactions with them in the following session. What he failed to anticipate, or even suspect, was the mass exodus prompted by his seeming neglect of the group. What we don't know is the reaction of the course director to these events, though it isn't difficult to imagine the dismay generated by the loss of so many students from the module.

It is important to make one last point here about the procedure used by the facilitator in this Case study: if the students on the module had previously studied group dynamics, it is likely that they would have understood what was happening. With prior experience and some knowledge of theory they would have been able to tolerate the anxiety and frustration that accompanied the opening session of the group. The principal mistake made by the lecturer was that he misjudged the group and their needs, and he did not have sufficient experience to conduct his experiment in a safe and educative way. It is also possible that he was more concerned to conduct an experiment for research purposes, than he was for the welfare of the students.

CONFIDENTIALITY

Throughout this book we have referred to the subject of confidentiality and its significance in both individual and group counselling. In chapter four we saw how important the assurance of confidentiality is, especially at the beginning when group members are meeting for the first time. Confidentiality is, of course, important at every stage of a group's life, so it is worth looking at some of the ways it may be accidentally, inadvertently, or even deliberately violated.

Confidentiality between two people in individual therapy is obviously much easier to maintain than it is when a number of people are interacting closely in a group. In chapter two we discussed the use of a contract to which all members of the group subscribed and observe. Confidentiality is the cornerstone of this contract, and it is probably true to say that when the contract is initially drawn up every member is dedicated to observing it.

Unfortunately, however, group members may, over time, forget the terms of the agreement, or they may simply trip up or become casual in their references to the group in their everyday life. One way to avoid such mistakes is to highlight the contract at various stages throughout the group's duration. The group counsellor can do this by exploring the nature of the contract, so that members are reminded of its terms and the reasons for agreeing to these in the first place. In the next Case study we can see just how easy it is for group members to slip up and forget their agreement about confidentiality in relation to group discussions.

CASE STUDY: GAVIN

Gavin, a member of a men's therapy group, told two people outside the group about the weekly meetings. He did not talk about confidential matters in relation to the group, but he did say that he was a member. The two people he spoke to were trained professionals, and both had some past experience of working with others in this context. As the conversation continued, Gavin inadvertently referred to another member of his group (Ellis) who was also known to both the professionals. The discussion petered out after this and nothing more was said. However, after the next group meeting Gavin talked to Ellis and told him what he had revealed to their two friends. Ellis didn't think too much about it at the time, but later on the incident began to bother him a great deal. He wouldn't have chosen to tell his two friends about his membership of the group, and he was now angry that Gavin had done so in such a casual way.

During the next group meeting Ellis broached the subject of confidentiality, and indicated to Gavin that he felt it had been violated indirectly. This led to a general discussion about the group contract and the terms it laid out. Several group members took the view that the contract could have been more specific, so that the possibility of an indirect breach of confidentiality could be addressed. This was now addressed, clarified and explored in the group, so that everyone knew exactly what was expected in relation to matters of confidentiality. In addition to the discussion about confidentiality, group members were keen to explore Gavin's reasons for talking to his two friends in the way he did. This was a difficult subject for Gavin to address, since he was not quite sure himself why he did it. On reflection, however, he could see that he wanted to impress his friends, both of whom were very interested in this kind of groupwork.

There are several points worth highlighting in this Case study. The first concerns the initial contract, which did not provide sufficient guidelines about confidentiality and its limitations, if any. Group members need to know what is confidential for the group, and what isn't. In addition the contract had been mentioned only once, at the beginning. This made it easier for members to 'forget' about it, hence Gavin's careless reference to Ellis and his membership. The second point concerns Gavin's admission to Ellis. This clearly indicates some measure of guilt and concern on Gavin's part about the indiscretion. He should have raised it in the group, however, since it was, in fact, a group issue. It was not something that Ellis and Gavin could sort out between themselves, with no regard to its importance for the group as a whole. Ellis, whose initial impulse was to challenge Gavin individually, decided later that it was a group issue, and this is why he addressed it in the group. The last point concerns Gavin's reasons for talking outside the group. It was important to explore this, and to understand the various ways that confidentiality can be broken. It was also important for Gavin to talk about what happened, and to feel that his indiscretion was not something that would be held against him indefinitely, by Ellis or the other group members. However, it should be added here that breaches of confidentiality always expose feelings of vulnerability among group members. This is why it is essential to discuss any violations that occur, and to establish trust and confidence in the group in its aftermath.

EXERCISE 52

WHAT IS CONFIDENTIAL?
Time: 1 hour.

If you are currently a member of a group with a counselling or training focus, you will have some experience of drawing up a group contract. It is most likely that confidentiality is an important component of your contract, and in this exercise you are asked to consider the exact nature of the group's agreement in relation to it. Working individually to begin with, read the following list of statements and indicate whether you agree or disagree with them. Afterwards, discuss your views along with members of the whole group.

1   It's all right to tell people outside the group about our contract. Agree / Disagree

2   I would be happy to discuss our teaching methods with people who are not in the group. Agree / Disagree

3   If someone outside the group asked for the names of members, I would tell them. Agree / Disagree

4   If someone in the group disclosed a personal problem I would regard it as totally confidential. Agree / Disagree

5   If someone in the group disclosed their abuse of another person, I would feel obliged to tell someone outside. Agree / Disagree

6   If another member of the group confided in me outside the group, I would raise this in the next meeting. Agree / Disagree

7   I would not talk about my family members in the group without their permission. Agree/Disagree

8   I would be happy to talk to people outside the group about the administrative details of the course. Agree / Disagree

9   If a group member talks about someone we both know at work, I would never refer to it again outside the group. Agree / Disagree

10 If my partner or best friend asked me if I would recommend the course, I would be happy to discuss it. Agree / Disagree

11 When group members worked together on earlier courses, it is unethical to refer in this group to what was discussed back then. Agree / Disagree

12 For a training group to be effective, the leader/trainer should not provide student evaluations for anyone outside the group context. Agree / Disagree

13 Shapiro (1999) suggests that an effective training contract includes a leader's commitment 'to having no administrative role' in relation to the group. Agree / Disagree

14 I would be happy to socialise with other group members in between meetings. Agree / Disagree

15 Meeting for drinks after sessions is likely to lead to breaches of confidentiality. Agree / Disagree

16 I would feel comfortable talking to someone who completed this course earlier, about the work they did then. Agree / Disagree

17 When two members share information privately, there is something wrong with the group's functioning. Agree / Disagree

18 If I want to talk in the group about one of my client's at work, I should ask for the client's permission first. Agree / Disagree

19 I feel happy to talk to work colleagues about my progress on the course. Agree / Disagree

20 It is important that everyone in the group agrees about the terms of the contract, especially in relation to confidentiality. Agree / Disagree

The statements listed here are meant to stimulate discussion in your group. Each will have its own individual contract, so what is right for one may not necessarily apply to another. During discussion about the statements you will see just how complex the issue of confidentiality actually is. We seldom think of its complexity when we initially subscribe to it. Unfortunately, it is usually only when an agreement about confidentiality is violated that we are forced to clarify its precise terms, its meaning and limitations.

CONFIDENTIALITY IN THE COUNSELLING GROUP

It goes without saying that group counsellors and therapists should be well versed in any requirements concerning confidentiality in their own geographical area, agency or organisation. On the other hand, as Barnes et al. (1999) stress, the provision of safe and confidential group therapy does not imply 'having a siege mentality'. When group therapists are excessively secretive they may cause problems within their working environment and organisation. There are often areas of information that need to be shared with other professionals, but when this is the case, group members should be told about it. One example of this is when a group member threatens to harm another person, or him/herself. This is especially important when there is a threat to children or other vulnerable people who would find it difficult, or impossible, to enlist help or support for themselves.

In our discussions about group planning and preparation in chapter two, we stressed the importance of sharing information with prospective group members. Individual members need to know what they will be expected to do in the group. This involves stating what can and cannot be discussed outside the group. Detailed clarification like this serves to reassure new members who are often preoccupied with worries about confidentiality. Indeed it is probably true to say that members of any new group need details about what is expected in relation to confidentiality. In student training groups, for example, it is usually a good idea to detail the terms of the agreement so that everyone knows what is regarded as confidential and what is not. If this kind of detail is not included in the group contract, members may become excessively worried about actually saying anything about the group outside.

An important point made by Corey (1995:32) is that even when group counsellors guarantee and model confidentiality on their own part, they cannot give an absolute guarantee that other members will provide the same assurance and commitment. At the beginning of this section we noted that confidentiality is much easier to establish and keep when just two people are involved. It is clearly much more difficult in a group, especially if there are conflicting ideas about what actually constitutes confidentiality. This emphasises the point once again that clarification and discussion are essential from the beginning, and at intervals thereafter in the life of a group.

Discussions about the group and records of meetings

When records of group sessions are kept (either written or recorded) group members should be aware beforehand that this is the practice. In addition, records should be securely kept, and shared only with authorised personnel who must also subscribe to a code of confidentiality. When discussions are routine within an agency group members need to be told about this too, and their agreement sought.

Some of these guidelines are especially applicable to young people and children, who, like everyone else, should know exactly where they stand in relation to confidentiality. There is no doubt that groupwork with teenagers and children is aided considerably if confidentiality and accountability are discussed and agreed upon between everyone involved in their care. Those involved may include social workers and other professionals whose cooperation and support are essential for the welfare of young group members. When confidentiality is discussed and agreed upon between professionals there is less likelihood that boundaries will become blurred, and the possibility of manipulation is reduced. Parents too need to know where they stand in relation to confidentiality, and what it is they are entitled to know about a young person's progress in a group. Corey (1995:33) stresses that group counsellors should aim to work cooperatively with parents, and this means discussing confidentiality and its limits with them. In her discussion about children in residential care, West (1992) suggests that it is usually a good idea to maintain confidentiality about the detail and content of group sessions, but she adds that it is also important to communicate with other involved adults about a child's general progress in group therapy. This sharing of information is essential if other key workers are to give the right kind of support a child needs in the wider environment. West also adds that the group counsellor or therapist needs to explain confidentiality in terms that are understood by children as well as adults. In addition, appropriate agreement should be reached about written records, video and audiotapes (if these are to be used), and about what might be communicated by the group counsellor in supervision sessions (West (1992:34)).

GROUP MEMBERS AND THEIR RIGHTS

In any group, therapeutic or otherwise, members have a right to be supplied with certain basic information about the overall purpose and function of the group. When the group is a therapeutic or counselling one, details about the leader's qualifications and training should be made available to all members. In chapter two we stressed the need to give prospective members any information they need and request, but it is worth restating here that a pre-group interview is necessary if this is to be done well.

Issues that need to be highlighted

It is easy to underestimate the fundamental importance of basic information for new members, many of whom are unacquainted with therapy groups, their ethos and their particular mode of functioning. New members need to have details of cost and payment (if applicable); what will happen if they are unable to attend some of the meetings; holiday breaks and when these occur; information about the therapeutic approach to be used in the group, as well as some detail about techniques or programmes to be used during sessions. Another subject to address here is the possibility of an alternate group meeting. This is a meeting that takes place between members when the leader is absent or on holiday, though it should be stressed that this is not mandatory and will only take place if it seems ill advised or unsuitable for the group or individual members. Tudor (1999:86) points to the value of such group meetings, and suggests that the alternate format provides a 'bridge between group therapy and the wider social context' of the outside environment.

It is also a good idea to point out to new members that the group is, in fact, a therapeutic one where people are gathered for therapeutic reasons, and not to socialise or make friends in the usual sense. Group counsellors might make the mistake of assuming that prospective members already know this, when often the opposite is the case. In addition, participants in a counselling or therapy group must be told that involvement in the group may be uncomfortable for them at times. The difference between a group that makes you feel good (as a social group would) and one that helps you should be highlighted in the pre-group interview. In giving this kind of information, however, the group counsellor should add that each person in a group is entitled to go at his or her own pace. It is important to emphasise that no undue pressure will be put on individuals, that members are not forced to self-disclose or speak when they don't wish to, and that one of the group leader's tasks is to ensure that the group is a safe and fair place to be. Hoffman (1999), in his review of necessary and salient issues for people entering therapy groups, points to the importance of giving exact details on all these matters during pre-group interviews with all new members. A consequence of not doing this is that some group members are likely to experience the group in a negative, as opposed to a therapeutic way. If group members are not told about the possibility of psychological discomfort they may find the experience intolerable and leave the group prematurely. When, however, they are prepared for some discomfort, and are also assured that this will not be *deliberately* inflicted, they are more inclined to stay until the reasons that brought them to the group in the first place are addressed and clarified. In other words, when people are told that they may be uncomfortable, frustrated or troubled at times in the group, they are at least prepared to talk about their difficulties, instead of acting them out through an impulsive departure from the group.

Giving appropriate feedback

The degree of discomfort is obviously commensurate with each participant's personal involvement in the work of the group, and the level of self-disclosure and commitment individuals are willing to invest. These are the details that should be communicated to prospective members, though, in reality, they are often forgotten, or not fully understood until experience in the group highlights them. It is possible, for example, to inform prospective members that giving and receiving feedback is an integral component of the therapy group, but when individuals are given such feedback it is often uncomfortable, even difficult for them to accept it. At the end of chapter three we referred to feedback, and the importance of giving it correctly. In any consideration of the psychological risks entailed by any feedback received, it is essential to stress the point that the leader/counsellor must model appropriate ways of using this skill. Furthermore, it is sometimes necessary to intervene when feedback in the group is unsolicited, or when it is destructive, inappropriately timed or lacking in sincerity. It is also important for the counsellor or leader to monitor feedback at all times, and to intervene when it is aggressive or punitive. Feedback, if it is to really benefit group members, should be specific rather than general. It should, moreover, be presented in an atmosphere of trust, in a descriptive as opposed to evaluative way. Edelwich & Brodsky (1992:135). If these basic guidelines relating to feedback are not observed there is a chance that someone in the group will experience psychological harm as a result. In the following Case study, the group member receiving feedback perceived it as a judgemental attack, and was later tempted to leave the group prematurely.

CASE STUDY: MAUREEN

Maureen, who was a member of a student training group, spent a residential weekend with her colleagues. The aim of the residential course was to examine group processes and students' experiences within the group. There were six people present, including three men and two women, along with their group leader. During an afternoon meeting one of the men (Ralph) unexpectedly confronted Maureen as she listened to another group member who was describing her difficult relationship with a teenage son. Ralph accused Maureen of insincerity and of simply pretending to listen. Before anyone could speak, he went on to accuse her of general insincerity in the group and of ignoring him when he spoke on a previous occasion. Other members of the group, and the leader, were silenced by the vehemence of Ralph's attack. It was not long before his verbal attack became personal, at which point Maureen became emotionally distressed and started to cry. This continued for some time until the leader finally intervened in order to process what was happening in the group. Several other members were extremely shaken by the very judgemental confrontation, and Maureen resolved to leave the group. In the end she did not do this, but she continued to feel very vulnerable, right up until the end of her six months course and afterwards. It was not until she completed a higher level course that she was able to make sense of what had happened in the meeting. Even then, she felt resentment and some anger that the group leader had not dealt with the situation in a more competent way.

There are several aspects of this Case study that deserve further attention and comment. The first point to make is that the leader failed to intervene at an early stage to process what was happening in the group when Ralph launched his unsolicited tirade against Maureen. The episode was not, in fact, clarified in a satisfactory way for the benefit of the whole group at the time, although Maureen, Ralph and the group leader were later able to make sense of their own contributions in the group. In the next group meeting Ralph talked about his experience, and added that Maureen reminded him of a bossy and overbearing aunt who looked after him in childhood. He was then able to establish that his had been a transference response, based on resentments left over from the past. Once this was clarified Ralph could see that the confrontation had much more to do with his own difficulties, than it had to do with the person he confronted.

In examining her very emotional response to what was said, Maureen discovered that there were similarities between that and the way she responded to criticisms from her strict and authoritarian father in the past. This process of analysis and discussion proved beneficial for both Ralph and Maureen, though the latter still felt resentment towards the leader for his ineptitude at the time. Because the leader was also her trainer, and had some responsibility for assessing her work, Maureen felt unable to challenge him about his role during the confrontation. This highlights an important point about students in training who, according to Shapiro (1999), should not be subjected to evaluations of their 'work, talents or limitations' by the person leading the group. Though this is a very difficult scenario to achieve in reality, it still remains the ideal. Shapiro also emphasises the fact that training groups focus on the nature of group process and the effects of these processes on group members. This means, in effect, that the trainer should not be 'influenced by therapeutic considerations' but should focus on helping students understand the dynamics of the group and their individual contributions (1999:65).

The trainer in the Case study (Gwyn) was certainly dissatisfied with his inability to intervene effectively, and at the right time, during the meeting in question. He talked about his experiences in supervision, and by doing so was able to reach some understanding about his own responses at the time. Ralph was a student he admired a great deal. In fact, as he spoke about him, Gwyn came to see that he was in awe of Ralph whose impressive academic qualifications were in philosophy and theology. Once he understood the basis of his countertransferential response, Gwyn was in a better position to identify the meaning of his inhibition in relation to what happened in the group. It is possible to elaborate even further on the content of this particular Case study (Maureen's feelings of being let down by a negligent or inadequate carer, for example) but the subject of transference and countertransference have already been highlighted in chapters five and seven. The point to make here is that without real understanding (or even with it) and regular supervision it is possible for anyone leading a group to encounter difficulties like those described in the previous Case study.

SUPERVISION

Supervision is an integral part of working effectively with groups. This applies even when two leaders work together in a system of co-leadership. In fact, it is probably true to say that co-leadership arrangements probably make regular supervision essential. There are a number of reasons for this, some of which have been indicated in chapter two and chapter five.

Included in the difficulties encountered by co-leaders are issues of status, the possibility of unhealthy alliances, different expectations, loss of individuality, or even overt competitiveness. To monitor these and other potential pitfalls, co-leaders should organise regular supervision before the group starts. Group workers who work within agencies sometimes find it difficult to organise suitable supervision. Indeed, they may even have problems convincing managers or senior personnel that supervision is necessary in their work. In spite of these difficulties, however, it is important to persevere, so that supervision is established as a norm for all group workers.

Although it may be stating the obvious to say so, groupwork is demanding, and group counselling in particular makes its own unique demands on leaders. The next exercise encourages you to consider the challenges of groupwork. It specifically asks you to think about supervision and how it might help group counsellors become more effective in their work.

EXERCISE 53

SUPERVISION
Time: 40 mins

Look at the following list of statements and give your responses to them. You are not asked to agree or disagree with them, but simply to use them as a starting point for reflection and discussion. When you have done this, discuss your responses with other members of your group.

1 Supervision is a process that helps group counsellors identify their own attitudes and values concerning groupwork.

2 Group counsellors need to be able to discuss their concerns in supervision even before the group starts.

3 Supervision can help group counsellors deal with their anxieties when planning the group. These anxieties include fears that members may not turn up, or that they will not find the group useful.

4 Good supervision should provide other opinions as well as encouragement, confirmation and support.

5 Supervision helps group counsellors maintain standards of service for members, and for the agency (if applicable) with overall responsibility for the group.

6 When co-leaders are supervised together, someone else (the supervisor) can observe their interaction, and help them understand how this might be manifest in the counselling group.

7 Group counsellors who prefer to work singly should explore this preference in supervision.

8 Supervision represents a commitment to professional growth and the development of knowledge and skills.

9 A group counsellor needs to state clearly what his or her expectations of supervision are. The supervisor should also be clear about expectations.

10 Supervision is quite different from personal therapy, but sometimes it does indicate to the supervisee that personal therapy would be beneficial.

These statements highlight some very important points about supervision and the reasons for having it. The beginning stage of a group is likely to generate special anxieties for the group counsellor concerned, and supervision can help to identify these and put them in perspective. Previous experiences of supervision can also be discussed at an early stage, and any difficulties encountered in the past analysed and understood. To do this effectively, however, it is necessary for both supervisor and supervisee to discuss their beliefs about supervision, and what it is they both expect from it. Group counselling can generate anxieties at the termination phase too, and here again supervision provides an opportunity to explore these feelings. Although supervision is not the same as personal therapy, the process of supervision can certainly highlight a need for personal therapy, when such a need exists. It is important that both supervisor and group counsellor understand the nature of their relationship, and that they both agree to focus on the development of the insights and skills that are essential for effective group counselling.

Standards

Supervision also ensures that standards are maintained in the group, and a valuable therapeutic experience is provided for all members. Different training organisations stipulate their own requirements in relation to supervision, and some provide supervision, or at least help students to access it. Group counsellors working in the health service, social work or the voluntary sector are often provided with supervision as part of their work. How much say they have in the choice of supervisor is another matter, and often the allocation of supervision depends on the availability of trained and suitable workers in a particular area.

Trainee supervisors should have at least one and a half hours of supervision a month with a trained practitioner of group counselling. Organisations that provide their own specialised courses in group therapy often lay down guidelines or requirements about supervision for trainees. Some of these are listed at the end of this chapter, so if you are interested in further training it is worth contacting them for details.

Co-leaders and supervision

We noted earlier that co-leaders need supervision as much as, if not more than, someone working alone. Barnes et al. (1999:174) indicate that co-leaders should be supervised together. This is because the style of interaction used by them in the therapy or counselling group is likely to be mirrored in Supervision. Clearly, there are advantages when this kind of replication occurs, and co-leaders can see at first hand both the positive and negative aspects of their relationship and the effects this might have on the counselling group.

Working alone

When a group counsellor prefers to work alone, it is worth discussing this in supervision. Preston-Shoot (1987:121) suggests that there are many reasons for solo leadership, including experience and confidence, inability to find another co-worker, a preference for personal autonomy, or a belief that 'role clarity' is facilitated in single leadership. Regardless of the reasons for working alone, however, they are still worth exploring. It might be, for example, that a preference for autonomy is really a preference for power and control. If this is the case group members may feel constrained or inhibited by the unspoken control they sense in the group leader. Sole leadership of a group is a heavy responsibility, since there is no one else to share ideas and concerns with in an ongoing way. Supervision is obviously essential in such circumstances because it provides a forum in which to discuss anxieties about working alone. It also ensures that skills and interventions used in the counselling group are subject to appraisal, review and assessment. Effective supervision, for either co-leaders or the solo leader, should provide encouragement, support and opinion, as well as the time and opportunity to try out fresh ideas and explore new approaches or techniques.

Methods of supervision

Edelwich & Brodsky (1992:164) list four main methods of conducting supervision. They refer to 'blind supervision' in which the supervisor discusses the counselling group with the facilitator, concentrating on what actually happened in the group and the his/her's responses to these events. Using this method, the supervisor may also keep written notes of the counselling sessions, detailing seating arrangements in the group, member interactions, interventions by the leader and any themes that emerge during meetings. There are some disadvantages in using this method, since the supervisor has no direct contact with the group and must therefore rely on the facilitator's overall interpretation. Edelwich & Brodsky also suggest the use of audiotape to record sessions, though they point out that though the method is easy to use, it cannot show the non-verbal communication taking place in the group. On the other hand, videotape can record both verbal and non-verbal communication, and is therefore an effective way of providing material for observation in supervision. The fourth method suggested by Edelwich & Brodsky is observation through a one-way mirror. The advantage of this method is that it enables the supervisor to note all interactions, both verbal and non-verbal, *as they actually occur* in the group, thus providing the kind of immediacy not possible with any of the other three methods described. However, this last approach does have some disadvantages. In the first place, it does not provide a permanent record in the way that a video recording does, and secondly it is time consuming for supervisors, especially those who are working with a number of supervisees.

Peer supervision

It is possible for a number of group therapists or counsellors to set up and conduct their own peer supervision group with no permanent supervisor taking overall responsibility. Barnes et al (1999:176) point out that though peer group supervision is less challenging than a group with a designated supervisor, it is, nevertheless, preferable to no supervision at all. However, the peer supervision model can be adapted so that members take turns to act as group leader, thereby giving some formal structure to the proceedings. Such an approach needs to be discussed beforehand, and agreement should be reached about rotation of leaders.

Co-leaders and post session processing

Two leaders working together can analyse their work during processing sessions, which usually take place after each meeting of the group. During these sessions co-workers review what happened in the last meeting. They can also discuss how members seem to be doing, and how they themselves are functioning in the group and as a partnership. Conyne (1989:70) describes this practice as one that provides qualified professionals with an 'ongoing, mutual supervision experience' and is the reason that many group counsellors prefer co-leadership. This is obviously something that single leaders are denied, since they do not have the opportunity to process their work in this way. It is interesting to note that Conyne refers specifically to 'qualified professionals' when he discusses the benefits of processing sessions. Most trainee group counsellors would probably agree that they need something more formal and directive than this approach if they are to develop their groupwork skills and knowledge. In the following Case study a group counsellor describes his relationship with his co-worker and the processing sessions they had.

CASE STUDY: PROCESSING

Yvette and I were co-leading a counselling group and we kept a record of our processing sessions as we went along. We knew from the start that we would have to share our feelings in a very open and honest way if we were really to learn from each other, and we had planned these sessions beforehand. We both kept individual notes about the sessions, and at an appointed time we met together to discuss and share these. Sometimes we found it difficult to communicate effectively, and on these occasions we were tempted to stray into other, less demanding topics of conversation. It took us some time to realise that we seemed reluctant to address and monitor real issues relating to the group, and it was not until we identified this reluctance that any real progress was made.

Conyne (1989:82) himself refers to co-leaders' reluctance to come to the point during some processing sessions. He goes on to suggest that co-leaders are avoiding their work on these occasions, and unless this 'blocked responsibility' is identified the flow of discussion about other extraneous matters will go unchecked. Conyne also highlights the importance of understanding group developmental theory, and of linking any blocks that occur in processing sessions with possible unacknowledged blocks or conflict in the group itself. Processing sessions between co-leaders are fruitful, informative and revealing, but they are also demanding and require risk taking and a total commitment to honesty and sharing.

PERSONAL THERAPY

Throughout this book we have stressed the importance of the personal experience of group membership. Theory alone cannot possibly enlighten students of group counselling (or indeed any other form of groupwork) about the intense and often unsettling experience of group participation. Personal therapy goes one step further than mere experiential learning, however, because it addresses a deeper need, often identified through training, for individual help through interaction with other group members. Yalom (1995:526) suggests that 'some extensive self-exploratory venture' is desirable for trainee group therapists, and an increasing number of training programmes require a personal therapy component. Yalom goes on to detail the reasons for personal therapy, including increased self-knowledge, insight into personal motivation, attention to countertransference issues, and the identification of attitudes to confrontation, conflict and intimacy (1995:527).

EXERCISE 54

EXPERIENTIAL GROUPS AND PERSONAL THERAPY GROUPS
Time: 30 mins.

This is a group exercise that should encourage discussion about the differences between experiential training groups and personal therapy groups. Working together as a group, brainstorm all the differences you can identify between these two group models. List your ideas under two headings: 1) Experiential groups and 2) Personal therapy groups. Example: experiential groups explore here and now group processes.

TRAINING IN GROUP COUNSELLING

As far as counsellor training is concerned, there still seems to be a bias in favour of providing training for individual counselling work. Tudor (1999:211) highlights this point, and suggests that employers, practitioners and course designers often assume that knowledge of counselling skills and theory is in some way 'transferable to working with groups.' Rowan (1997:124) makes a similar point when he highlights the poor provision for groupwork training. Tudor also goes on to intimate that the special status given to training in individual counselling probably reflects the 'primacy of the individual over the group' in Western societies generally (1999:212). However, there is some reason to suspect that this situation may be changing, as more and more counselling courses now include a group component or module as part of their training. Once students are introduced to group counselling they begin to see its unique advantages. These advantages include cost effectiveness, since a number of clients can be helped (and help each other) together.. As well as this, certain interpersonal problems, many of which have been discussed throughout this book, are addressed more effectively in groups. Wessler & Wessler (1997:174) refer to some of the opportunities uniquely provided in groups. These are opportunities for feedback about personal presentation and behaviour, the possibility of corrective emotional experience, and the chance to learn new social skills. Wessler & Wessler also predict that counselling in the future will comprise more groupwork.

For information about training:

British Association for Counselling
1 Regent Place, Rugby CV21 2PJ   email: <u>bac@bac.co.uk</u>   Website: www.counselling.co.uk

British Association for Behaviour and Cognitive Psychotherapies
PO Box 9, Accrington BB5 2GD   email: <u>membership@babcp.org.uk</u>

Cambridge Group Work
CGW Administrator, 4 George St, Cambridge CB4 1AJ

The Group Analytic Society
90 Belsize Village, Belsize Lane, London NW3 5BE

The Institute of Group Analysis
1 Daleham Gardens, London NW3 5BY

Group Analysis North
79 Fog Lane, Didsbury, Manchester M20 6SL

The Training Department
Westminster Pastoral Foundation, 23 Kensington Square, London W8 5HN

Westminster Pastoral Foundation
Goldsmith College, Sheffield University

UK Council for Psychotherapy
167–169 Great Portland St, London W1N 5FB

Minster Centre
1 Drake Court Yard, 291 Kilburn High Road, London NW6 7JR

The Gestalt Psychotherapy Training Institute
2 Bedford St., London Road, Bath BA1 6AB

Centre for Rational Emotive Behaviour Therapy
156 Westcombe Hill, Blackheath, London SE3 7DH

References
Barnes, B., Ernst, S. and Hyde, K. (1999) *An Introduction to Groupwork: A Group-Analytic Perspective.* London. Macmillan.

Conyne, R. K. (1989) *How Personal Growth and Task Groups Work.* London. Sage.

Corey, G. (1995) 4th Ed. *Theory and Practice of Group Counselling.* California. Brooks/Cole Publishing Co.

Edelwich, J. and Brodsky, (1992) *Group Counselling for the Resistant Client: A Practical Guide to Group Process.* New York. Lexington Books.

Hoffman, L. (1999) 'Preparing the Patient for Group Psychotherapy' in Price, J. R. Hescheles, D. R. and Price, A. R. (eds) A *Guide to Starting Psychotherapy Groups.* California. Academic Press.

Preston-Shoot, M. (1987) *Effective Groupwork.* London. Macmillan.

Rowan, J. (1997) 'The Future of Primal Integration' in Palmer, S. and Varma, V. (eds) *The Future of Counselling and Psychotherapy.* London. Sage.

Shapiro, E. (1999) 'Special Groups' in Price, J. R. Hescheles, D. R. and Price, A. R. (eds) *A Guide to Starting Psychotherapy Groups.* California. Academic Press.

West, J. (1992) *Child-Centred Play Therapy.* London. Edward Arnold.

Wessler, R. L. and Wessler, S. H. (1997) 'Counselling and Society' in Palmer, S. and Varma, V. (eds) *The Future of Counselling and Psychotherapy.* London. Sage.

Yalom, I. D. (1995) 4th Ed. *The Theory and Practice of Group Psychotherapy.* New York. Basic Books.

Glossary

Acting out
This term refers to the use of action as a replacement for verbal communication. For example, a member of a therapy group may walk out of a meeting instead of saying why s/he feels under stress at that particular time. One of the aims of group counselling and therapy is to encourage members to bring their concerns into conscious awareness and articulate them.

Actualising tendency
The actualising tendency is, according to Carl Rogers, present from birth in every person. It is an impulse to grow and develop towards maximum human potential. Rogers believed that the actualising tendency is present in all living things, including plants and animals.

Anima and Animus
These are terms used in Jungian psychology. The word Anima refers to the unconscious female archetype in the male psyche, while the word Animus refers to the unconscious male archetype in the female psyche. An important focus of Jungian therapy is to examine the roles that these archetypes play in both interpersonal and intrapersonal behaviours in the group.

Alternate Group
An alternate group is one that meets without the presence of the therapist or counsellor. There are several advantages for members meeting in this way. For example, an alternate group often helps members experience independence and to help one another. In addition, group members can try out different behaviours in an alternate group, and then compare these with how they behave when the counsellor is present.

Altruism
Yalom (1995) describes the therapeutic factors that, in his view, help people in groups.

Altruism is one of these factors, and refers to the help that members receive through the process of helping others. When group members realise that they can actually help and support others, they become more confident and their self-esteem is enhanced.

Archetypes
These are unconscious universal images and ideas that all human beings in all societies recognize. According to Jung's theory, archetypes determine the way human beings function and their patterns of behaviour. Mental functioning, therefore, follows an inherited pattern in the same way that physical functioning follows an inherited pattern.

Auxiliary Ego
This is a term used in psychodrama to describe the use of improvisational actors chosen by the protagonist (the person whose story is being enacted) to represent other people in his life.

Boundaries
A boundary is an imaginary line that the leader draws around the group. This gives a sense of structure and holds the group together. Boundaries include practical details like times of meetings, venue, number of meetings, and ground rules relating to the expected behaviour of members. When there are secure boundaries, group members feel safe enough to engage in the therapeutic work of the group.

Brainstorming
Brainstorming is a group performance technique designed to encourage creative thinking. Group members are asked to come up with as many ideas as possible, regardless of how ridiculous or sensible they may seem. Group members do not criticize each other's contributions, but allow the free flow of ideas in the hope that new solutions may emerge.

Boredom
A leader who experiences feelings of boredom during meetings, may take this as a clue that the group is failing to thrive or make progress. Group members may also experience boredom or helplessness at times, and this too is usually a sign of impasse or deadlock. Boredom may be a factor when there is a pattern of lateness or absence in the group, or when emotional topics are avoided. Long periods of silence may indicate that boredom affects the group.

Breaks
Counselling and therapy groups do not usually include breaks during meetings. This is because breaks tend to interrupt concentration and may encourage the development of a social, as opposed to a therapeutic, focus. Group meetings are normally one and a half hours long, so it is not unreasonable to ask members to remain together for that time.

Case Notes
Members of a group may have received individual therapy or some other form of help prior to joining the group. Group leaders may sometimes wish to read case notes relating to these earlier experiences. Reading case notes may bias the leader, though they might also provide

valuable information about certain prospective members and their ability to function as effective members.

Catharsis

This refers to the expression of feelings, either in one to one counselling or in the group. Often these feelings have been buried for a long time, and when they are expressed can provide members with a sense of relief and closure. In the group context, one person's experience of catharsis may be contagious, so that other group members are prompted to address their own emotional problems.

Cohesion

The joining together and bonding of a group is referred to as cohesion. When group cohesion is strong, members work more effectively together and the therapeutic potential of the group is enhanced.

Collusion

Groups, and the group leader, may sometimes 'collude' or agree not to address certain issues that are present in the group. It should be added that these issues do not go away just because they are ignored. In fact, when something important is ignored it tends to have a negative or subversive effect on everything else in the life of the group.

Co-therapy

This refers to two leaders working together in the group. Such an approach has many important advantages, including the provision of different perspectives, the opportunity for a wider range of transference responses, a model for expression of feelings, conflict resolution and problem solving. Two leaders can also support each other, engage in group process analysis together, and provide continuity in the group when one is absent. On the other hand, there are some disadvantages, including failures in communication, irreconcilable personality differences, and the question of status and levels of training.

Debriefing

Debriefing refers to a process whereby group members talk about any roles they have taken on in the group. In psychodrama, for example, people may use role play to highlight or illuminate personal conflicts or problems. When the role play is over, it is necessary to de-role or debrief so that the here and now of reality is once again apparent.

Developmental Stages

These are the stages of group development, variously described by theorists and writers on the subject. Central to all these descriptions is the idea that groups experience patterns of behaviour that depend on a variety of factors, including how long the group has been in existence, and the tasks that members have to address at specific points.

Differentiation Stage

This term refers to a group stage that is characterised by independence from the leader, mutual support among members, and a greater ability to relate to others in a rational and objective way. This is obviously a mature stage of group development, and is analogous to the kind of independence that young people achieve when their parents have provided the support and structure necessary for them to grow into adulthood.

Diversity
Members of any group are all different, regardless of how similar or homogeneous the group may appear on the surface. It is important for the group leader to encourage the sharing of differences, including those of sexual orientation, belief systems and past experience. Along with the rest of the group, the leader should be open to learning about diversity and the experiences of other people, and should encourage an ethos of acceptance and sharing in the group.

Dreamwork
This term describes the process of recounting a dream in the present tense, in order to shed light on its meaning and content. The process also includes conducting a dialogue with its various elements, and talking to people who appear in the dream. In any group where there is a focus on the unconscious dreamwork is likely to feature.

Eclectic Groups
The word eclectic refers to the use of different theoretical and practical approaches in a group. A group leader might, for example, use techniques or ideas drawn from various schools, including Gestalt, Psychodrama or Transactional Analysis. To do this successfully, however, it is essential that the group leader be properly trained in these different models.

Ego
The Ego, which is a Freudian concept, refers to the 'I' part of the individual. Freud defined the structure of personality as consisting of the Id, the Ego and the Superego. The Ego is concerned to mediate between the Id and Superego, and to stay in touch with reality. In order to do this without incurring too much anxiety, people often use ego defence mechanisms. One of the objectives in group counselling is to help members develop a healthy ego, or sense of self. The group itself has an ego, which over time, develops and becomes stronger and less dependent on the leader.

Emptiness
This is one of the stages of group development described by Peck (1987:94). Emptiness occurs after Peck's stages of pseudo-community and chaos, and describes a crucial phase of growth in a group or community. During this time, members 'empty' themselves of all barriers to true (as opposed to pseudo) communication. To do this, they need to stop trying to fit others, and their relationships with them, into a preconceived model. When members empty themselves in this way, they are able to relate to one another in a genuine and congruent way. Peck's stage of emptiness is similar to Tuckman's description of Norming in groups, when members develop increased levels of commitment, spontaneity and involvement.

Facilitation
The word facilitation is frequently used to describe a style of leadership that is democratic, member centred and concerned to promote autonomy and independence.

Family Sculpting

This is a technique used in some groups, especially those with multifamily members. When people are uncomfortable or unable to express themselves verbally, they can learn a great deal through a programme of family sculpting. Individuals who are unable to articulate feelings can ask family members to pose in certain ways to illustrate aspects of their relationships. A group member who perceives another member of the family as angry or sad, for example, may suggest a sad or angry pose to highlight this point.

Feelings

The exploration of feelings has a high profile in counselling and therapy groups. One reason for this is that people are seldom given the opportunity to explore and discuss their feelings in any other context outside the group. Many people feel out of touch with their feelings, and group members often experience great relief when they are given a chance to identify their feelings and the relationships or events that accompany them. People who have little experience of therapy or groupwork sometimes think this emphasis on feelings is excessive. However, their reluctance to acknowledge the importance of feelings is often an indication of anxiety or fear about actually experiencing their own.

Flight

Flight is a defence mechanism often seen in groups, and is used when members avoid confronting certain issues that they find difficult or painful. Flight is evident when group members talk about people or events outside, or when discussion is confined to generalities or abstractions. For example, when members talk in abstract terms about general topics, such as the causes of drug addiction or the difficulties of raising children they usually do so to avoid considering their own difficulties in relation to these issues.

Games

Games are sometimes used in groups to help members explore or address specific issues, often in relation to the particular group phase. A group of people coming together for the first time may feel less anxious if an ice-breaking game is used, for example. In therapy and counselling groups, though, games may be viewed as counterproductive, even anti-therapeutic. This is because the game itself may serve to mask group members' feelings, or to make them less accessible for identification, acknowledgement and discussion.

Groupthink

The term groupthink refers to a phenomenon whereby individuals fail to express their own views because they are influenced by the views expressed by other group members. This can have serious consequences in many situations, especially those that require a consensus of opinion honestly expressed. The word groupthink was first used by Janis (1972) who was interested in the process of decision making in groups. According to Janis, dissent is often stifled in groups, especially if the leadership style is directive, and other group members seem impressive in some way. Although groupthink is not directly applicable to counselling and therapy groups, it does tell us something important about the kind of dynamics that might operate in an inhibiting way for certain members.

Holding Environment

The concept of 'holding' was introduced by Winnicott (1971) to describe the kind of environment that a mother provides for her baby. In this environment the infant feels securely held until s/he has sufficient confidence for a sense of self, or personal identity to develop. The concept of a holding environment can be applied to groups too. In this context it means the provision of a safe place in which members can explore their relationships and other issues. Because the exploration of difficult material is threatening and difficult, a holding environment is necessary to facilitate the process.

Humour

Humour is often used as a defence mechanism in groups, and is especially evident at times of stress. When group members feel uncomfortable, or unable to face difficult issues, they may resort to humour. Humour is obviously pleasant for everyone concerned, and helps to relieve tension in social or task groups. In counselling and therapy groups, however, humour may prevent members from clarifying and confronting personal issues.

Id

In Freud's theory of personality the Id is the most primitive and pleasure seeking component. It is present from birth, and contains everything that is instinctual and inherited in a person's personality.

Ideal (Self)

This is a term used by Carl Rogers to describe the true inner person that each of us aspires to be. Often, however, people are unable to acknowledge or express the ideal self, but are forced, usually because of the expectations of others, to adopt a 'false self' instead.

Identity Crisis

Erikson (1995) coined the term identity crisis to describe the confusion that accompanies the transition from childhood to adult life. Often during this time there is major conflict, and young people become excessively preoccupied with relationships, roles and personal image. However, an identity crisis can occur at other life stages too, and this phenomenon is often demonstrated in groups when members reflect on the difficulties they have experienced at key points in their lives.

Individual Roles

In the group context, these are roles that people adopt in relation to others. It is common in most groups to find at least one person who is a joker, for example, another who asks questions and so on. For further discussion about individual roles in groups, see chapter three.

Journals

Some group members keep a journal in which they record their progress, especially in relation to the emotional life of the group. Feedback received may also be recorded in the journal, as well as any special insights gained. The group journal is confidential, and no one need see it unless the particular member wishes to discuss it with the leader. Keeping a journal like this has some advantages for members, since it is possible to monitor individual changes that have occurred over time. In addition, some groups use journals to very good effect. These include groups with a cognitive or behavioural focus where it is important for members to note changes in thinking and behaviour over time. However, there are some disadvantages too. Keeping a journal may mean that important issues are not discussed in the group, but are recorded in the journal instead.

Key Issues

Key issues are common themes that emerge in a group from time to time. If we think of a group as a living organism, with its own impetus and momentum, we can see how a groundswell of feeling, preoccupation and concern, will surface at different times. A key issue could be on any theme, but may relate to confidentiality, safety in the group, fear of expressing strong feelings and so on. It is important for the leader to comment on key issues as they emerge. This helps members to understand the underlying concerns and to acknowledge them.

Lateness

When members are late for group meetings it is usually seen as a flight from personal issues that are difficult or threatening. When lateness is evident, the leader can use process statements to address what is happening. When just one member is persistently late or disruptive however, it is probably an indication that he/she does not really want to be there.

Latent Content

Groups operate on two levels, the conscious and unconscious. At a conscious level, members are aware of what is happening in the group, but they may not be aware of the latent or unconscious content that motivates this. In a psychodynamic group, or indeed any group concerned with unconscious motivation, much attention is paid to latent content. A task for the group leader is to uncover the latent issues of the group, and of the individual personalities within it.

Learned Helplessness

In some groups, especially where members suffer from addiction or depression, manipulative dependency may be evident. Seligman (1975) describes the kind of helpless role that people sometimes use to elicit help or assistance from others. Quite often the helpless group member appears vulnerable and assumes the role of victim, and other members tend to respond to this. Once again, the group leader needs to highlight (through process observation) what is happening in the group.

Loss

Group members usually experience feelings of loss and a fear of separation at the termination stage. Sometimes the feeling of loss is for the end of the group as a whole, but it may also occur when one member (or a leader) is leaving. When group members experience loss, it is reminiscent of earlier losses in their lives, so they need time to prepare for, and adjust to it. In addition, members need to acknowledge what has been gained in the group, even though they may be in the process of breaking away from it.

Manifest Content

The term manifest content refers to the communication that is expressed openly in the group. However, open communication tends to mask latent themes, most of which can only really be understood when the leader pays close attention to non-verbal cues within the group.

Mourning

Mourning and loss are characteristic of the final stage of the life cycle of a group. During this time, members need help and support to acknowledge and deal with their feelings, and to anticipate separation from the group.

Non-counselling responses

Even in counselling and therapy groups, counsellors sometimes respond in ways that are not strictly speaking counsellor responses. A cognitive or behavioural group might, for example, include strong teaching elements such as giving information, and evaluating homework assignments. Establishing norms and explaining the nature of confidentiality are all non-counselling, though essential responses in all counselling groups.

Normalism

The word normalism describes an attitude or expectation that everyone should fit within a certain average range. Any difference, whether in physical appearance or behaviour, is often frowned upon, and those who appear to be different are often discriminated against, often covertly.

Object Relations Theory

Object relations theory is a psychodynamic theory of relationships. It emphasises the early mother/child relationship, and stresses the significance of this in personality development, and in later relationships too. The mother is the object, and parts of her body, including the breasts, are referred to, as 'part objects' while the infant is the subject who needs to relate to objects in order to form a sense of self or identity.

Objectivity in Group Leadership

When two leaders are present in a group there is usually enhanced objectivity as well. Group processes are likely to be more thoroughly observed, and transference and countertransference responses can also be monitored more effectively.

Other focus

The term other focus is sometimes used to describe a defence mechanism used by group members when they do not wish to confront personal issues. When members use this defence they focus on other topics, usually generalities or people outside the group.

Ownership of Feelings

Group leaders need to be prepared to own their own feelings in the group. If a leader withdraws emotionally, members get the message that it is a bad idea to express feelings. Ownership of feelings relates to group processes, and not to personal issues that the leader has outside the group.

Paradox in Group Counselling

There are several interesting paradoxes intrinsic to group counselling. Included here is the paradox that diversity equals creativity, as well as the possibility of more conflict. Another paradox relates to boundaries, since these both encourage members' actions, yet limit them as well. It is important for the group counsellor to feel comfortable with the various paradoxes and to be aware of them at all times.

Power Issues

Supervision is important for group counsellors for a variety of reasons, and the issue of power is one of them. It is not acceptable for counsellors to use the group for power, prestige or ego gratification. Members should be empowered through their participation in the group, so control in the group needs to be shared with them.

Process Groups

In process groups, members are active rather than passive, since they take the initiative and raise the issues that concern them. There is a distinction between process groups and programme groups where there is a much more directive approach.

Programme Groups

Programme groups are usually educative in their approach and in the procedures they use. Information is imparted to members on a range of subjects, and is tailored to meet their specific needs. Group leaders have a prepared agenda or programme that may include exercises, assertiveness training or didactic teaching.

Reciprocal Model

A reciprocal model of groupwork is one that includes everyone on equal terms. Group members reach a contract by agreement, and the facilitator encourages a democratic process and mutual support. In addition, members set the goals, and the facilitator remains in a non-directive but supportive role.

Reframing

This is a skill that is used in groups to give members another view of particular issues. Reframing refers to an invitation by the group counsellor to look at something in a different way. It is intended as a challenge, but because it comes from the counsellor, and is an interpretation, it should be offered tentatively. One example of reframing is the following: 'You say you felt devastated by the experience, but is there some challenge to change too?'

Rehabilitative or Remedial Model

This model is in direct contrast to the reciprocal and places the leader in a superior role. The approach suggests that members need a great deal of help to develop skills. The leader will, therefore, give instructions and exercises, teach, model certain behaviours and actively guide the group. The rehabilitative or remedial model might be used with a group of children, or with young people needing learning support.

Rescuing

Occasionally one group member may act as a 'rescuer' to others in the group. The role of rescuer is developed over many years, and is usually adopted in response to early relation-ships and the demands that these have made. Group leaders need to be vigilant about their own impulses to rescue which often stem from feelings of importance and fantasies of being superhuman.

Safety in Groups

Therapy groups do incur some psychological risk for members. However, group members need reasonable assurance that efforts will be made to conduct group counselling in a safe environment. Though confrontation is usual in groups, it needs to be conducted in a respectful way. These are concerns that the leader should address, and good preparation of members is one way to do this. Another way is for the leader to model respectful con-frontation for the benefit of the group.

Scapegoating

Scapegoating and inappropriate confrontation often go hand in hand. Confrontation that is invasive, unsolicited, or disrespectful is usually indicative of scapegoating.

Screening of prospective members

Screening members before the group starts ensures that they understand what participa-tion in a group will actually be like. In addition it will ensure that members benefit from group therapy, and that they are sufficiently psychologically minded to make use of the group for personal growth.

Superego

In Freud's theory of personality the superego is concerned with moral judgements that are absorbed through socialisation and parental influence. It begins to develop at about three years of age, and its main function is to curb the demands of the id. In group counselling, it is not unusual for some members to feel dominated by a harsh or punitive conscience or superego.

Therapeutic Groups

It is possible for almost any group to be therapeutic if it helps members address problems or difficulties in their lives. The sharing of experiences and information is in itself thera-peutic, as is the realisation that other people have problems too. Yalom (1995) identifies eleven factors that he believes will produce therapeutic benefits in groups.

Translating

This is a skill used by the group counsellor to clarify, for the benefit of the group as a whole, something that has been either said or otherwise indicated. For example, the group coun-sellor might say to the group – 'I think Kim is trying to tell us that she feels the group is not listening.'

Unconscious

Psychodynamic group theory takes as a starting point the idea that there is a concealed part in each person's mind that remains outside awareness for most of the time. One aim of psy-chodynamic groups is to help members become more aware of unconscious motivation and processes.

Universality
This is one of the therapeutic factors described by Yalom (1995), and refers to the experience of similarity and sharing that group members find beneficial.

Ventilation
The word ventilation refers to the expression of feelings, and is often used interchangeably with the word catharsis.

Working Through
This is the process of gaining insight and self-knowledge in the course of therapy. It also implies a willingness to overcome resistance and to engage in change. The term originates in psychoanalytic theory, and was first used in relation to clients in individual therapy. However, it also applies to participants in group counselling and therapy.

References

Erikson, E. (1995) *Childhood and Society.* London. Vintage.

Janis, I. L. (1972) *Victims of Groupthink.* Boston. Houghton Mifflin.

Peck, S. (1987) *The Different Drum.* London. Rider & Co.

Seligman, M. E. P. (1975) *Helplessness: On depression, development and death.* San Francisco. W. H. Freeman.

Winnicott, D. W. (1971) *Playing and Reality.* Harmondsworth. Penguin.

Yalom, I. D. (1995) 4th ed. *The Theory and Practice of Group psychotherapy.* New York. Basic Books.

Index